Columbia Books on Architecture, Engineering, and Materials
A series edited by Michael Bell and Craig Buckley

Other books in the series:

Engineered Transparency—The Technical, Visual, and Spatial Effects of Glass
978-1-56898-798-9

Solid States: Concrete in Transition
978-1-56898-895-5

Post-Ductility: Metals in Architecture and Engineering
978-1-61689-046-9

Published by
Princeton Architectural Press
37 East Seventh Street
New York, New York 10003

Visit our website at www.papress.com.

Front cover image:
© Phillips de Pury Company
Thyssen-Bornemisza Art Contemporary, Vienna

Back cover image:
© Uwe Walter

This book was made possible through the generous support of:
The Vinyl Institute

Editor: Megan Carey
Associate Editor: Meredith Baber
Designer: Jan Haux

Special thanks to: Sara Bader, Nicola Brower, Janet Behning, Carina Cha, Andrea Chlad, Barbara Darko, Benjamin English, Russell Fernandez, Will Foster, Jan Hartman, Diane Levinson, Jennifer Lippert, Katharine Myers, Lauren Palmer, Jay Sacher, Rob Shaeffer, Sara Stemen, Andrew Stepanian, Paul Wagner, and Joseph Weston of Princeton Architectural Press —Kevin C. Lippert, publisher

Library of Congress Cataloging-in-Publication Data
Permanent change : plastics in architecture and engineering / Michael Bell and Craig Buckley, editors. — First edition.
pages cm. — (Columbia books on architecture, engineering, and materials)
 ISBN 978-1-61689-166-4 (hardback)
1. Plastics in building. I. Bell, Michael, 1960– editor of compilation. II. Buckley, Craig, editor of compilation.
T A668.P46 2014
691'.92—dc23
                                                                    2013029567

Permanent Change

Michael Bell and Craig Buckley, editors

Plastics in Architecture and Engineering

Princeton Architectural Press

New York

Contents

Structure and Energy

Cultural Effects

Preface

Plastics are a crucial dimension of our material world. They are everywhere, all the time, integral to almost any construction, device, or event. They handle countless basic physical responsibilities but also the most extreme demands for high performance. Plastic has an unprecedented range. As a synthetic polymer—a formula that can be endlessly reconfigured—it has a massive bandwidth that allows it to infiltrate, support, or protect almost any situation. Plastic is never a simple material. It is not so much a set of properties as a capacity to transform. Its ability to adopt any shape and level of performance is itself transformative. Our world is not just filled by plastic. It has become a plastic world. Even those who want to leave our industrialized environment behind, going as far from cities as possible to bond with nature, are usually wrapped in high-performance plastic fabrics, sleeping in a plastic tent tied down with plastic ropes, eating food in plastic bags, drinking from plastic containers, looking at nature through their plastic sunglasses, and carrying plastic-encased electronics in a plastic backpack. You can escape from cities but not from plastic.

Yet plastic remains largely invisible, particularly in architectural discourse. We act as if our cities and buildings have no plastic. This blindness is no accident. Plastic is a deep, even traumatic challenge to our field. The first generation of building materials were found: stone, wood, animal skin, mud, dung, and ice. Architecture was a matter of cutting, stacking, stretching, weaving, pressing, pounding, smoothing, drying, and tying. The next materials were made or, more precisely, cooked: concrete, metal, and glass. New physical properties were engineered with heat in factories. Finally, with plastic, it is all chemistry. Born in test tubes, plastic is the quintessential twentieth-century material. If modern architecture is associated with the freedom and efficiency offered by concrete, metal, and glass, then it is not so modern after all. It remains cooked and cut. A more modern architecture would be incubated in laboratories rather than in furnaces, quarries, and mills. With plastic, architecture becomes a laboratory experiment. In the late 1920s, Buckminster Fuller was insisting that real building materials were the ninety-two chemical elements and that the force of architecture lies not in what you see but in chemical bonds and their geometry. What we see is just the tip, and Fuller insisted that the visible tip, especially the building envelope, was destined to be made of plastic.

Perhaps this is starting to be realized. The high-performance plastics in yachts, airplanes, cars, shoes, and skis are increasingly found in buildings. The range of possible performance of plastic is now so great that it can be argued that buildings are assembled within that range. Architecture now lies within plastic rather than plastic within architecture. Plastic has become a fundamental material that changes the roles of all other materials. Concrete, metal, and glass arrive at any building site with a long history and a responsibility to represent ancient values of stability and security, but they are now asked to behave in new ways, brought into the laboratory to greatly expand their capacity. Architecture has become a branch of chemistry. Even stone and wood, the natural materials celebrated by architectural tradition, have been transformed by plastic. To preserve and protect old structures and values, plastics are deployed in specialized gaskets, fibers, impregnations, and films. Even plastic itself now has to be preserved using other plastics. Plastic now has history.

For the first time, plastic is not just the material of the future. It is fully embedded in our present and past. It is time to acknowledge, archive, and analyze it. The research in this book is the fourth in a series reexamining our basic materials across a broad range of scales, from the nano to the global. After thinking about glass, concrete, and metal, it has again been a privilege to invite such a density of remarkable minds to forge this picture of the state-of-the-art in plastics. Our collaboration with the Fu Foundation School of Engineering and Applied Science at Columbia and the Institute for Lightweight Structures and Conceptual Design (ILEK) at the University of Stuttgart has been a delight in incubating new paradigms of reflection and action. As we think through plastic, the field must reboot to reengage its oldest and deepest aspirations with the latest ideas, techniques, and chemistries.

—Mark Wigley, Dean

Introduction

Plastic Space: Plastic Material

Michael Bell

In architecture and engineering the term *plastic* has historically referred to aspects of space and form; that is, how building forms become virtually active, complex in shape and contour, or visually compelling and completed as form. In engineering *plastic* refers to a material's ability to sustain itself and recover at the limits of its elastic capability. Both aspects of the term are deeply historical, if not ancient—they are fundamental aesthetic and technical aspects of architecture, engineering, and materials.

Yet during the second half of the nineteenth century, these broader artistic, cultural, and technical meanings of the term were essentially transformed, if not fully replaced. *Plastic* literally came to mean a new and engineered synthetic material rather than the aesthetic or technical attributes of a material. Polymers dramatically affected the historic, i.e., "plastic" modeling of form, shape, and color but also garnered the technical capacity afforded by centralized research and development. They are simultaneously old and unprecedented: the hybridization of plastic as quality and as engineered material conflates experience and material science, leaving both terms inadequate to describe their social meaning and potential. The advent of polymers and the one-hundred-year evolution of the chemical engineering of polymers prior to the 1950s met with a mid-twentieth-century strain of commercial mass media, mass production, and social upheaval that today is quasi-historical but also still evolving and shaping both culture and production. Polymers are everywhere in construction, but they are not yet evident in architecture in ways that were prophesized by critics and practitioners well into the 1950s. What is the state of plastics as both a broader term and also as the more specific strains of polymers that are embedded in building today, and how do the current manifestations relate to the waves of promise that drove much of our last century's fascination with the material? Is plastic the first material for which it is possible to claim that material precedes concept? Did plastic emerge without a mandate or with seemingly eased constraints compared to wood, stone, glass, or metal, materials imbued with architectural meaning or at least overt structural capability? Embodied in plastics, the aspects, effects, and qualities of luster, reflection, surface, or even weight all seem to have often been seen in light of other more historically qualified materials: plastics have signified every other material and finish, but have also heralded their own new advanced forms and flexibility. The writers who have contributed to *Permanent Change* at times suggest that plastics need an entirely new language; that they exist without an intrinsic architectural concept, even as they have become some of the most omnipresent materials in contemporary construction.

With any shape possible, plastics have often reproduced or mimed existent forms rather than deliver new shapes. Aspects of imitating forms already known (imagine a 1970s car dashboard molded in thermoplastic simulating a jet-fighter cockpit) have contributed to plastics being the bearer of artificial or contrived experience. But conversely, plastics have also allowed, and at times prompted, newly responsive and ergonomic experiences. Easily molded with new efficiency, lightness, ease of production, and often durability, they drive a consortium of industrial design devices that have become newly personal, bearing private experience.

If the cultural connotations of *plastic* include artificiality and at times superficiality, the term also connotes all manner of technical innovation, if not new levels of authentically original modes of experience. Plastics are ubiquitous and have increasingly become essential to construction and to the entire built world, from transportation and architecture to electronics and equipment. They are as likely to be part of a medical or food production process as they are to be embedded in industrial procedures, but they have almost never delivered a capability to shape architecture in a holistic sense. In fact, they have seemingly become more invisible and have enabled architecture to sublimate technical concerns to a substrata of performance (weatherproofing, insulation, electrical casing) and transfer overall figure and design to a host of often unanchored linguistic signifiers. That is, polymers are doing work beneath the surface while the surface is free to represent whatever the designer (its sponsor) chooses. Yet this is once again changing, as composites—polymers fused with carbon and other materials—are increasingly reshaping the production of planes and other results of technologically sophisticated industrial production—highly capitalized processes. In these cases we are again at a threshold where polymers are perhaps beginning anew to reshape their own cultural and technical legacy: to revise their promise in ways that challenge both the design and technical capacities of other materials but also the initial waves of design and engineering that polymers have activated since the mid-nineteenth century. Composites promise change not only in how things are made and what they can do but also in what they look like and what they connote; the Boeing 787, for example, as a composite structure is often discussed in light of the network organization of its global production and assembly. Composites help instigate this capacity and yet often seem to be a background story to the network itself.

The more precise annotations for the subset of polymers—specifically vinyl, PVC, and resins, and more broadly, composites and the processes that define their formation—are a stark contrast to the easy use of the term *plastic* and the complex range of capabilities for specific materials. Plastics have reshaped construction, yet the ways in which architects and engineers employ them in construction has been the subject of less scholarship than with materials such as glass or concrete. One reason for this may be the gap between the midcentury promise of plastics and their later implementation. The lack of a technical understanding of the chemical engineering and specific "plastic" behavior of polymers has further slowed related architectural design and scholarship.

Plastics still constitute an essentially new genre of materials and while they are perhaps the most deeply engineered building materials today, they are still in their nascent

stages of understanding for potential applications and uses. When coupled with a commensurate rise in research and development, they become the recipient of a focused and tremendously sophisticated range of innovations.

Permanent Change brings these materials to a new light: materials that promised tremendous flexibility and complex modeling are now becoming the most permanent materials in construction. From silicones to sheathing to electrical casing and plumbing to vinyl and PVC, plastics of all types are often the most long-lasting warranted and tested materials in construction. They also portend a deep set of ecological issues that are only recently becoming fully addressed. Plastics remain the most easily contoured and aesthetically and functionally formed materials, but they are not alone in complex modeling or innovations in chemical engineering; fiber-reinforced concrete and new modes of laminated glass, glazing, and coatings, as well as new metal alloys, all have acquired more elastic capabilities; they begin to be less easily identified as discrete materials as their properties overlap or become more specifically comparable. What then is the future of plastics in design? How can we begin a more comprehensive project of segregating the complex aspects of polymers and the host of issues that they create, and learn from either their recent history or from the historical meaning of the word *plastic* in art and architecture? To do this, one must begin by addressing a series of aspects of plastics: their basis in nature, their historical periods of implementation and at times propaganda, and more so their future in regards to chemical engineering and environmental capacities, that is, for returning postconsumer polymers to nature. *Permanent Change* traces a history of polymers as a means to chart a future of their role in architecture and engineering.

Natural Material—Industrial Material
The emergence of polymers since the middle of the nineteenth century occurred in specific phases of development and within a broad range of relationships to natural sources, as well as to the inorganic aspects of the urban and

industrial world. The natural origins of polymers seem to be virtually forgotten today, at least in terms of the popular perception of plastics as artificial or lifeless, but at the outset polymers such as vulcanized rubber existed at a crossroads, conflated between industry and nature. Is it possible to still see polymers as natural, or have they migrated so far from these beginnings that they have become something else altogether? What is the outcome of how these materials are understood historically; has the history of polymers been irrecoverably lost? *Permanent Change* takes on these questions and in the context of these essays, plastics are not only renewed but also often revealed for being barely understood from a chemical as well as social vantage. Such a ubiquitous material at this point is considered in its infancy; the term *plastic* is often characterized as overused, if not meaningless, yet it is still the term that most fully engages the issues of what are more technically known as *polymers*.

Charles Goodyear's patent on vulcanization in 1844 set the stage for a new industrial procedure for rubber that would lie at the heart of the automobile industry and pave the way for vulcanized rubber to become intrinsic to urban landscapes. The aspects of the history of polymers that have been deflected, undervalued, or misrepresented, if not simply lost, are the key focus in *Permanent Change*. The period leading up to the 1950s, one hundred years after Goodyear's patent, was when plastics were first encountered as both material and as a spectacular component of modernization, but it was in the postwar period that plastics became a semiotic presence in everyday life. That is when plastics became a signifier as much as a material; it was this conflation of chemical engineering and social significance that drives much of theory around plastics but it is also a division that in part thwarts a deep understanding of plastics' material future. Polymers, if understood as inorganic, have often been seen as almost without history—separate from the life of nature and from historical processes of change. Yet plastics were natural in their origin and this scenario is a key issue of their renewal: they exist between industrial engineering

and natural material. In this regard, they are ripe for renewal again as technology broadens the capacity to engage and work with all materials.

Permanent Change: How Long Does a Flexible Material Last? Plastics have promised deeply engineered parameters that assure material stability and describe warranted degradation over time. Plastics are considered disposable but they are also seen as inert and more stable than other materials. Yet plastics also offer a component of aesthetics or stylistic change—any shape is achievable, with tremendous flexibility and rapid moldability. Plastics have very different life spans from other materials in building; they are tested, documented, and adhered to for safety and investment parameters in ways that are generally seen as short term. Yet plastics are also in some ways the sustaining material in countless commodity items; they assure the permanence of the market if not the commodity itself. They are also an essential component of countless commodity items that are guaranteed against failure. *Permanent Change* explores these issues in examining how the public understands plastics not only in terms of implementation and waste but also in terms of gauging their safety, their uses, and their postconsumer potentials.

Degradation, loss of elasticity, loss of coloration—these are all aspects of a material's commodity value, and help to determine its liability. What are the design limits of plastics in this realm? They seem to assure everything other than their own material effect. Is there a cleft between life span engineering and formal pliancy that one assumes with plastics? Do we see them as materially pliant but also automatically disposable? Are there long-term attributes of plastics that alter their environmental determinants; or applications and quantities of use and implementation that register in how they relate to public health, reuse, or recycling? How do these attributes come together in plastics in ways that are unique or different from concrete, wood, metal, or glass, whose life span and design potential are also often highly managed?

Permanent Change describes futures in which the malleability of polymers allows one to alter their chemical structure after production; that is, to reengineer polymers by either returning them to their original atomic origins or remapping their molecular makeup and rerouting their postconsumer uses and thus environmental impact. Similarly the authors examine how polymers gain structural capacity—strength—and are shaped by way of initial thermal processes. Exhibiting properties of entropy prior to the application of heat, thermoplastics can be heated, shaped, and then melted again to be re-formed. Thermosetting of polymers induces molecular cross-linking; once formed the molecular structure becomes permanent, giving the material strength, but it cannot be reshaped after its initial formation. The thermosetting and its inherent cross-linking effectively block the flow of one molecule past another, thwarting potential reuses or reengineering capabilities. Plastics have far more specific limits in terms of postproduction reshaping than broadly assumed and this has limited the theorization of meaning and capacity in design. Plastics have promised a unique relationship to history, altering the life span of building components, but also engaging with other materials in ways that alter otherwise known architectural/engineering assemblies, such as curtain walls: polymer gaskets and silicone pull insulated glazing units (IGU) inward, reversing years of curtain walls as mechanical assemblies. Today an IGU is chemically pulled inward as opposed to a midcentury assembly within which a plate of glass is mechanically pushed in. Likewise metals sustained by polymers in acrylic paints have altered the relationships of given materials and thereby reengendered their properties and architectural meaning. Within *Permanent Change*, plastics are reexamined in the context of their own chemical capacities and in light of their own reengineered futures.

Architectural Plastic

In the mid-1950s the promise of plastics took on a utopian guise but also often they assumed a fully fledged image of total design. Plastics heralded an era of synthetic and ultimately engineered design whose semiotic image and form at times seemed to betray the flexibility and dexterity that plastics represented at a chemical level. If the image of the fifties utopian house of the future at times became unilateral and effectively closed (literally as a hardened surface and social image) even as it was first envisioned to signify the torrents of heterogeneous practices that were beneath society, how do we today approach plastics? What newly engineered materials and forms of practice do we find operating in an architecture of change, fusing differences or harvesting potentials? Plastics are agents in an era of harvesting energy or recovering lost energy, convening as a new means of cross-fertilization to conflate disciplines. Here plastics add a particular value—one of a range of newly liquid materials in the fields of design and engineering. The architectural value is still evident, yet the overall role of plastics as a semiotic icon—a signifier of change and simultaneously a comprehensive solution—has been replaced by a wider sense of plastics as the nomenclature of engineered environments, which today includes all building materials.

Like the Monsanto House of the Future, other 1950s and 1960s iconic images of plastic architecture had a corollary in the far more pervasive yet nonfigural uses of plastics in plumbing, electrical wiring, and waterproofing. If this was a functional versus aesthetic divide that some saw in advance, it seems to have also cast the project of a plastic architecture—a figural plastic/plasticity—into a kind of nostalgic kitsch approached as a signal of a nascent but unrealized former future. That is, we approach plastics in a way that is inhabited by the former vision of the material as a precursor of change and in doing so miss a closer look at what made the material radical in the first place. The House of the Future seems to be received today as a figural as well as material prophecy come undone before it even began—a trajectory that lost ground in light of other imperatives. In its place, we have realized a world of plastic versions of previous building components—vinyl-clad wood windows, vinyl wood siding, et cetera—now employed in ways that sustain former vernaculars (histories rather than futures), simultaneously casting our gaze forward materially and backward formally.

There seems to be little overt proclamations for a plastic architecture today even as the capacity of plastics is present in a wide body of practices. Polymers such as vinyl are increasingly called upon to abet an array of design strategies and are intrinsic to both experimental and commodity driven practices. The deep and pervasive use of polymers in building mechanics and discrete systems—from paint and coatings to wire casing, plumbing, windows, and siding—seems to continually reveal a divide where plastics migrate to pragmatic architectural functions rather than expressive proposals of form or shape. As opposed to being the manifest strategy of both meaning and form, as in the House of the Future, plastics often are called on to enclose uses and needs in airtight containers.

Permanent Change mounts a case for the future of plastics with an eye to history. The book examines the social histories of midcentury experimentation; the early histories of chemical engineering; and a new future in which the chemical structure of discarded polymeric materials is reengineered to resolve environmental implications of unusable polymers. To link the terms *permanent* and *change* is a slight of hand in one regard, but within the words of this volume it is also an unsettling fact. Here, the techniques that will keep polymers out of landfills are a form of permanent change; a process that is perhaps financially untenable today but is possible with a reallocation of political will and economic power. Can these efforts transform the expectations and begin to rewrite the presence of plastics' natural and industrial origins?

Metal, concrete, and glass have all challenged their original nomenclatures. The evolution in their chemical engineering has altered what we thought were finite materials with known limits. *Permanent Change* aims to do the same for polymers, perhaps the most chemically engineered material of them all. Yet metal, concrete, and glass have not been seen as critically distant from architecture. While similar recycling issues (grinding, melting, reuse) have to be considered for polymers, it is the capacity to reengineer them that is perhaps the defining aspect of their future. That is, if polymers have struggled to find footing and to evade their own apparent shapelessness, in this new context, *Permanent Change* instead shows that this struggle was in some sense a false start. Plastics are about change—yes—but that change was perhaps more poignantly at the molecular level rather than the formal level. Plastic in this regard is not about shape, nor is it a material itself, but is a chemical workshop that has been inadvertently cast as a disposable commodity. Now plastic is in search of a built economy that appreciates its chemical capacity.

History and Theory

Neither: Plastic as ~~Concept~~, Plastic as ~~Material~~

Sylvia Lavin

Plastic has generated more conversation and less precision than perhaps any other word used in architectural discourse to the extent that it now seems both tiresome and tired. Producing more than just the ennui caused by the constant repetition of buzzwords, *plastic* itself seems to be exhausted by the balancing act the word has been forced to perform since antiquity, when it was placed atop a crevasse between concept and material. From the very first descriptions of the plastic arts, the term has referred to both an active means of form making and the passive matter from whence form arises. When, in the 1960s, *plastic* also came to mean a new class of material—invented and conceived as well as found and molded—*plastic* went into overdrive, becoming a massively important cultural cipher that, at the same time, anticipated its ultimate collapse into exhaustion.

During the 1960s, *plastic* invaded language itself and became a model for the semiotic turn of that era. Rather than hold together fundamentally opposed epistemologies and ontologies, the word constantly threatened to expose these conflicts. The result was that plastic became a super sign—a sign for signs themselves, molded in the idea that all things can be substituted for something else and, through this process of abstraction, become elements in the established chain of signification and integrated into a system of cultural signs. *Plastic* became the sign of the arbitrary relationship between signifier and signified, always on the verge of collapse. Everybody who was anybody famously said something about plastic during the 1960s and all of these statements together reflect a broad desire to exert control over the fluidity of meaning and to stave off permanent semiotic regress. In a perfectly circular logic, asserting that plastic lacked an essential nature became a means of asserting that the essential nature of all things was to lack an essential nature. As Andy Warhol said, "I want to be plastic."

The usefulness of plastic today does not lie in an essentializing discourse on its material properties or a critical examination of its semantic value, but rather in an investigation of the way plastic can be used to model a resistance to having to choose between the two—between the specificities of matter and the cultural vectors through which these specificities are inevitably shaped on their way to becoming perceptible. Here I will focus on the 1960s, when the project of plastics as both cultural sign *and* material was widely evident—when the facets of plastic's double identity converged. Not content to merely witness or simply contain this convergence of semiotics and material, the decade was manifestly shaped by the plastic objects and forms that began to overtake the visual landscape and was haunted by the ease with which plastic seemed to equally trigger a catastrophic transformation in cultural values and certainties. When Charles Moore—one of the first architects to embrace what in the 1960s was considered to be the pop aesthetic of plastic—noted that the "plastic on your sandwich really doesn't have to be made to last fifty years," he was not only recognizing the challenge plastic posed to architectural time but was also expressing anxiety that this shift in cultural life span could challenge the very difference between culture and biology, then understood to be axiomatic. The active response to these concerns was either to produce so much chatter that the term could be reduced to cliche (always a good way to neutralize anxiety-provoking notions) or to force plastic's potential as a material, on the one hand, and its nomination as ideal free-floating signifier, on the other, to appear as an incompatible opposition.

A pivotal episode in this drama of plastic playing between signifier—material without content—and signified—meaning without content—is the word "Plastics!" as famously uttered to Dustin Hoffman's character in the 1967 film *The Graduate*. The single word recalls plastic's heroic rise into a material of utopia and simultaneously announces the false idol's imminent collapse into semiotic dystopia. With exquisite economy, it expresses the primal power attached to the notion of materiality as such, as well as the duplicity of an

*Reyner Banham, in taking stock of the impact of **tradition** and **technology** on architecture today, finds it necessary to re-define these terms. For his purposes both words are used in a specialized sense.* **Tradition** *means, not monumental Queen Anne, but the stock of general knowledge (including general scientific knowledge) which specialists assume as the ground of present practice and future progress.* **Technology** *represents its converse, the method of exploring, by means of the instrument of science,* **a potential** *which may at any moment make nonsense of all existing general knowledge, and so of the ideas founded on it, even 'basic' ideas like* **house, city, building.** *Philosophically it could be*

1960
STOCKTAKING 1
1
vi

argued that all ideas, traditional or otherwise, are contemporaneous, since they have to be invented anew for each individual, but the practical issue is not thereby invalidated. For the first time in history, the world of **what is** *is suddenly torn by the discovery that* **what could be,** *is no longer dependent on* **what was.**

tradition

Architecture, as the professional activity of a body of men, can only be defined in terms of its professional history—architects are recognized as architects by their performance of specific roles that have been assigned to the profession in previous generations. Any significant attempt to extend or alter those roles will be dismissed, by most of the profession and even more of the public, as something other than the business of architects as architects. As James Cubitt wrote recently 'Designing roundabouts or doorknobs is not architecture. The idea that it is arises from a misconception of the purposes of the Bauhaus, primarily a school of industrial design. Architecture is, and always will be concerned, roughly speaking, with "carefully balancing horizontal things on top of vertical things".'.

technology

Architecture, as a service to human societies, can only be defined as the provision of fit environments for human activities. The word 'fit' may be defined in the most generous terms imaginable, but it still does not necessarily imply the erection of buildings. Environments may be made fit for human beings by any number of means. A disease-ridden swamp may be rendered fit by inoculating all those who visit it against infection, a bathing beach may be rendered fit by removing land-mines left over from the last war, a natural amphitheatre may be rendered fit for drama by installing lights and a public address system, a snowy landscape may be rendered fit by means of a ski-suit, gloves, boots and a balaclava. Architecture, indeed, began with the first furs worn by our earliest ancestors, or with the discovery of fire—it shows a

tradition—that of communicability. No one doubts that Ed Stone's Delhi Embassy, or Saarinen's in London, look like representational government buildings, but the argument over what Ronchamp looks like is still proceeding, the only basis of agreement being that it does not look like a church.

The attempts to explain why Ronchamp is as it is, and how it is connected with the true nature of modern architecture, bring out the other way of regarding the Modern tradition itself—not as a man-to-man communication of attitudes and concepts, but as an immutable and scientifically ascertainable succession of historical facts. Such an approach is in direct conflict with the 'traditional' view of the modern tradition, and has been described as 'using facts to pervert the history of modern architecture' by supporters of that view. It has also led to persistent allegations of modern eclecticism being levelled against younger architects who hold to the 'scientific' view of recent history. Very often this is true, particularly at student level where the formal vacuum of half-trained minds can as easily be filled with pickings from the Twentieth Century as from other centuries. But much of this alleged eclecticism has been the stimulus, mask, or vehicle of radical attempts to establish 'what really happened in modern architecture.'

The most important aspect of this view of the tradition is its all-inclusiveness. The other type of tradition proceeds by what might be called 'selective amnesia', each generation forgetting anything that had ceased to be of interest in order to find room for new matters of interest that had come up in its own time. The new view, on the other hand, demands total recall—everything that wasn't positively old-fashioned at the time it was done s to be regarded as of equal value. The Futurists must be discussed in the same breath as the Deutscher Werkbund, de Klerk must be put alongside Rietveld, Maybeck alongside Wright. The guardians of the Modern tradition, such as Sigfried Giedion, have been called in question for forgetting too much, and—it is claimed—distorting the truth by over-selectivity. In revenge, every discarded formal and functional device that was dropped or ignored by the developing mainstream must now be re-examined and, wherever applicable, re-used.

Much of what results—projects and a few finished buildings—is, indeed modern movement revivalism, the resurrection of usages (though rarely of total building forms) of the architecture of the Twenties, or even the Forties—David Gray's house at Lowestoft can serve as an example of the former, the Smithson's school at Hunstanton of the latter. But Hunstanton—the building by which the much-battered term 'New Brutalism' is commonly defined—immediately raises another problem altogether. Wherever the scientific and all-inclusive attitude to recent history is found, it is nearly always accompanied by a similar attitude to the use of materials. The mystique of materials 'as found' involves (a) a resolute honesty in their use (paralleling the refusal to allow a selective attitude to historical fact) and (b) an insistence that all the qualities of a material are equally relevant.

Thus, in the Hunstanton School, steel is given a far higher valuation than the rather abstract one implicit in Mies's work. Its visual quality as a rolled product with makers' trade marks embossed on it is given value, the nature of its ultimate performance under stress is acknowledged in the use of plastic theory by the engineer

tradition

technology

Fibreglass, ARCHITECTURAL REVIEW, December 1969)—... the fabrication of components large enough to be effective determinants of functional volumes. Thus, the Monsanto House has only four large components to form the whole of one of its cantilevered rooms (bar the lateral windows) while some of the products envisaged by the French group around Coulon and Schein call for the off-site fabrication of complete functional volumes such as bathrooms and kitchens, a procedure which both has structural advantages and makes it possible to complete most of the fabricating work under controlled, laboratory conditions. The result seems likely to be a house put together from large non-repeating units—except for the joiners which, like railway corridors, must be universal fits. In larger structures room-units might be carried in an independent frame, but in either case the result should be that service-rooms, which need to be connected to the public mains, might be treated as expendable clip-on components, thus obviating some of the difficulties of

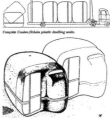

Complete Coulon/Schein plastic dwelling units.

the Appliance House project, which runs the risk of degenerating into a series of display-niches for an ever-changing array of domestic machinery.

However, such ideas have hardly touched the general body of architecture at all as yet. Much of the most painstaking and valuable research that can be shown, has been undertaken in conditions that presuppose the existence of rectangular buildings. Much of this work has been structural, concerned chiefly with prefabrication techniques, a field in which, for instance, the Ministry of Education and independent commercial experimenters can be found advancing, from the other end, into territory already being prospected by the Modular mathematicians. Elsewhere, as with the Nuffield Trust, a great deal of solid, plodding work, that most architects would rather not undertake, has been accomplished in the fields of space-requirements and the physiological effects of daylighting and colour. The fruits of such work, because of the 'logical formalist' connection discussed above, often wear a characteristic air of grid-like simplicity which, it should be noted, derives more from the mental disposition of the men involved than from the findings

98

98

fig. 1 | "Stocktaking: Tradition and Technology," by Reyner Banham, *Architectural Review*, February 1960

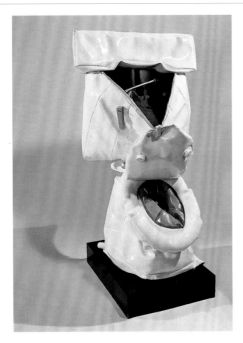

fig. 2 | *Soft Toilet*, by Claes Oldenburg, 1966

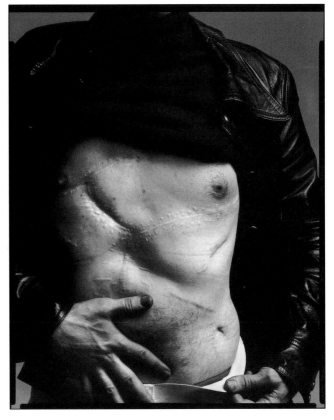

fig. 3 | *Andy Warhol, artist, New York, August 29, 1969*, by Richard Avedon, 1969

endlessly malleable signifier able to take on the impressions and desires of any given moment.

The fact that this word, which once contained not one but two radical sets of assumptions, has now become a quip or a cliche is an urgent call to rethink plastic beyond either of these regimes. Perhaps when plastic moved into the chain of signification, prodded as it was by architecture to do so, it was not as positively, passively, and permanently integrated into the semiosphere as Roland Barthes and others argued.[1] Some trace of plastic might have been left on the plane of experience, a plane that by now should include both questions of matter and questions of sense. In which case, the real question becomes whether or not the peculiar double history of plastic can today be asked to yield something singular.

The architecture critic Reyner Banham famously wrote a lot about plastic and contributed significantly to the resonance of its chatter. But Banham was perhaps more forceful in determining its fate when he did not write *about* plastic, but rather wrote *around* plastic, avoiding the term but managing its implications. The best of many examples of this redirection via indirection is his 1960 essay "Stocktaking"— the only piece in his massive oeuvre in which the essay itself is treated as malleable.[2] | fig. 1 He splits the text into two columns, one devoted to "technology," or architecture as performative structure, and the other to "tradition," or architecture as signifying structure. The two columns are side by side, much like an art historical slide comparison. The essay is, in effect, a writerly intermedia project that uses technology transfer to plasticize the history of architecture. The shape he chose to give the history of then-recent architecture was generated (and limited) by the split between the flip sides of plastic—the liberty of form and the potential of performance. In neither column does he use the term *plastic*, even though the images clearly embed the formal column within the traditions of what was generally called plastic form and the technological column with the development of product and commodity design. In this essay, plastic has no place in either tradition or technology, and yet it is the matrix that

allows these two elements, set in opposition to each other, to reside together, to negotiate existence on the same page. To form, you might say, a composite.

Every step in the history of contemporary plasticity is full of these accidents and reversals of fortune between plastic as material and plastic as concept. Leo Baekeland claims he discovered plastic on his way to looking for something else, like Marco Polo. Baekeland wanted something soft but got something hard. Unlike Baekeland, Fernand Leger said, "Enormous enlargements of an object…give it a personality it never had before…[making it able] to become a vehicle of entirely new…plastic power." For Leger, shifts in scale and the plasticity of formal transformation could enable everyday objects of negligible importance to radically transform the cultural hierarchy in which different kinds of objects were classified. By the time the artist Claes Oldenburg had enough plastic to produce massive enlargements of toys and toilets, the notion of power was turned back into its critique: Oldenburg's series of plastic "softies" may have begun with Leger's interest in granting plastic power to everyday artifacts, but when confronted by the fact that everyday modernist objects associated with labor and value had become just consumer objects, his softies instigated limpness instead. | fig. 2 The 1969 photograph of Andy Warhol's scars by the photographer Richard Avedon reveals all of the plasticity and refashioning that the human body can tolerate. | fig. 3 Despite Warhol's claim that "everyone is plastic…I love plastic, I want to be plastic," his body's lumps and hairy stitches introduce a radical aporia in the flow of plastic toward the state of being a free-floating signifier. His bulging striations make Tia Carrere's claim that "beauty lasts [fifteen] minutes. Maybe longer if you have a good plastic surgeon" seem oddly nostalgic. His own body got in the way of material artifice's complete dissociation from the real and his desire to be plastic.

In architecture, even those who are considered great enthusiasts show some anxiety regarding plastic. For example, both Eero Saarinen and Charles Eames, often described as masters of plastic design, warned architecture to approach plastic's malleability with extreme caution. They found in its formal softness a dangerous lack of virility—a flaccidness that made them uneasy. They both worried that they could not master the collision of modernist fantasies of pure material performance—what the plastic wants to be—with what was already an emerging postmodernist fantasy of pure semiotic play—that plastic can be anything it wants to be.

By the 1970s a semiotic logic was fully taking over the cultural landscape just as plastic—shiny, furry, puffy, squishy plastic—was taking over the domestic landscape. And it is precisely in this moment of convergence of the semiotic and the material that we can today uncover the beginning of new forms of defiance and desire, a desire for plastic and all it stands for to push back and resist, rather than offer itself up as endlessly supple and compliant. The 2002 exhibition Mood River at the Walker Art Center in Minneapolis, curated by Jeffrey Kipnis, offered a look at what such a plastic would look like, what it would feel like. While Mood River was an explicit reflection on Philip Johnson's Machine Art exhibition of 1934, it contained every bit as much plastic as did the exhibition Italy: The New Domestic Landscape at the Museum of Modern Art, curated by Emilio Ambasz in 1972. Today it is more productive to compare Mood River to the Ambasz exhibition, and to recast the role of plastic in theories of materials and meaning. Both exhibitions had a productive "shopping trip" ethos, a concern with systems of classification, and environmental milieus with rivers and landscapes. Both catalogs used "cool" dust jackets to proclaim that their ideas were encapsulated above all by a new sense of material culture. And it is precisely in this sense, this sensation, that their very convergence makes available the most dramatic disparities in what plastic has been asked to do.

The architect and designer Ettore Sottsass described his contribution to Italy: The New Domestic Landscape as an orgy of plastic, by which he meant not an environment designed for excessive immersion in libidinal activity, but precisely the opposite: a deployment of the material so complete, so totalizing and overwhelming, that it would induce

absolute detachment and disinterest. | fig. 4 He wanted "plastic overload" to perform as a disaffection machine, extracting what he called "psycho-erotic indulgence" out of the subject until nothing was left—no feeling, no plastic, no matter, only the now-exposed interminable chain of signification. Mood River restaged this party and invited ubiquity and excess once again, but the orgy of plastic behaviors in the show frustrated rather than satisfied Sottsass's wish for a future disaffection.

Kipnis called the Panton chair the "avatar and *eminence colorée*" of Mood River, not because it was the first chair in production made entirely of plastic—or even because it was marketed, according to a 1970 ad campaign in the magazine *NOVA*, as an essential tool for "properly undressing in front of your husband"—but because infinitesimal changes in the makeup of its plastic and modes of manufacture, which caused small variations in shine, bounce, and hue over its thirty-year production run, created not disaffection and apathy but uproars. | fig. 5 The public reaction to the slight alteration in the chair's polymers presents a powerful counterargument to Roland Barthes's myth that you can substitute every single molecule in an object with a different molecule and still end up with the same thing. With difference and particularity restored to each material variation, with both the affective and behavioral effects of these variations on explicit view in Mood River, the result was not a lesson on the chair as indifferent semiotic system but a veritable chair-on-chair orgy.

One thing for sure is that today everyone is doing it in every conceivable position: We are surrounded by a plastic orgy. And the most interesting players are precisely, if perversely, the flaccid ones, as in an inflatable without enough air, where plastic is not the perfectly buoyant and free-floating signifier, released from all material burden or pressure or specificity, but an almost heavy sign collapsing under its own weightless weight, a prone and vulnerable bubble of existence hoping neither to burst nor to utterly detumesce. A plump attraction between facts of matter and figures of

concern, between material behavior and disciplinary meaning, a gravitational pull between signifier and signified operating as a means of survival is also evident in the Succulent
House, designed by the Los Angeles–based firm Murmur in
2011. Like a cow or a desert plant, the house has heavy-duty
polyurethane-coated nylon udders, which, along with the
shape of the roof, capture and store water. The house is organized spatially and physiologically by the rise and fall of
these sacs, which have shape and produce material effects
but are not simple indexes of water containment. The droopy
udders and the logic to which they belong cannot simply be
reduced to their function as signs: the udders behave rather
than signify.

Everyone from Baudrillard to Barthes, from Sottsass
to the semiotic turn as such, desired plastic to take the shape
and assume the role of good sign—"good" meaning perfectly empty and endlessly, indifferently malleable, the sign
of matter lying prone and passive under the dictates of the
signifying chain. But through a velvet (or, rather, succulent)
revolution, architecture is swelling up to confound the difference between plastic as idea or form and plastic as material or force. Or, rather, to reveal architecture as a *confound*
wherein the facts of matter and the matters of concern, while
discrete and separately describable, are, in the moment of
perception, in the moments of the heave and of the swell,
utterly inseparable. The result is a cultural logic whereby
materials interact and engage conceptual pressures with
abandon and thereby suggest a way of being in the world
that is neither empty nor dominating but rather something
like a well-tempered orgy.

What more can be said about plastic? There are so
many famous quips, quotes, and comments about plastic
that the word seems almost used up. And this despite the
fact that plastic in its common usage is a relatively recent
material invention with a short but thick history about which
there ought to be much more to say. Yet at the same time, it
seems too soon to say much of anything about plastic, which
in its less common usage refers to an emerging paradise of

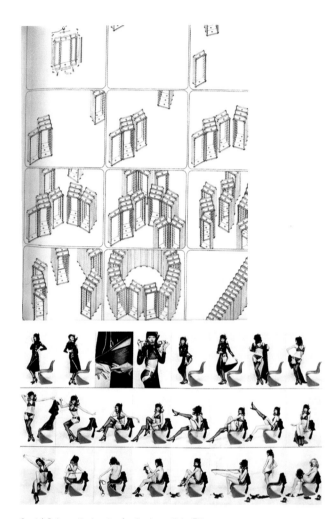

fig. 4 | Schematic drawing for display unit, by Ettore
Sottsass, Italy: The New Domestic Landscape, Museum of
Modern Art, 1972

fig. 5 | Ad campaign for Panton chair, *NOVA* magazine, 1970

mutable form, proliferating products, and endless types of newly plastic plastics. These shapes and materials are so fresh out of the oven that it's hard to imagine anyone has had the time to formulate a proper statement about them. And, furthermore, all these novelties really shouldn't be called "plastic" at all; the word's surprising historicity has become so overdetermining that its faintly old-fashioned sound is at odds with the vanguard of contemporary composites and extreme form.

Plastic, more than any other material, is but the sum and force of the things that have been said about it. And of those things that have not yet been said, it is an exemplary product of many discourses—scientific, aesthetic, cultural, philosophical, material—but their product rather than their object. The primary symptom of this fact is that rather than thinking about plastic through adjectives or adverbs ("glass" becomes "transparency" in the blink of an eye, "steel" almost immediately slips into "strength"), to think about plastic is to recall quotations. If plastic began as the perfect emblem of modernity, an absolutely raw and totally pure material without a trace of cultural convention, youthful, ephemeral, radical, supple, new, and socially transformative, it is because Pete Townshend said, "I was born with a plastic spoon in my mouth." If plastic then became the privileged postmodern signifier, a sign of representation, of counterfeit, of infinite regress, of immanent and inevitable critique, we recognize this fact because Cate Blanchett said, "You know you've made it when you've been molded in miniature plastic. But... what children do with Barbie dolls—it's scary actually."

Add in a few of Guillaume Apollinaire's plastic virtues and a couple plastic surgery jokes by Joan Rivers and suddenly the only thing to say about plastic becomes: Is there anything left to add? The most extreme evidence for the plasticity of plastic is the fact that the word that once could mean anything has now ceased to signify. And yet while utterly exhausted of meaning, converting depletion into a new beginning is perhaps the most important challenge the plastic arts have ever faced.

1 | See, for instance, Roland Barthes's well-known article "Plastic," *Perspecta* 24 (1988), 92–93.

2 | See Reyner Banham, "Stocktaking," *Architectural Review* (February 1960).

Pollution, Plastics, and the Sealed Interior

Jorge Otero-Pailos

Louis Kahn asked a brick what it wanted to be and apparently got an honest answer. We know by now, however, not to expect such truthfulness from plastic. | fig. 1 If psychoanalysts were asked to classify plastic, they would probably label it as psychotic. Plastic does not know what it is. It finds itself becoming every other material around it. Introduced to industry and culture long before Sigmund Freud was born and before the *Sweets Catalog* was compiled, plastic was marketed as a miracle material precisely because of its mimetic capacity. | fig. 2 It could assume the appearance of almost any natural material. By 1862 Alexander Parks was advertising that he could turn Parkesine into ivory, tortoiseshell, and even wood. If a cheap substance such as plastic could be turned into some of the most valuable materials of the time, it must have seemed as if humanity was surely within close reach of Jesus's miracle of transubstantiating water into wine.

Plastics emerged in the mid-nineteenth century, at the same time as other cost-saving industrial substitutes such as terra-cotta and cast iron, both of which were first introduced as cheaper replacements for stone. But, as with these other substitute materials, lower costs did not necessarily guarantee that they would be adopted in practice. Aesthetic considerations—does the mimetic material look and feel like the original; cultural pressures—will it be perceived as fake; political hurdles—trade unions and installers of traditional materials could lobby to prevent new materials from entering the market; scientific challenges—could plastic pieces be made large enough for architectural applications; and environmental concerns—could the new material resist weathering better than the old—all played a role in determining a material's viability. While remaining attentive to the interplay between these domains, I want to focus on the environmental pressures that influenced the adoption of plastics within the building industry. In particular, I want

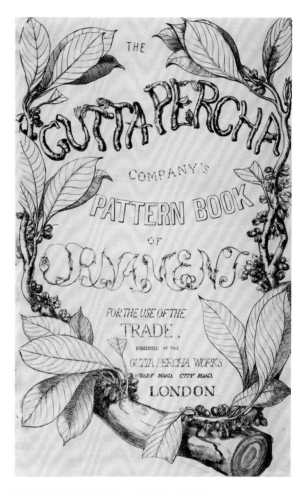

fig. 1 | *The Gutta Percha Company's Pattern Book of Ornament*, London, 1800

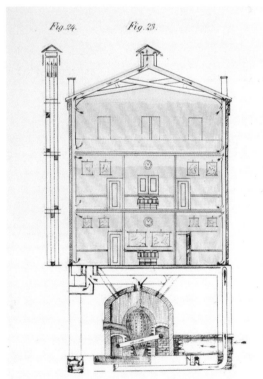

fig. 2 | Illustration of microcosm of the *"Monster Soup" of the Thames River*, by William Heath, 1828

fig. 3 | Illustration from the *Uses and Abuses of Air*, by John H. Griscom, 1850

to examine how plastics helped redraw the conceptual line between the exterior and the interior of buildings into a far more hermetic boundary than ever before. | fig. 3

Plastics promised to solve two of architecture's most difficult problems: how to keep buildings from decaying and how to maintain healthy indoor air quality. Decay seemed so intractable that preservationists such as John Ruskin and many after him thought it to be architecture's "natural" state. Beginning in the early nineteenth century, a market of protective architectural paints emerged in Europe, spurred by competitions such as one convened by the Bath and West of England Society, which offered a prize for the invention of a cheap and durable paint.[1] Durable patented protective coatings had existed since the early seventeenth century, including the special formulas developed by shipbuilders for the preservation of wood.[2] But they were expensive and cumbersome to prepare and apply. Late eighteenth-century pharmacists—who were some of the most knowledgeable chemists during the infancy period of modern chemistry—prepared and sold more affordable paints in their pharmacies.[3] Some, like pharmacist Johan Julius Salberg, even tried to improve on traditional paints with new formulas that would preserve building materials for longer.[4] In the United States, pharmacists or "druggists" sold paint pigments and binders well into the nineteenth century.[5] The development of these cheaper, more durable paints in the early nineteenth century occurred simultaneously with debates between European architects on whether ancient Greek temples had been painted or not. Significantly, those arguing the case of polychromy, such as Jakob Ignace Hittorff and Gottfried Semper, speculated that paint had been used to protect stone against decay.[6]

The new rubber paints of the late nineteenth century were mass-produced and premixed, having the advantages of color consistency over the pigments and binders on offer in pharmacies, and eliminating a dependence on the costly craft of wall painters. | fig. 4 However, the most significant change in materials was due to the decay of building materials, which became related to interior air quality with the advent of industrial smoke pollution during the latter half of the nineteenth century. Exposed to acid rain, stone facades that had withstood centuries of damage began to rapidly dissolve, especially in the regions where the industrial revolution first took root, such as England, Northeast United States, and Germany's Ruhr valley. The chemically inert plastics seemed impervious to the new aggressive chemical makeup of the air. "Indestructible" early materials such as Ingersoll's Rubber Paint, Parkesine, gutta-percha, Linoleum, and Lincrusta suggested a future in which architecture would triumph over decay. | fig. 5 Significantly, Linoleum and Lincrusta, patented in 1860 and 1877, respectively, by the Englishman Frederick Walton, were advertised as "sanitary" materials meant to improve indoor air quality, because they could not be eaten by insects or worms, and did not absorb moisture and therefore did not produce mold. In our contemporary parlance, early plastics were the first nonbiodegradable materials, at least in theory. And if that victory over nature and labor was not astonishing enough, these new materials also purported to improve human health standards. Lincrusta was awarded a gold medal at the 1884 International Health Exposition in London for its sanitary qualities. Plastics became the material of choice in spaces identified with infectious contagion, such as kitchens, bathrooms, nurseries, and hospitals.[7]

While the chemical composition of early rubber paints and plastics varied greatly from their twentieth-century successors, early research and development of organic polymers played an instrumental role in the introduction of fully synthetic plastics before the first World War.[8] Unlike chemistry, our understanding of modern architecture has yet to fully account for the lessons learned in the latter half of the nineteenth century. The history of plastic paints in buildings offers us one fertile line of research for addressing that lacuna, and stakes claims about modernism's "radical break" from its predecessors in the context of some important continuities. In particular, plastic paints were instrumental in developing the modern notion of the tightly sealed hygienic

interior, free from the dust-collecting cracks of wood or plaster and the mold-prone mortar joints of glazed tiles.

It is worth remembering that bacteria, viruses, and hormones did not "exist" in the mid-nineteenth century, as they did not enter into people's common conception of reality. Our contemporary understanding of biology is dependent on the emergence of microbiology in the 1860s, when Louis Pasteur identified microorganisms, such as bacteria. Microorganisms were a new form of pollution: invisible, odorless, and tasteless, but potentially deadly. Plastic paints appeared in the decade following Pasteur's discoveries, and their resistance to insects, worms, and mold spurred their swift adoption into architecture, and especially interiors that had to be kept free of microorganisms that transmit illness. By the early twentieth century it was common to hear claims such as one 1913 report by a German scientist, who suggested that the oxidation of linseed oil in Linoleum gave off a beneficial germicidal gas.[9] Plastic off-gassing does not have such positive health connotations today. What was deemed salubrious at one historical moment is considered poisonous in another.

Until the mid-nineteenth century, disease was thought to be transmitted by inhaling miasmas or corrupted air, especially air polluted by gases from the incomplete decomposition of organic matter. Pasteur's discovery caused a controversy over whether miasmas or bacteria were the main pollutants of human health. Building on the seminal work of Joel A. Tarr, historians of urban pollution have focused attention on the long drawn-out debates—lasting into the late nineteenth century—that followed Pasteur's discoveries, well before modern sanitary infrastructures were adopted by municipalities.[10] If we shift the focus from municipal infrastructure to residential construction—from the political and administrative to individual responses to perceived sources of disease—we see that the miasmatic theory of disease was in crisis even before Pasteur's contributions. By the mid-nineteenth century, manuals of residential construction—particularly those specialized in health—identified industrial airborne pollution, mostly produced by coal combustion, as a far more deadly "air" than naturally occurring miasmas. These texts reveal that the miasmatic theory of disease had already begun to lose its grip well before Pasteur—a weakness that he and his followers exploited.

Take for instance John Griscom, a physician at a New York hospital and a Fellow of the College of Physicians and Surgeons, who fully subscribed to the miasmatic theory of disease. In 1850 he wrote the *Uses and Abuses of Air*, a treatise on how to combat illnesses through "healthier" architecture, whose design called upon what we would today call biomimicry.[11] Buildings, he argued, should be designed to mimic human breathing: inhaling unbreathed air and exhaling consumed air. | fig. 6 He proposed that buildings be sealed from outside air via a skin like our own, with discrete openings to let air in and out, and ducts like our trachea serving to move air around within the architectural body. His notion that a tightly sealed interior increased its hygienic level preceded the discovery of bacteria by more than a decade.

The idea of sealing the inside was radical because buildings had not previously been so hermetically closed. For centuries they had been designed with numerous operable windows precisely for health reasons, to circulate fresh air in and out. In the winter, when windows were mostly kept shut to save energy, physicians suggested releasing healthful gases within buildings to push out miasmas such as the plague. In 1665 London's College of Physicians published a pamphlet recommending that infectious air within homes be pushed out by burning coal and allowing its smoke to fill the home, to which might be added any of a list of fragrant combustibles, such as cedar and spices. The college also recommended the frequent discharging of guns indoors to purify the air.[12]

The lack of operable windows in Griscom's design is evidence of a reversal in the medical profession's perception of coal smoke, from purifying agent to the worst air pollutant of the Industrial Age. Griscom made a series of terrifying claims about the hazards of inhaling coal smoke,

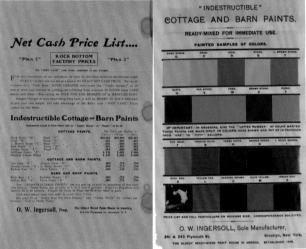

fig. 4 | Advertisement for Ripolin Peinture Laquée

fig. 5 | Rubber Paint Sample Colors, by O. M. Ingersoll, 1891

fig. 6 | Illustration from the *Uses and Abuses of Air*, by John H. Griscom, 1850

including blaming it for the biological degeneration of modern Westerners. Inhaling coal smoke, he said, produced quarrelsomeness, intemperance, pusillanimity, cowardice, deformity, imbecility, idiocy, cretinism, a general decline of morality, and even depression in young girls, leading them to drink in order to regain their spirits, and thus down a slippery slope to alcoholism and prostitution.[13] The ancients, he argued, breathed cleaner air and therefore were healthier. Since it was impossible to return the atmosphere to its ancient state, Griscom presented a solution in the form of a new architectural ideal: the self-contained building. It could keep polluted air out and serve as a prosthetic lung for its inhabitants. The controlled entry of air into the building would also eventually permit it to be filtered and cleaned. To achieve a completely sealed building, without cracks that let in dangerously polluted drafts, required painting the interior shut. The elimination of cracks and drafts would have the additional benefit of reducing heat loss, which would in turn reduce the amount of coal burned to heat households (and thus the smoke produced).

As a physician Griscom subscribed to miasmatic theories, but working as an architect led him to question that way of thinking. Miasmas were not just gaseous emanations of improperly decayed nature; they could also be man-made, such as coal smoke, a type of artificial air that mimicked the noxious health effects of natural miasmas. Griscom's focus on the perils of man-made smoke suggests that the idea of natural miasmas had already begun to lose its hegemony as the single explanation of disease.

During the decades of controversy in which miasmatic theories of disease coexisted with Pasteur's theory of invisible, odorless, tasteless microorganisms, uncertainty about proper household hygiene fueled the paranoid pursuit of the self-enclosed house as a means to keep organic, living, decaying nature at bay. It is in this cultural context that the first plastic paints made their successful entry into the marketplace. Ingersoll's Indestructible Rubber Paint promised never to decay. It contained no oil, and thus deprived molds and bacteria of nourishment. It also seemed to make

possible the idea of a continuous architectural skin, because its viscosity covered over small cracks, preventing air and small organisms from penetrating a building while also sealing the building materials against water infiltration. "These paints," advertised Ingersoll, "are the most durable money can produce. They will not 'chalk' like White Lead and Oil hand-mixed paints, nor fade, scale and crumble off like the cheap mixed paints sold in retail stores. The Ingersoll Liquid Rubber Paint is the only Paint made, that will resist the action of the Sun, Moisture, Coal Gas, Salt Air."[14] Many other manufacturers, including the Rubber Paint Company of Cleveland, the Plastico Paint Company, and the Averill Chemical Paint Company, made similar claims about rubber paint. They also claimed that rubber paint was "washable," an important advantage in the fight against microorganisms.

Rubber paints were an entirely new architectural material, meant to replace the older oil-based paints by providing customers with a product that looked and felt like the old. They were among the first modern organic polymeric "plastic" materials to be adopted in mass construction, along with molded rubber-based materials such as gutta-percha, which was used in imitations of natural wood bas-reliefs, and Linoleum, which was meant to emulate stone tile floors. Rubber paints were advertized as being the same but better than oil-based paints. Their main point of differentiation was their manner of decay—rubber paints did not decay, at least according to their manufacturers. | fig. 7

The business of rubber paints continued to grow inexorably into the twentieth century, and developed into the business of today's more sophisticated latex paints, which have entirely replaced older oil-based paints (except for some niche applications, such as high-end wood flooring). By contrast, molded rubber products, like Lincrusta, began to lose market share in the 1920s and 1930s, when the taste for elaborate ceiling bas-reliefs began to wane and historicist eclecticism began to give way to the cleaner lines of modernist aesthetics. Molded rubber products continued to be produced, but those that survived, like Linoleum, adjusted their

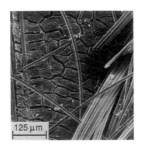

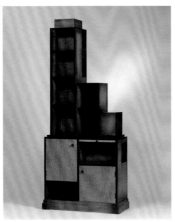

fig. 7 | Glass Fiber Reinforced Plastic after twelve years outdoors showing breakdown in the glass-resin interface resulting in fiber pop-out and surface microcracking of the matrix

fig. 8 | Skyscraper Cabinet, by Paul T. Frankl, c. 1927–28

aesthetics to appear more like a jointless painted surface.

The success of organic polymeric paints led to the invention of fully synthetic plastics. Leo Baekeland was looking for a substitute for shellac paint (made from the excretions of lac beetles) when he stumbled upon Bakelite and inaugurated the age of phenolic plastics. The Bakelite Company presented the first synthetic plastic product to the architecture and design industry as a replacement for shellac paint. But Bakelite was not paint; it was rigid and had to be molded into thin sheets and shapes so that it could be glued on surfaces. In the hands of Art Deco designers, Bakelite was adopted in interior design, and it was made famous by Paul T. Frankl's Skyscraper Cabinets of the late 1920s. | fig. 8 The important distinction to make is that the first plastic-laminated woods were not attempts to mimic wood, but rather attempts to copy the effect of paint on wood.

Of all the competitors in the manufacturing of phenolic laminates, Formica became the most famous within architecture. The company was astute enough to advertise its products not simply as painted wood, but as more hygienic than other painted woods. Formica's focus on hygiene came partly from the fact that the company began as a pioneering manufacturer of plastic sewer pipes and electrical conduits. Plastic paints were excellent sealants for building above ground, but they were less suitable underground, where leaks between the segments of traditional glazed terra-cotta sewage pipes could pollute drinking wells. Businesses, such as the Fiber Conduit Company in Orangeburg, New York, experimented with coating pipes with viscous paints as a way to seal leaky joints. In 1893 they introduced the Orangeburg pipe, made of pressure-molded cellulose fibers impregnated with coal-tar pitch, and it became an overnight success. It was used for sewers and in the growing market of electrical conduits, including in the Empire State Building. In 1910 George Westinghouse, whose main business was to provide electricity, entered the sewer and conduit market with a new pipe called Micarta that replaced coal-tar pitch with Baekeland's new formula for phenolic resins. Two years

Pollution, Plastics, and the Sealed Interior

Jorge Otero-Pailos

fig. 9 | Exterior view, Statler Hotel, by Holabird and Root Architects, Washington, D.C., 1943

fig. 10 | Brochure for the Statler Hotel showing the Formica paneling and window details

IN AMERICA'S FINEST NEW HOTEL

Formica Tops

Formica Cigarette-proof Red Gum "Realwood" Table Tops in the Men's Bar

In view of the steadily growing confidence of top flight hotel organizations in Formica as a surfacing material, it is not surprising that the splendid new hotel of the Statler system just completed in Washington, D. C. made a greater use of Formica than any previous hotel. It was the last big job of the kind that Formica handled before it became necessary to devote all Formica resources to the war effort for the duration.

Figured Red Gum Realwood was used for table tops in the men's bar and Grey Formica tops in the Veranda Lounge. It was also extensively used in the Embassy Room, restaurants and guest rooms.

Formica was specified by the Statler design staff and Holabird & Root, architects.

FORMICA ARMY E NAVY

Veranda Lounge with Grey Formica Cigarette-proof Table Tops

THE FORMICA INSULATION COMPANY, 4612 SPRING GROVE AVENUE, CINCINNATI, OHIO

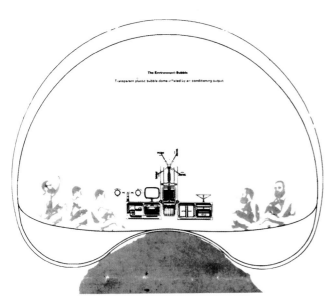

fig. 11 | Un-house, Transportable Standard-of-Living Package:
The Environment Bubble, by François Dallegret, 1965.

later, Westinghouse's engineers Daniel J. O'Conor and Herbert A. Faber thought of replacing the cellulose fibers with Kraft paper, also impregnated with resin. Their breakthrough, however, was to add color to the outermost layer of Kraft paper, creating a decorative effect that imitated paint and was also protected with melamine. They quit their jobs and launched the company Formica, offering a line of products that included electrical insulation as well as the plastic-laminated boards that became their signature product.

By the late 1920s and early 1930s, Formica lined the interiors of Radio City Music Hall, Woolworth stores, cafeterias, diners, cocktail lounges, hotels, residential kitchens, and bathrooms everywhere.[15] It came to replace plastic paint as the material of choice in places that needed to be washed frequently for hygienic reasons. Formica's flawless smoothness contrasted with the gritty reality of the Depression era and made surfaces seem, in the eyes of designers such as Raymond Loewy, like self-contained dream worlds, encapsulating a more polished, orderly, and healthy future.[16] Formica thus helped to further the architectural tradition of sealed interiors as the hygienic answer to a decayed and degraded environment.

Because of the promiscuity of their beds, hotels were places in which designers had to answer guests' hygienic anxieties, and here the architectural pursuit of the sealed environment found its most intense expression. The owners of the Statler Hotel in St. Louis, designed by George C. Post in 1917, had to address the city's notoriously bad air quality and the progressive groups that were fighting to clean it up. Post's answer was to build the first air-conditioned hotel in the United States.

The Statler formula was perfected by 1943, when the office of Holabird and Root Architects designed the chain's hotel in Washington, D.C. It was completely sealed off and air-conditioned. For the guest rooms the architects specified Formica's Realwood panels, plastic-laminated veneer of quartered walnut. | **figs. 9–10** The company touted the fact that even though they looked remarkably like real varnished wood, the panels had all the advantages of nondecaying plastic: "They are non-absorbent, cigarette-resisting, chemically inert. They are not stained or injured by conditions that would ruin wood." The hotel touted its hygienic use of laminated plastics throughout: in the restaurant tables, the front desk, the kitchen, and the laundry rooms. In their advertisements, Formica presented this totalizing use of laminated plastics as the future of hotel design. With its combination of Formica and mechanical ventilation, the D.C. Statler represented the apotheosis of the now modernist architectural pursuit of hygiene through the sealed interior.

Plastics made the self-enclosed interior possible long before the 1960s avant-gardes discovered plastic films and turned them into inflatables. In turning plastics into the ventilating tube itself, the 1960s avant-gardes reduced the architecture of the squeaky-clean interior to its layer of plastic, something their precursors—the nineteenth-century hygienist architects who had begun the quest to seal off interiors with plastic paints—could only dream of. | fig. 11

1 | James Crease, *Hints for the Preservation of Wood-Work exposed to the Weather. Applicable to all kinds of fences, gates, bridges, ships &c.* (London: Letter to Dr. Parry of Bath, 1808), 3. Rare books section, the British Library. See also: Lydia Kallipoliti, "Dry Rot: The Chemical Origins of British Preservation," in *Future Anterior* 7, no. 1 (Summer 2010): 1–19.

2 | The first coating recorded explicitly as a protection against the fouling of wood appears to be a composition patented by William Beale in 1625, which was composed of powdered iron, cement, and probably a copper compound. Possibly, this was the first use of copper as an anti-foulant. Two other patents for unknown compositions for "gravings against the worm" were also granted in the seventeenth century, and a third was granted in 1670 to Howard and Watson for a coating composed of tar and resin in a varnish of beeswax, crude turpentine, and granulated lac dissolved in grain alcohol. The fourth, granted to William Murdock in 1791, was for a composition of iron sulfide and zinc roasted in air and mixed with arsenic. See: Woods Hole Oceanographic Institution; United States Department of the Navy, Bureau of Ships, *Marine Fouling and its Prevention* (Annapolis: United States Naval Institute, 1952).

3 | Antoine Lavoisier's *Traité Élémentaire de Chimie* (Elements of Chemistry, 1789) is considered to be the origin of modern chemistry.

4 | Salberg's 1742 formula improved on the traditional technique to coat wood with falun red (red ochre) and tar by adding iron vitriol to it. See Marita Jonsson and E. Blaine Cliver, "Coloring Historic Stucco: The Revival of a Past Technique in San Juan, Puerto Rico," in *APT Bulletin* 33, no. 4 (2002): 31–36.

5 | Susan Louise Buck, "Paint Analysis," Inquiry HP lecture series, Graduate School of Architecture Planning and Preservation, Columbia University (March 27, 2008). See also Susan Louise Buck, *The Aiken-Rhett House: A Comparative Architectural Paint Study* (Ph.D. Dissertation: University of Delaware, 2003).

6 | Gottfried Semper, *Vorläufige Bemerkungen über bemalte Architectur und Plastik bei den Alten* (Altona: J. F. Hammerich, 1834).

7 | Carly Mae Bond, "Lincrusta-Walton: History of a Versatile Embossed Wallcovering" (master's thesis, Columbia University, 2006): 23–24.

8 | Colin J. Williamson, "Victorian Plastics: Foundations of an Industry," in *The Development of Plastics,* eds. S. T. I. Mossman P. J. T. Morris (Cambridge: Royal Society of Chemistry, 1994): 1–9.

9 | Ibid., 23–24.

10 | Joel A. Tarr, *The Search for the Ultimate Sink: Urban Pollution in Historical Perspective* (Akron, Ohio: University of Akron Press, 1996). See also Martin V. Melosi, *The Sanitary City: Urban Infrastructure in America from Colonial Times to the Present* (Baltimore: Johns Hopkins University Press, 2000).

11 | See John H. Griscom, *The Uses and Abuses of Air* (New York: J. S. Redfield, 1850).

12 | Barbara Freese, *Coal: A Human History* (Cambridge, MA: Perseus, 2003): 39.

13 | Griscom, *The Uses and Abuses of Air*, 145–60.

14 | Ingersoll Rubber Paint trade catalog, Avery Library, Columbia University.

15 | Jeffrey L. Meikle, "Materia Nuova: Plastics and Design in the U.S., 1925–1935," in *The Development of Plastics*, ed. S. T. I. Mossman, P. J. T. Morris, (Cambridge: The Royal Society of Chemistry, 1994): 40.

16 | Ibid., 40.

Plastic Atmospheres, 1956 and 2008

Beatriz Colomina

.1956

Outside it was a wooden rectangular box of almost blank walls. The words "House of the Future" flashed on and off, projected onto one of the longer walls. A small opening to one end of the wall acted as an entrance. Inside was another blank box. Visitors would circle around it, peeping in at ground level through a few openings that had been cut in the walls for that purpose before ascending to an upper level, where a viewing platform circled the inner box again—allowing a bird's-eye view into its interior—before leaving the outer box through another discreet opening on one of the short sides before finally descending to the ground of the vast Olympia exhibition hall in London. The mysterious structure had been commissioned by the *Daily Mail* for its Jubilee Ideal Home Exhibition and displayed there for twenty-five days in March 1956. | figs. 1 and 2

How are we to understand Alison and Peter Smithson's House of the Future? How can we discuss today a 1956 project that tried to imagine the house of 1981? How can we look back at a forward-looking house? For years it was considered, or ignored, as an anomaly in their career, the project that didn't fit with anything else. Much discussed at the time, the House of the Future faded away from everybody's memory, almost disappearing, until the last few years, when it has regained some currency. After half a century the house seems almost impossible to ignore. Is it because its sinuous curves resonate with a renewed interest in biomorphism, and the growing sense that new moldable materials are a driving force in architecture? | figs. 3 and 4 Or is it the contemporary fascination with the 1950s and British Pop in particular? Or is there perhaps something about the house itself that, as it were, forces itself back upon us? To echo Richard Hamilton's famous collage from the same year: Just what is it that makes this house of the future so different, so appealing?

If there is one word that comes to mind when thinking about the H.O.F., it is *plastic*. The building was all plastic and filled with plastic objects. The chairs, especially designed by the Smithsons for this house, were all experiments in the new material: the folding "Pogo" chairs—seen by the Smithsons as "relics of the previous constructed technology"—were in steel and transparent Perspex, while the "Egg" chairs (one honey colored and the other citrus yellow), the "Petal" (in pimento red and honey color), and the white "Saddle" were molded in reinforced polyester resins—and seem to share the character of the doubly curved modeling of the house itself. | figs. 5 and 6 The kitchen sink, like the sunken bath, the hand basins, and the cubicle for the shower and dryer were a Bakelite polyester and fiberglass molding in pimento red. | figs. 7 and 8 The mattress and headrests for the bed were made of latex foam and covered with nylon. | fig. 9 The bedclothes consisted of a single red nylon fitted sheet. The cushion in the living room was covered in royal-blue nylon fur. The curtains were made of orange colored fiberglass. A never realized suspended cloud was envisioned in pale-blue nylon stretched over a light metal structure. The working surfaces and cupboard doors in the kitchen were in Pitch Pine WareRite. Even the food had been packed in airtight plastic containers. | fig. 10 *House Beautiful* described the house as a "Wellsian fantasy in plastic," with "herrings wrapped in polythene" and eggs without shells individually packed in little plastic sachets, the whites separated from the yolks.[1] The H.O.F. was a veritable showcase of plastic and the showcase itself took its logic from plastic. The exhibition catalog describes the structure of the house as "a kind of skin structure…[with] floor, walls, and ceiling as a continuous surface."[2]

Is that all that the H.O.F. was: a plastic house with curves? A skin structure, the smooth rounded look of mid to late 1950s architecture and design, of the Monsanto House of the Future of 1956; of Ionel Schein's Maison plastique and Cabine hoteliers, both of 1956; of Eames and Saarinen

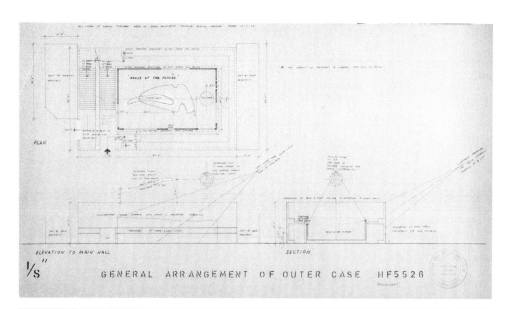

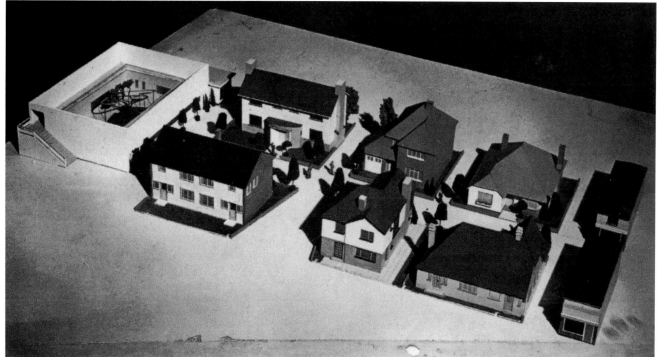

fig. 1 | Drawing of the Outer Case, House of the Future
for the *Daily Mail* Jubilee Ideal Home Exhibition, by
Alison and Peter Smithson, London, 1956

fig. 2 | Model as part of the layout of traditional houses,
House of the Future, 1956

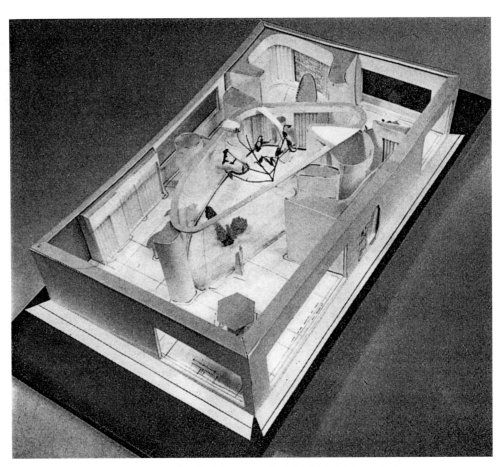

fig. 3 | Model, House of the Future, 1956

fig. 4 | Dressing room with Saddle Chair and two "inhabitants," House of the Future, 1956

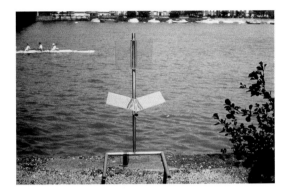

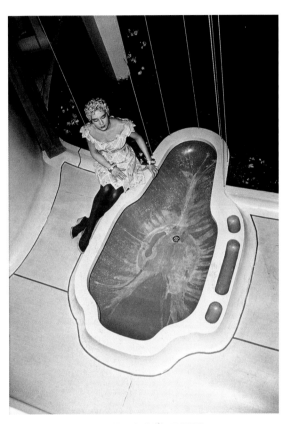

fig. 5 | Pogo Chair prototype, House of the Future, 1956

fig. 6 | Living room with hexagonal table in raised
position, serving trolley and Pogo, Petal, and Egg Chairs,
with back-projection television on the wall, House of the
Future, 1956

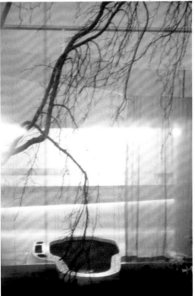

fig. 7 | "Inhabitant" operating the self-cleaning bathtub,
House of the Future, 1956

fig. 8 | The bathtub as seen from the patio, House of the
Future, 1956

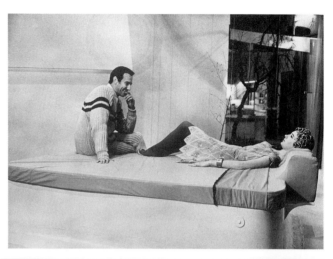

fig. 9 | Bedroom with "inhabitants," House of the Future, 1956

fig. 10 | Prepackaged food on the kitchen counter, House of the Future, 1956

fig. 11 | Model, Maison Plastique, by Ionel Schein, 1956

fig. 12 | Tupperware products displayed on a highway

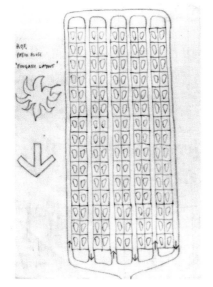

fig. 13 | "Fougasse" layout of a neighborhood of Houses of the Future, with a density of seventy houses to an acre, by Peter Smithson, 1955

fig. 14 | Drawing of clothing design for the "inhabitants," House of the Future, by Teddy Tinling, 1956

fiberglass chairs; of Tupperware bowls; and so on? | **figs. 11 and 12** A house that looks like a plastic consumer product and is meant to be mass-produced, easily transported on the back of a truck, and arrayed in a "dense mat of similar dwellings"—a "mat-cluster," as Alison put it?[3] | **fig. 13** A plastic version of the 1920s dream of the industrialized house then—but the dream was no longer of a series of standard elements that can be combined in different ways to produce different houses. Rather, the dream was of a series of unique molded shapes that could fit together in only one form.

The H.O.F. learned from plastic. It had the aura of plastic, the dream material of the time. Popular magazines had been heralding the arrival of the new material in the house for some years. A 1952 article in *Life* magazine entitled "House Full of Plastics," for example, cataloged the endless plastic contents of an American ranch style house. A house, any house, could be turned into a dream house simply by filling it with dream material. Four years later, experimental architects were turning the container, the house itself, into plastic.

The H.O.F. was received by the press as a plastic polemic. Article after article points to every plastic feature, from the translucent walls and chairs to food packaging and even the clothes, which a journalist described as follows:

FOR HIM. A Superman space outfit of nylon sweats and tights with foam rubber fitted soles
FOR HER. The Pixie look—a sort of nylon skirt with scalloped edge, and tights with high-heeled fitted soles.[4] | **fig. 14**

But in fact this plastic house was not made of plastic. It was a simulation, a full-scale mock-up in plywood, plaster, and emulsion paint, traditional materials collaborating to produce the effect of a continuous molded-plastic surface. As Peter put it: "It wasn't real. It was made of plywood. It was like an early airplane, where you make a series of forms, then you run the skin over them....It was not a prototype. It was like the design for a masque, like theatre."[5]

It was "make believe." Even the transparent plastic wall to the garden of the house was fake. Thin chromium wires tensioned between the floor and the ceiling created for the viewer the illusion of the curved transparent wall molded in metal-reinforced plastic described in the brochure of the house, when in fact the opening was left unglazed.[6] The Smithsons saw the tradition of such temporary theatrical structures as a centuries-old tradition in architecture:

> The architects of the Renaissance established ways of going about things which perhaps we unconsciously follow: for example, between the idea sketchily stated and the commission for the permanent building came the stage-architecture of the court masque; the architectural settings and decorations for the birthday of the prince, for the wedding of a ducal daughter, for the entry of a Pope into a city state; these events were used as opportunities for the realization of the new style; the new sort of space; the new weight of decoration; made real perhaps for a single day…the transient enjoyably consumed, creating the taste for the permanent.[7]

Like in the Renaissance, the H.O.F. was staged architecture, a shimmering masque, which doesn't make the proposal less provocative but perhaps more: "Like all exhibitions, they live a life of a few weeks, then they go on and on forever. Like the Barcelona pavilion before it was reconstructed."[8] The temporary turns out to be permanent.

.2008

> We decided to use acrylic to make transparent curtains.
>
> We imagined an installation design that leaves the existing space of the Barcelona Pavilion undisturbed.
>
> The acrylic curtain stands freely on the floor and is shaped in a calm spiral.
>
> The curtain softly encompasses the spaces within the pavilion and creates a new atmosphere.
>
> The view through the acrylic will be something different from the original with soft reflections slightly distorting the pavilion.[9]

SANAA in the Barcelona Pavilion. The ultimate encounter, since SANAA is widely considered the inheritor of Miesian transparency—a "challenge," as Kazuyo Sejima admitted, a return to the scene of the crime, one could argue. The installation carefully marks off a part of the pavilion with an acrylic curtain acting as a kind of crime scene tape, leaving, as SANAA put it, the "space of the Barcelona Pavilion undisturbed." | fig. 15

But what crime has been committed here? What has been cordoned off? Is it the freestanding golden onyx wall at the center of the pavilion and the two Barcelona chairs where King Alfonso XIII and Queen Victoria Eugenia of Spain were supposed to sit during the opening ceremonies of the building on May 26, 1929, and sign the golden book? Or is the space outside the spiral that has been marked off, preserved, "undisturbed?"

In any case, the cordon is loose. The spiral is open. We can walk in, but not so easily. First we have to find the entrance, slide around the outside of the curtain. Only when we are in the other side of the space of the pavilion, having squeezed between the acrylic curtain and the front glass wall of the pavilion, can we suddenly fold back into the spiral by making a 180-degree turn, which echoes the two 180-degree turns already required to enter the Barcelona pavilion. Just as Mies van der Rohe narrowed the entrance down, subtly constraining the visitor with a folded path, SANAA spins and

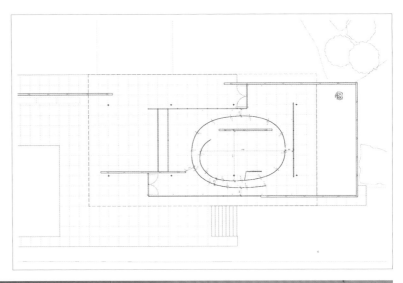

fig. 15 | Plan of Barcelona Pavilion with SANAA spiral
curtain, by SANAA, Barcelona, Spain, 2008

figs. 16 and 17 | Mies's Barcelona chairs and SANAA's
acrylic curtain and chair, Barcelona Pavilion, 2008

squeezes the visitor between the narrow planes of acrylic that curve around until suddenly one is inside, facing the two Barcelona chairs, or rather the chairs are facing us, as if the King and Queen were still there, sitting down, presiding over everything. | fig. 16

There is a new chair beside us, as if for us. It is a SANAA plywood chair with two asymmetrical bunny ears: whimsical, childlike, fragile, uncomfortable, funny. A kind of inexpensive school or cafeteria chair facing at an angle the wide, ceremonial, orthogonal, plush, leather and chrome chairs of Mies as if in some kind of playful challenge. | fig. 17 Another SANAA chair is placed outside the acrylic curtain, behind the Barcelona chairs, as if guarding the scene. The new chair represents SANAA just as much as the old one represents Mies. The new chair belongs to the acrylic curve while the old chairs belong to the marble.

What do they mean, the pavilion is "undisturbed?" Something has changed. In fact, everything seems to have changed. The simple spiral makes a new pavilion out of the old one—a pavilion inside a pavilion, each transforming the other to produce a whole new architecture. The most famous pavilion of the twentieth century becomes something else. All the classic images embedded in the brain of every architect now have additional layers of reflections.

SANAA returns the curtain to the pavilion, or is it the pavilion to the curtain? The acrylic freestanding curtain recalls the Velvet and Silk Cafe—a brilliant collaborative work of Lilly Reich and Mies for the *Exposition de la mode* in Berlin, two years before Barcelona, where draperies in black, orange, and red velvet and black and yellow lemon silk hung from metal rods to form the space. | fig. 18 The Cafe is a kind of prototype of the pavilion, in its radical approach to solely defining the space by suspending sensuous surfaces. In the pavilion the richly veined marble surfaces take over the role of the curtains—the hard surfaces absorbing softness. In fact, Mies pretends that they are curtains, denying that they have a structural role, even if we now know they did. That the walls are curtains may also explain why we don't enter the

Barcelona Pavilion frontally, but at an angle, as if entering behind a glass curtain on a stage.

SANAA's project reminds us that the Barcelona Pavilion comes from curtains, from a soft material. The beginnings of architecture were textile. It is a Semperian idea of architecture, beautifully adopted by Adolf Loos, who wrote:

> The architect's general task is to provide a warm and livable space. Carpets are warm and livable. He decides for this reason to spread one carpet on the floor and to hang up four to form the four walls. But you cannot build a house out of carpets. Both the carpet on the floor and the tapestry on the wall require a structural frame to hold them in the correct place. To invent this frame is the architect's second task.[10]

The space that SANAA has wrapped by the new transparent curtain is precisely the center of the pavilion, the throne room, the space the King and Queen of Spain would have occupied. In old pictures the space is marked by a black carpet on the floor, which nobody dares to step on. | figs. 19 and 20 SANAA's curtain is the invisible cloak, which further protects that space—a royal transparent cloak. The garment is moving. It billows outwards, allowing us to enter between its folds. Space is defined in a kind of invisible movement, neither limited nor unlimited, a paradox that the spiral has always communicated.

> "My house," writes Georges Spyridaki, "is diaphanous, but it is not of glass. It is more of the nature of vapor. Its walls contract and expand as I desire. At times, I draw them close about me like protective armor....But at others, I let the walls of my house blossom out in their own space, which is infinitely extensible." Spyridaki's house breathes. First it is a coat of armor, then it extends ad infinitum, which amounts to saying that we live in it in alternate security and adventure. It is both cell and world. Here geometry is transcended.[11]

fig. 18 | Velvet and Silk Cafe, Women's Fashion exhibition, by Lilly Reich and Mies van der Rohe, Berlin, 1927

fig. 19 | The throne room, Barcelona Pavilion, by Mies van der Rohe, Barcelona, 1929

fig. 20 | Woman on the edge of the carpet, Barcelona Pavilion, 1929

fig. 21 | Mies van der Rohe greeted by King Alfonso de Borbón on the inauguration day, Barcelona Pavilion, 1929

fig. 22 | Rendering of the Glass Pavilion at the Toledo Museum of Art, by SANAA, Toledo, Ohio, 2006

fig. 23 | Installation in the Barcelona Pavilion, by SANAA, Barcelona, 2008

SANAA's diaphanous curtain preserves the pavilion by allowing it to breathe. It is a kind a life support in a moment in which the subtlety of Mies might so easily be forgotten precisely because the building is so insistently celebrated. The single curtain slows us down, allows us to enter the pavilion again, as if on the day of its opening. | fig. 21 Once again, the fact that Mies did so little, when asked so much, can be appreciated. Yet what allows SANAA to take us back, or bring the pavilion again forward toward us, is that the curtain is precisely not transparent. What is added is not a clear window but a delicate veil. SANAA's acrylic, like its glass, is never neutral.

SANAA's vision is far from crystal clear. In fact, its architecture appears to be more interested in blurring the view, and softening the focus, than sustaining the transparency of early avant-garde architecture. | fig. 22 If Sejima is the inheritor of Miesian transparency, the latest in a long line of experiments, she is the ultimate Miesian, deepening the transparency logic into a whole new kind of mirage effect. The temporary acrylic curtain in Barcelona intensifies the Miesian effect. A plastic lens is placed inside a glass lens to intensify and therefore prolong the Miesian effect, the masque of modern architecture.

The ghost here is unambiguously modern architecture, preserved rather than transformed by subtle deflections. If the theatrical performance of the Smithsons looks forward to the plastic future, the theater of SANAA uses plastic itself to look tenderly backwards. It is the disturbance of the plastic that allows things to return to us undisturbed. | fig. 23

1 | "House of the Future," *House Beautiful,* May 1956; clipping in A&P Smithson Archives; and "House of the Future," *The Scottish Daily Mail Ideal Home Exhibition, Waverley Market,* June 29–July 14, 1956, 6; manuscript in A&P Smithson Archives.

2 | Alison and Peter Smithson, "The House of the Future," *Daily Mail Ideal Home Exhibition, Olympia, 1956,* exhibition catalog, 97.

3 | Alison Smithson, "The House of the Future, Ideal Home Exhibition, Olympia, end August 1955 to March 1956," manuscript in A&P Smithson Archives.

4 | The clothes for the actors' daily enacting the inhabitation of the house were designed by Teddy Tinling, a prominent designer of sportswear who designed tennis outfits for Wimbledon.

5 | Beatriz Colomina, "Friends of the Future: A Conversation with Peter Smithson," *October* 94 (Fall 2000): 24.

6 | Trevor Smith (exhibition architect), "Technical specifications" for the construction of the H.O.F., November 11, 1955, manuscript in A&P Smithson Archives.

7 | Alison and Peter Smithson, "Staging the Possible," in *Alison + Peter Smithson, Italian Thoughts* (Sweden: A&P Smithson, 1993): 16. See also the earlier version of the same argument in "The Masque and the Exhibition: Stages Toward the Real," *ILA&UD Year Book* (July 1982).

8 | Beatriz Colomina, "Friends of the Future," 24.

9 | Kazuyo Sejima and Ryue Nishizawa, *Intervention in the Mies van der Rohe Pavilion,* (Barcelona: Actar, 2010).

10 | Adolf Loos, "The Principle of Cladding," *Spoken into the Void: Collected Essays 1897-1900,* translated by Jane O. Newman and John H. Smith (Cambridge, Mass., and London: MIT Press, 1982): 66. Compare with Gottfried Semper's statement: "Hanging carpets remained the true walls, the visible boundaries of space. The often solid walls behind them were necessary for reasons that had nothing to do with the creation of space; they were needed for security, for supporting a load, for their permanence, and so on. Wherever the need for these secondary functions did not arise, the carpets remained the original means of separating space. Even where building solid walls became necessary, the latter were only the inner, invisible structure hidden behind the true and legitimate representatives of the wall, the colorful woven carpets." Gottfried Semper, "The Four Elements of Architecture: A Contribution to the Comparative Study of Architecture," *Gottfried Semper, The Four Elements of Architecture and Other Writings*, transl. by Harry Francis Mallgrave and Wolfgang Herrmann (Cambridge: Cambridge University Press, 1989): 104.

11 | Gaston Bachelard, *The Poetics of Space*, transl. by Maria Jolas (Boston: Beacon Press, 1969): 51. Bachelard is quoting Georges Spyridaki, *Mort lucide* (Paris: 1953): 35.

Structural Experiments in Inflatability

Chip Lord

The Boston City Hall was a highly influential building when
I was a student at Tulane School of Architecture from 1962
to 1968. | fig. 1 The building is a classic of Brutalism, and,
as such, it represents the dominant style of that decade.
Of course there were other influences during my student
career, including Archigram, Andy Warhol, and Marshall
McLuhan. The era ended with worldwide student protests
and rebellions that grew out of the civil rights movement, the
protest movement against the Vietnam War, and a general
sense that our parents' generation was on the wrong path to
the future. *The Graduate*, released in 1967, made famous the
one-word line of dialogue, "Plastic!" which was funny and
ironic because by 1967 plastic no longer held the promise of
the future that it had in the 1950s. It was a scene that also
spoke to the cultural gap between generations.

When I graduated in 1968, it seemed that no one in
my class wanted to take a job in a corporate architecture
office and design branch banks. A branch bank in Chula
Vista, California, had just been burned to the ground as a
protest against the Vietnam War. I moved to San Francisco
and founded an alternative architectural practice with Doug
Michels. To a friend we once described what we were doing
as "underground architecture," because you had "underground radio," "underground newspapers," and a sense
of an underground culture in San Francisco. The friend
replied, "Like the Ant Farm toy I had as a kid?" Yes! We now
had a name that was a perfect metaphor, and it also provided
a logo and an official color (green being the only color that
Ant Farms came in). | fig. 2

We moved to Houston in late 1968, when the University
of Houston College of Architecture offered us an invitation to
teach. Our first experiments used surplus cargo parachutes
as structures. They were extremely limited in their utility, as
they only provided shelter from the sun, but as architecture
these wind-supported single-membrane structures were the

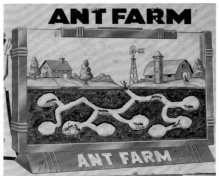

fig. 1 | Boston City Hall, by Kallmann McKinnell and
Knowles, Boston, Massachusetts, 1968

fig. 2 | Ant Farm toy, by Uncle Milton, 1956

fig. 3 | First architectural experiments that used surplus cargo parachutes as structures to provide shelter from the sun

fig. 4 | Interactive inflatables—a good wind would lift the user off the ground

fig. 8 | Clean Air Pod, by Ant Farm, at University of
California, Berkeley, 1970

fig. 9 | The inflatable dubbed "Ice 9" functioned as a
mobile life-support unit during the Truckstop Tour.

fig. 5 | Image technology combining photo documentation
with superimposed collage images

fig. 6 | The first giant pillow enclosed ten thousand square
feet of space.

fig. 7 | Demonstrating inflatables at the free Rolling
Stones concert at Altamont Speedway, December 1969

fig. 10 | Four point net holding down reinforced vinyl pillow, 1970

fig. 11 | Image showing the accident in which one of the earth augers failed, ending the reliability of the inflatable

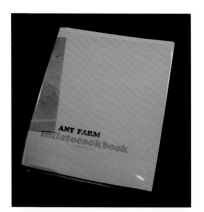

figs. 12 and 13 | Ant Farm's do-it-yourself manual *Inflatocookbook*, 1971

fig. 14 | House of the Century, by Ant Farm, Houston, 1972

symbolic opposite of Brutalism: lightweight, easily transport-able, ephemeral. | fig. 3 They were also interactive. They could be shaped by a user, and it was even possible to ride them; a good wind could lift you off the ground. | fig. 4 They were made of plastic-derived nylon, and thus they signaled an acceptance of technological solutions, in contrast to the back-to-the-land ethos of the counterculture. The fact that these parachutes began life as military hardware, and were being repurposed for pleasure and collective play, was not lost on Ant Farm.

We also engaged in a form of "image technology," combining photographic documentation with superimposed collaged images to expand the idea of what these struc-tures could do and represent. | fig. 5 These image works were shown as multiscreen projections and given illusion-ary names like *Dreamcloud, Electronic Oasis, Enviroman,* and *Plastic Businessman Meets Space Cowboy.* The naming of the projects was often accomplished by making a rubber stamp or Kwik Kopy stationery and then presenting it via publi-cation in *Architecture and Design, Domus,* or *Progressive Architecture.*

By late 1969 we had met Charley Tilford, a Columbia Uni-versity engineering graduate, who arrived in Houston with a black egg-shaped inflatable. Working with Tilford, we added inflatable structures to our repertoire. The first giant pillow enclosed ten thousand square feet of space with a polyethyl-ene skin anchored against the wind by a rope netting. | fig. 6 In its portability and temporality, it seemed like a high-tech circus tent, and it required a crew to erect and maintain it. The group expanded at this point, and the name "Ant Farm" was even sometimes suppressed in favor of the name "Pneu-mads." We spent much of our time on the road, demon-strating this and other structures at countercultural events, including the notorious December 1969 Rolling Stones con-cert at Altamont Speedway and a 1970 *Whole Earth Catalog* Demise party at the Exploratorium in San Francisco. | fig. 7

For the first Earth Day in April 1970, we were invited to the University of California, Berkeley campus, where we were proud to perform on the site of the Free Speech Move-ment. The Clean Air Pod was presented as a solution to the daily problem of smog and unhealthy air quality in the Bay Area. Dressed in lab coats and wearing gas masks, the Ant Farm crew announced, "There is an air emergency, every-one into the Clean Air Pod." This performance was derived from "die-ins" and other theatrical protest actions, but it is important to note that it also preceded serious techno-logical attempts to alleviate the air quality problem in, for example, Tokyo, as well as the amendments to the 1970 U.S. Clean Air Act.[1]

We moved on to somewhat more complex structures, incorporating vinyl as the primary material and acquir-ing a radio-frequency welder so that we could design and construct prototypes. These were tested in the field on the Truckstop Tour 1971, in which the inflatable dubbed "Ice 9" functioned as a mobile life-support unit. | figs. 8 and 9 The most strenuous test was a two-month summer residency in the woods at Goddard College in Vermont, where we lived in an inflatable named "Turbodome."

We also had a countercultural architectural commis-sion. A rock festival promoter hired us to design inflatable tents for a music event in Japan. (He disappeared once the prototype had been fabricated.) This was a fifty-by-fifty-foot pillow with reinforced six-millimeter vinyl on the bottom, transparent ends, and a translucent top. We designed a sim-ple four-point net using four hundred-pound webbing and employed giant earth anchors to hold it down. | fig. 10 The strength of the vinyl allowed for more vigorous usage. We often climbed on top as the inflatable was filling, and kids loved to throw themselves against its walls and bounce back. This structure was the central meeting space for the 1970 Freestone Conference, a gathering of architects and design-ers interested in alternative methods.[2]

In late 1970, Stewart Brand rented the fifty-by-fifty-foot pillow for the production of the *Whole Earth Catalog* Supple-ment, which involved a sojourn to the Saline Valley, west of Death Valley in Southern California. The blowers were powered by a gas generator. Midway through the three-week trip, one of the earth augers failed, ending the reliability of the inflatable space for editorial writing.[3] | **fig. 11** Although the only casualty was an IBM Selectric typewriter, which suffered fatal damage, this disaster underscored the limitations of inflatables. They had originated to be symbolic buildings and to create architectural experiences, but they fell short in situations requiring dependable climate control and stable functional space.

The inflatable period ended for Ant Farm with the publication of *Inflatocookbook* in 1971. This do-it-yourself manual was inspired by Steve Baer's *Dome Cookbook* and *Zome Primer,* as well as the motto of the *Whole Earth Catalog*: "access to tools." | **figs. 12 and 13** We were not interested in making inflatable products per se; rather, our mission was to share information in order to empower other builders and inflators. The *Inflatocookbook* was self-published in a first run of one thousand and sold for $3. It was so successful that we printed a second edition a year later with the comic book producer Rip Off Press. Today you can find it online as a PDF, and it has been instrumental in at least one commercial product: in 2003 the American film and music video director Roman Coppola used the *Inflatocookbook* to build a 150-foot-long inflatable in which he shot the television advertisement introducing the Toyota Prius to the California market.

In 1972 Ant Farm secured an architectural commission for a weekend house for Marilyn and Alvin Lubetkin on a man-made lake in the swampland thirty-five miles southeast of Houston.[4] It was in exasperation that Alvin named this design-build project the House of the Century, but we thought the name made sense. We were using ferrocement as the primary material, and surely it would last one hundred years. The finished house reflects the influence of the inflatable years, but the design is equally inspired by the bulbous shape of the fenders of early automobiles, especially the 1938 Cord. | **fig. 14** We had arrived at a "permanent" material that could be plastically and sensually expressive while still being symbolically opposed to Brutalism.

1 | In 1992, to cope with NOx pollution problems from existing vehicle fleets in highly populated metropolitan areas, Japan's Ministry of the Environment adopted the Law Concerning Special Measures to Reduce the Total Amount of Nitrogen Oxides Emitted from Motor Vehicles in Specified Areas, or "The Motor Vehicle NOx Law" in short. The regulation designated a total of 196 communities in the Tokyo, Saitama, Kanagawa, Osaka, and Hy go prefectures as areas with significant air pollution due to nitrogen oxides emitted from motor vehicles. Under the law, several measures had to be taken to control NOx from in-use vehicles, including enforcing emission standards for specified vehicle categories.

2 | For a more complete description of this conference, see Felicity D. Scott, *Ant Farm: Living Archive 7* (New York: Actar, 2008), 73. An issue *of Progressive Architecture* was devoted to this conference and included pages designed by the participants.

3 | Ibid., 81.

4 | The architect and builder Richard Jost partnered with me and Doug Michels to realize this project. It was designed in late 1971 and built by Nationwide Builders (Jost, Lord, and Michels) throughout 1972. The project won a *Progressive Architecture* Awards citation in 1973. When completed, it was published in *Progressive Architecture* magazine.

Plastic Man Strikes, Again (and Again)

Felicity D. Scott

In March 1968 the critic John Perreault reported in *ARTnews* on the recent work of the Irish-Canadian artist Les Levine under the title "Plastic Man Strikes." "Mild-mannered, soft-spoken Les Levine, wearing his horn-rimmed glasses," Perreault began, "steps into a telephone booth, orders a new plastic dome and almost everyone is infuriated."[1] | fig. 1 In his use of this communications technology, Levine is referencing László Moholy-Nagy, who in the 1947 edition of *The New Vision* famously claimed to have ordered the fabrication of a set of enamel-on-metal paintings in 1922 by dictating instructions by telephone to a sign manufacturer; each party was equipped with a piece of graph paper and an industrial color chart. Forging new stakes for artistic engagement with industry by staging a withdrawal of the "individual touch," Moholy-Nagy insisted that the manufacturer on the other end of the line had executed the so-called telephone paintings entirely in the artist's absence.[2] | fig. 2

Forty-five years later, it seemed such mediation by telephone was no longer critically in alignment with heroic modernist ideals. Perreault noted the "irrational fury and defensiveness" provoked by Levine's work, as manifest in statements such as "Les Levine is a science-fiction artist out to destroy Western Culture." He proposed that the key culprit was plastic, which, as he put it, had "negative overtones—plastic people, plastic food, etc." "Since his 'discovery' of industrial vacuum and pressure molding techniques," Perreault reported of Levine, "he has worked exclusively in plastic."[3]

By 1968 Levine did not, in fact, work exclusively in plastic, a detail Perreault later alluded to when he referenced the artist's "non-apologetic use of technology" such as television, computers, and print-based media. Yet something about the artist's engagement with the plastics industry, and hence with a material so identified with mass consumer culture, clearly resonated uncomfortably with

fig. 1 | Les Levine on the telephone

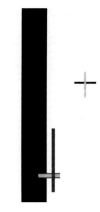

fig. 2 | *Em (Telephone Picture)*, by László Moholy-Nagy, 1922

fig. 3 | *The Clean Machine*, by Les Levine, Fischbach Gallery, New York, 1969

conventional ideas at the time regarding the role of artistic practice. Levine's work played with contradictions within long-standing modernist tropes (such as truth to materials and the benefits of collaboration between art and industry) and within avant-garde pursuits of the dialectical sublimation of art into life. Here, it seems, was a *too* comfortable fit. Moreover, these uncomfortable resonances, I want to posit, might have something to say about the object of my own discipline, architecture, which encountered a similar nexus of historical forces at this moment. To unpack the nature of Levine's provocation, I want to begin by looking at his work from 1968, and Perreault's reading of it, before turning back to the previous year and then to his shift away from plastics to electronics—or really to the desublimation of electronics—soon afterward.

The article "Plastic Man Strikes" appeared on the occasion of Levine's solo show at Fischbach Gallery in New York. The announcement for the show read: "Caution: Some Plastics May be Hazardous to Your Health." Levine presented two new plastic works: *Disposable Walls* and *The Clean Machine*. If the former exemplified his ongoing project of mass-producing cheap, disposable art—literally art objects intended to be thrown away by the collector once their aesthetic effects had worn off—the latter exemplified the other primary modality of his work: the production of "environments," or what Perreault referred to in his article as "epistemological environments." | fig. 3

Disposable Walls took the form of eight brightly colored, satin-finished, vacuum-formed metallic butyrate plastic units, their shape reminiscent of refrigerators. Levine posited in his press release—itself a creative work—that his walls were "conceived as anonymous objects to be arranged in sequence by the purchaser to his own specifications."[4] (Philip Johnson, it was later reported, purchased a whole wall.[5]) *The Clean Machine*, by contrast, was "composed of 60 plastic units with a glossy white finish arranged to form a passageway around the perimeter of the gallery space. Each of the plastic forms is four feet wide by six feet high by eighteen inches deep at the point of greatest projection and is made of pressure-formed Uvex, a cellulose acetate butyrate plastic."[6]

Levine continued in the press release: "I am concerned primarily with making a work not entirely reliant upon visual devices, but also a work that is physically experiential." He continued, in a manner reminiscent of Walter Benjamin's famous account of architecture being received in a state of distraction,[7] "I want the work to be free of visual references because they are related to the idea of contemplation and I want a work that one can experience as one goes through it without having to 'look' at it. The spaces in the piece are constantly opening and closing as the spectator passes through it, so that one is constantly being physically reminded of one's size, how one walks, and how one's senses react to space."[8]

Perreault also reviewed the exhibition for the *Village Voice* under the title "Plastic Ambiguities," noting that when one walks through this distinctly nonstatic piece, "nothing seems to happen."

It is only after you have walked through the glistening corridor of *The Clean Machine* and come out the other end, in perhaps two minutes flat, that you begin to realize that something very perplexing has just happened. All the modules are exactly the same, and so there is no reason to stop and look at any particular one of them. They are too close, in fact, to allow you to stand back and take a reading. They protrude almost dangerously and combine a cold hard look with an illusion of softness created by their surface reflections. The forced perspective created by the trapezoidal protrusions pulls you along at breakneck speed through this almost featureless circular maze. In a work that on the surface seems very simple and very empty, Levine combines several different ways we have of reading space and lets them rub up against each other and contradict each other in a way that is new and almost completely successful. The trapezoids

describe the single-point perspective used in traditional drawings, except here the vanishing point is continually elusive.[9]

After noting that this "high-speed work" prompted him to walk through its passageways five or six times, trying (unsuccessfully, it seems) to grasp what was causing the effect, Perreault concluded of its exhilarating impact, "All I know is that I found myself wishing that I could take off all my clothes and walk through it naked to get the full charge of its ambiguous tactility."[10]

In a landmark 1968 *Artforum* essay on postformalist art practices titled "Systems Esthetics," the critic Jack Burnham situated Levine's *The Clean Machine* within an artistic lineage traced from Moholy-Nagy's telephone works and continuing through Ad Reinhardt's black paintings, Donald Judd's concept of "specific objects," Robert Morris's L-beams, and Morris's recent earthworks and his steam piece for Willoughby Sharp's Air Art exhibition of 1968, to Carl Andre's modular floor pieces. The very scope of such systems-based work, Burnham argued, necessitated interdisciplinarity, or the refusal of "boundary concepts" through which modern art usually operated. "Consequently," as he put it, "some of the more aware sculptors no longer think like sculptors, but they assume a span of problems more natural to architects, urban planners, civil engineers, electronic technicians, and cultural anthropologists."[11] It was at this point Burnham turned to Levine, whom he called "methodologically...the most consistent exponent of a systems aesthetic." "Levine's *The Clean Machine* has no ideal vantage points," he noted, "no 'pieces' to recognize, as are implicit in formalist art. One is *processed* as in driving through the Holland Tunnel. Certainly this echoes Michael Fried's reference to Tony Smith's nighttime drive along the uncompleted New Jersey Turnpike. Yet if this is theater, as Fried insists, it is not the stage concerned with focused-upon events."[12]

In addition to Levine's having moved beyond the "boundary definitions" circumscribing conventional art mediums,

fig. 4 | *Electric Shock*, by Les Levine, University of
Michigan, Ann Arbor, Michigan, 1968

fig. 5 | *The Star Garden*, by Les Levine, Museum of Modern
Art, New York, 1967

Burnham noted that the artist's "visual disengagement" extended to the point where "in a recent environment by Levine rows of live electric wires emitted small shocks to passersby. Here behavior is controlled in an esthetic situation with no primary reference to visual circumstances. As Levine insists, 'What I am after here is physical reaction, not visual concern.'"[13] The work, titled *Electric Shock*, was indeed an extreme case of an artwork confronting the beholder and existing only through his or her participation. As the critic David Bourdon argued in a *Life* magazine article on Levine titled "The Plastic Arts' Biggest Bubble,"

> This "place" consists of a completely bare room equipped with a row of overhead wires, creating a false ceiling a few inches above spectators' heads. At regular intervals a high-frequency generator charges the wires with electrostatic energy, giving a jolt to any spectator who happens to touch the wires, as well as anybody they happen to be touching. People are drawn together (or apart) because they can hold hands and get a charge (or escape) from one another.[14] | fig. 4

Before I address the question of what might have motivated such a work, I want to return to several slightly earlier works that exacerbated the suspension of the observer within a matrix, or system, of information. Running concurrently with the Fischbach Gallery show was a second, related exhibition of Levine's work at John Gibson Gallery in New York, a sort of retrospective of earlier plastic pieces, now rendered somewhat allegorical in miniature. It included seven scale models of works comprising the *Star Series*, three of which indicated new possible arrangements of his clear plastic "bubbles," the other four recalling their organization within recent exhibitions: *The Star Garden (A Place)* (1967); *All-Star Cast* (1967), installed in the plaza of the Time and Life Building; *The Star Machine* (1965); and *Prime Time Star* (1967).

The modules for the *Star Series* were fabricated using a distinct technique, and unlike *The Clean Machine,* transparency was key to their operation. Consider, for instance, *The Star Garden (A Place)*, installed on the upper terrace of the sculpture garden of the Museum of Modern Art in New York. | fig. 5 Covering an area of forty square feet and standing about seven feet high, the work was composed of four sets of four modules arranged to form bubble-sided cubes, each mounted on aluminum uprights with two-foot aisles between them. With materials donated by the American Cyanamid Company's Building Products Division, each bubble derived from a clear Acrylite plastic sheet that, as the press release explained, had "been heated and then shaped by jets of air into rounded forms." The press release also noted that Levine referred to the work as an "architectural device." As with *The Clean Machine*, the artist insisted on the primacy of the viewer, explaining

> the piece has no importance without people—the viewer enters and becomes the "star." The piece is concerned with physical experience rather than visual contemplation, it has no validity until someone is inside it, not simply looking at it. The work is almost invisible—intentionally. The viewer is more aware of his own physiognomy and of the people and objects outside *The Star Garden (A Place)*, not in a visual way but in a sensory way, than of the piece itself. It is intended literally as a place to be in, rather than an object. It packages people in endless space and makes them look more beautiful, shiny, and new.[15]

Critics repeatedly mused over the fact that these bubbles were not the product of the artist's hand. Recalling Moholy-Nagy's earlier claims, Levine stated, "I simply phoned up the plastics company, told them to take 16 sheets of Acrylite plastic and free-blow it to the size I wanted, and filled in some other technical details. I never went to the factory—five minutes over the phone was all that was needed. I never touch my work at all.... Nowadays, all the artist has to do is think about the piece and tell the proper person what he wants.... The artist's real function is to conceptualize."[16] Such a hands-off

approach to fabrication is, of course, entirely familiar to architects, whose practice consists not of making buildings but of conceptualizing and issuing instructions for them; in other words, producing documents of mediation.

Key to the physical experience, or physical reaction, provoked by *The Star Garden (A Place)* was a feeling of weight-lessness, or what Levine called "the sensation of your body lifting up and down." Interviewed for *Art in America*, the artist offered a clue as to what might be at stake, noting, "People stretch their hands out, since they don't know where the edges are. They can't feel boundaries, and yet they know there's some kind of restraint."[17] On July 2, 1967, Levine and *The Star Garden (A Place)* appeared on WCBS-TV in the hour-long broadcast "Eye on Art: The Walls Come Tumbling Down." Speaking with Levine, the commentator Leonard Harris referenced the notion of breaking down the "wall...between you and your environment." Levine responded: "It also has the effect of bringing you the information immediately surrounding the area, in that, if you look at it as you pass through it, you see the buildings that are the surround [sic] here. So what you get is the sensation of your own physicality, plus the information around you. And you get a funny sensation, because for the first time in your life you see yourself moving in the environment in which you really move."[18] That is, right from these earliest works, the phenomenological dimension of reception was already understood to be inscribed within a perceptual and conceptual matrix derived from an information paradigm. The work aimed to produce the experience of time-based media, like closed-circuit television without affiliated equipment.

In addition to art press, *The Star Garden (A Place)* garnered significant chemical industry coverage. Tom Bross, customer relations manager for American Cyanamid Co., referred to it as "an attractive exposure vehicle for Acrylite," since it demonstrated the material's key properties: "toughness, weatherability, formability, light transmission and clarity."[19] That is to say, with plastic, the old modernist adage of truth to materials made smart business sense as well.

While *The Star Garden (A Place)* was on view at the Museum of Modern Art, Levine was installing another (and, to many observers, even more psychedelic) environment called *Slipcover* at the Architectural League of New York, where he served as vice president for sculpture. Previously exhibited in a slightly different configuration in an octagonal gallery at Toronto's Art Gallery of Ontario in 1966, the work in its new appearance was timed to coincide with the national convention of the American Institute of Architects, that year taking place in New York. *Slipcover* was a plastic environment whose floors, ceilings, and pulsating walls were covered, as the press release noted, with "Mirro-Brite, a mirror-finished metalized polyester film supplied by Coating Products, Inc., Englewood, New Jersey."[20] | fig. 6 "When you tire of it," the artist explained to the *New York Times* critic Rita Reif of his use of a "shimmering synthetic fabric" to create "disposable rooms," "you rip it off and throw it away."[21] As Levine noted when interviewed during the installation of the project in Toronto, "A slipcover is a very common object which is used by most people to change their world." Like a slipcover that gives a piece of furniture a new surface, this one could just as readily be removed and replaced.[22] | fig. 7

The most detailed account of the spatio-visual topology of *Slipcover*, with its mirrored surfaces, projected images, and "air-erections," was set out by Perreault for the *Village Voice*: "The Mirro-Brite material," he explained,

> dissolves, conceals and expands the actual space involved into a labyrinth of shiny textures and reflections....It is like being inside an iceberg that has no top, bottom, or sides. Slide projectors bounce colors and subliminal images off the mirroresque surfaces and increase the spatial dislocations brought about by the billowing, breathing, bag-forms that are inflated programmatically by concealed rotary-blowers and alternately expand and contract the space around them as they themselves expand and contract, at times almost filling the rooms and forcing the viewer up against his own reflection.

At once cool and calculated yet strangely "organic," Perreault said, "the effect of these dazzling vinyl-scented explorations of synthetic materials, concealments, and space manipulations...is eerie, fascinating, and coldly beautiful....It is like a cave of crystal that hovers dangerously between a beautiful daydream and a crazy nightmare."[23]

Levine insisted of the installation in Toronto that "visual and audio feedback is the most important aspect" and that "it creates extended human consciousness in the same way as sophisticated computers. The computer system is based on memory, and the computer extends its own memory by the feedback of information it produces. The simultaneous vision of what was there and the immediate memory will create a scary, peculiar sense of a reality which is more than real."[24] In this he was referring not only to the work's closed-circuit television component but also to the plastic. In addition to a reorientation of temporal structures and the uncanny exteriorizing of memory, there was another, perhaps more trippy dimension to this cybernetic experience, a sort of melting into the environment (familiar to psychedelic literature) born of the reflective plastic.[25] The use of plastic, that is, also mirrored the subject's dissolution into technological systems through the viewer's "integration" within information environments.

In this case, the plastic resulted from Levine's own industrial research. It was developed "from formulae he evolved after research at Kodak" and had been "especially made for him in New Jersey."[26] As the artist explained of its intended qualities:

> The shiny surface is not only clean and precise, but it also attaches itself to you. It draws you to it to some degree. Reflective things, highly shiny surfaces do attach you to them in a strange abstract way. Even though you are across the room from them, you still have some rapport with them.[27]

Levine seemed happy with the outcome. As reported by the *Toronto Globe and Mail*, the artist, wearing a reflective suit,

Plastic Man Strikes, Again (and Again)
Felicity D. Scott

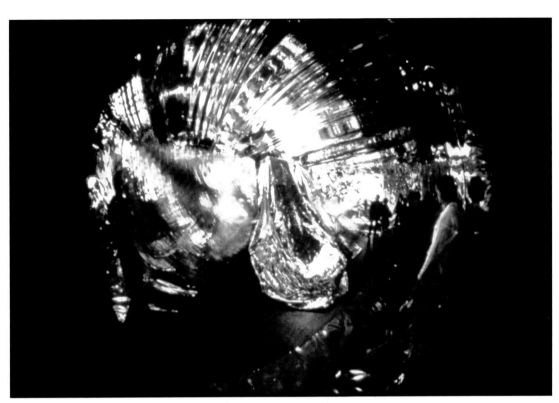

fig. 6 | *Slipcover*, by Les Levine, Art Gallery of Ontario, Toronto, 1966

fig. 7 | *Slipcover*, by Les Levine, the Architectural League of New York, New York, 1967

observed the piece with great pleasure. "'Oh God, isn't that fantastic?' he said. 'You see how it doesn't need me any-more? It has a mind of its own. Everything here has its own feedback. It's just like a computer, the more information you give it, the more it feeds back to you. You just can't keep up with it.'"[28]

Genuine Plastic

1968 was in many regards a watershed moment—even the apotheosis—of the art world's engagement with plastic. Levine's work appeared in the three key exhibitions that year addressing the material (or, as repeatedly suggested, the new medium) of plastic. On October 18, 1968, Made of Plastic opened at the Flint Institute of Arts in Michigan. Alongside works by Andy Warhol, Paul Thek, Hans Haacke, Robert Morris, Louise Nevelson, Claes Oldenburg, Donald Judd, Eva Hesse, and others, Levine presented *Mini-Star* (1967). The following month, the Museum of Contemporary Crafts in New York opened the show PLASTIC as Plastic. In addition to artworks, it included works categorized as architectural applications, furniture and interior accessories, housewares and appliances, packaging, historical (such as Bakelite), technological applications (for instance laboratory equipment, medical syringes, portable toilets, electronic equipment, prosthetic body parts), and toys.

In PLASTIC as Plastic, Levine's *Disposables* (1967) appeared alongside both mass consumer disposable arti-facts and also experimental architectural works, including Haus-Rucker Co.'s *Balloon for Two* (1967), *Yellow Heart* (1968), and *Room Scraper* (1969); a model of Yutaka Murata's proj-ect for the Fuji Group Pavilion at the upcoming 1970 Osaka Expo; Arthur Quarmby's inflatable domes produced for the 20th Century Fox film *The Touchables* (1968); Ugo La Pietra's installation for the 1968 Milan Triennale; a model of Matti Suuronen's 1968 Futuro house; and Felix Drury's experimen-tal foam houses for Union Carbide.

Finally, A Plastic Presence opened in November 1969 at New York's Jewish Museum. The exhibition attempted to address, or rather *redress*, the way in which plastic con-founded conventional notions of a material or a medium's specificity, since with plastic both the material and the optical properties—color, transparency, toughness, duc-tility, diffraction qualities, etc.—could be designed. It fea-tured a wide-ranging group of artists that notably included many women: not only Nevelson and Hesse but also Helen Pashgian, Susan Lewis Williams, Sylvia Stone, and Vera Simons. Levine presented *Body Color* (1969). The photo-graph he submitted for the catalog showed him on the telephone. *Body Color* would be Levine's last major plastic bubble work. It took the form of an approximately sixty-foot-long walk-through sequence of fifteen pairs of acrylic plastic domes, which varied in color and opacity. | fig. 8 As Bourdon explained in "The Plastic Arts' Biggest Bubble," "Everybody gets a physical reaction out of *Body Color*....Seen from the outside, people change color, then disappear from view as they pass through different opaque units."[29]

Environments

At the Architectural League, *Slipcover* was officially titled *Environment III: Slipcover*, as it was part of a series of exhi-bitions exploring concepts of environment.[30] The series was an initiative of the architect Ulrich Franzen, who had just become the director of the League and who, in 1967, was fea-tured alongside the architect and critic Peter Blake in one of Levine's early video works, simply titled *Architecture*. This video was exhibited at the League as part of the artist's televi-sion series *The Big Eye*.

As suggested by the critic Harold Rosenberg in October 1967, by this time the term *environment*—encom-passing both postobject practices and work engaging the spectator in a spatial unfolding—had itself become some-what ubiquitous, if not cliche. Referencing the series at the League, Rosenberg wryly noted, "To label a project an Environment qualifies it as significant and avant-garde." Yet to him it came with a subjection to control mechanisms that warranted interrogation. If, as he argued, one could

fig. 8 | *Body Color*, by Les Levine, New York University, Loeb Student Center, New York, 1967

recognize the derivation of environmental art from the functionalist aesthetics of the Bauhaus as well as its indebtedness to Happenings and mixed-media performances, there was an important historical distinction to be made. Stressing a shift from tropes of high modernism to paradigms of management and regulation, he explained:

> What separates the current art from Bauhaus constructions is the rise of Environments in a period when managed, or programmed, living space, from dwellings to metropolitan "cores," is envisaged by architects, engineers, and community planners as dominating the environment, the sensations, and, ultimately, the decisions of human masses. Space travel, too, has brought the necessity for a completely controlled environment, both within the vehicle of transportation and at the point of arrival. To Buckminster Fuller, the living conditions of the astronaut are the first instance in human history of totally regulated space occupancy, and to him the astronaut's cabin provides the ultimate model for planned utilization of the world's resources.…Responding to phenomena of this order, Environmental painters and sculptors carry their medium into the domain of architects and engineers.[31]

At stake for Rosenberg, and certainly for many historians and critics, including Burnham, was, as he put it, the need for a "renewed questioning of the viability of art and of the position of the artist as creator in the technological age." Indeed, we might recall, Burnham opened his essay "Systems Esthetics" by musing on the rise of technocracy and new paradigms of research. "Already in California think-tanks and in the central planning committees of each soviet, futurologists are concentrating on the role of technocracy, i.e., its decision-making autonomy, how it handles the central storage of information, and the techniques used for smoothly implementing social change. In the automated state power resides less in the control of traditional symbols of wealth than in information."[32] By "think-tanks" he was no doubt referencing the

RAND Corporation, which was soon to be a key protagonist in Levine's "service"-based conceptual works.

It is here that the key lessons of Levine's plastic work might lie, at least in the sense of the stakes it articulates for architecture. Of more consequence than the more literal association of his work with architectural and urban spaces under the rubric of *environment*, was his recognition and critical and conceptual interrogation of how the artist might operate within a contemporary society of computerized information and control mechanisms. This he understood very precisely as a systems environment subject to related forms of analysis. "Art in the future will be like a Think Tank experience," Levine wryly proposed in 1969.[33] And, later that year, "The ecology of the United States is technology."[34]

In his April 1970 *Artforum* article "Les Levine: Business as Usual," Burnham returned to the provocation of the artist's use of plastic.

> Levine's *The Clean Machine* is a most elegant summation of Minimalist esthetics, traditionally made palatable for some critics by the inclusion of various surface and spatial articulations relating to, or defying, older traditions. But Levine removed and transformed these allusions into sterile, vacuum-molded, plastic projections, forcing us to deal with the question, "Can you accept this as an esthetic experience, even if it is not prettied up with art historical allusions?" Few of us could.[35]

The unpalatable or discomforting nature of Levine's plastics works seems to have arisen in part from the sources of such commodified materials and what he considered to be a capacity of plastic: its ability to cleanse the visual environment of art historical allusions and visual referents. As Bourdon's comments make clear, to many, plastics exhibited an uncomfortable or too-obvious proximity to corporate capitalism; he noted in one article that critics "disapprove of his [Levine's] popularity with corporations, which have showered him with thousands of dollars' worth of materials."[36]

Moreover, as suggested in a work like *Electric Shock*, Levine's work spoke not only of the conventions of modernist artistic practice—its mediums and modes of reception (which it certainly attempted to breach, as had minimalism)—but also of the subjection of bodies and populations to emergent regimes of power, of the subject's inscription within a highly technologized spatial and temporal matrix through which he or she encountered—we might even say participated in—micropolitical techniques of control. Through its use of plastic, a material produced by multinational corporations and exhibiting an ever-more-capillary reach within mass culture and the everyday environment, the work perhaps alluded too directly to the supremacy of American capitalism in the 1960s and its role in forging new regimes of governmentality through technology. Recall the announcement for the Fischbach Gallery show featuring *Disposable Walls* and *The Clean Machine*: "Caution: Some Plastics May be Hazardous to Your Health."

I would like to thank Michael Bell for the kind invitation to speak at Permanent Change and hence for the opportunity to present publicly aspects of my current research on Les Levine. I would also like to acknowledge the generous support of an Arts Writers Grant from Creative Capital / Andy Warhol Foundation, which has helped fund my work on the artist, and especially I would like to thank Les Levine himself for his generosity in allowing me to undertake an extensive interview and in tracking down some rare articles and reviews on short notice. This text forms part of a broader exhibition and book project addressing his work from the mid-1960s to the mid-1970s.

1 | John Perreault, "Plastic Man Strikes," *ARTnews* (March 1968): 38.

2 | See László Moholy-Nagy, *The New Vision* (New York: Wittenborn, 1947): 79–80. See also Louis Kaplan, "The Telephone Paintings: Hanging Up Moholy," *Leonardo* 26, no. 2 (1993): 165–68.

3 | Perreault, "Plastic Man Strikes," 38.

4 | Les Levine, press release, "The Clean Machine," February 20, 1968.

5 | See Stewart Kranz, *Science & Technology in the Arts: A Tour Through the Realm of Science + Art* (New York: Van Nostrand Reinhold, 1974): 235.

6 | Levine, "The Clean Machine."

7 | See Walter Benjamin, "The Work of Art in the Age of Its Technological Reproducibility," in *Walter Benjamin: Selected Writings, Vol. 3: 1935–1938*, ed. Michael W. Jennings (Cambridge, MA: Belknap Press of Harvard University Press, 2002): 101–33.

8 | Levine, "The Clean Machine."

9 | John Perreault, "Plastic Ambiguities," *Village Voice*, March 7, 1968, 19.

10 | Ibid.

11 | Jack Burnham, "Systems Esthetics," *Artforum* 7, no. 1 (September 1968): 30–35. Reprinted in Jack Burnham, *Great Western Salt Works: Essays on the Meaning of Post-Formalist Art* (New York: George Braziller, 1974): 18. All page references are to the reprinted version.

12 | Ibid., 20. See also Michael Fried, "Art and Objecthood," in *Art and Objecthood: Essays and Reviews* (Chicago: University of Chicago, 1998): 148–72.

13 | Burnham, "Systems Esthetics," 20.

14 | David Bourdon, "The Plastic Arts' Biggest Bubble: Les Levine Bursts with Elusive Ideas—and Ego," *Life*, August 22, 1969, 66.

15 | Museum of Modern Art, press release no. 36, exhibition 825, "The Star Garden (A Place)," April 21, 1967.

16 | Les Levine, cited in Jane Margold, "And Now Bubbles Pop into the Art Picture," *Newsday*, May 9, 1967.

17 | Les Levine, cited in Thelma R. Newman, "The Artist Speaks: Les Levine," *Art in America* (November/December 1969).

18 | Les Levine, cited in Kranz, *Science & Technology in the Arts*, 69.

19 | Tom Bross, "When—and How—Should a Company Support Fine Art," 1967, clipping from the Museum of Modern Art Archives, PI II.A.223.

20 | Architectural League of New York, press release, "*Slipcover* by Les Levine Will be Presented at Architectural League," April 20, 1967.

21 | Rita Reif, "And the Walls Come Tumbling Down," *New York Times*, April 19, 1967, 32.

22 | Les Levine, "An Interview with Les Levine," by Brydon Smith, in *Slipcover: A Place by Les Levine* (Toronto: Art Gallery of Ontario, 1966): 2–3.

23 | John Perreault, "Stars," *Village Voice*, May 4, 1967, 13.

24 | Levine, "An Interview with Les Levine," in *Slipcover*, 2.

25 | On this trope in architecture, see Felicity D. Scott, "Acid Visions," in *Architecture or Techno-Utopia: Politics After Modernism* (Cambridge, MA: MIT Press, 2007): 185–206.

26 | Barrie Hale, "Slipcover: A Theatrical Place," *Toronto Daily Star*, 1966. Clipping courtesy of the artist.

27 | Levine, "An Interview with Les Levine," in *Slipcover*, 3.

28 | Les Levine, cited in Kay Kritzwiser, "Levine Returns with Wall-to-Wall Levine," *Globe and Mail*, April 1966. Clipping courtesy of the artist.

29 | Bourdon, "The Plastic Arts' Biggest Bubble," 62–67.

30 | The series also included *Environment II: Prisms, Lenses, Water, Light*, a collaboration between artist Charles Ross and USCO (a collaborative of artists, engineers, and filmmakers) and *Environment V: Vibrations* by the light artists Jackie Cassen and Rudi Stern.

31 | Harold Rosenberg, "The Art World: Lights! Lights!" *New Yorker*, October 21, 1967.

32 | Burnham, "Systems Esthetics," 15.

33 | Les Levine, "For Immediate Release," *Art and Artists* 4, no. 5 (May 1969): 47.

34 | Newman, "The Artist Speaks: Les Levine."

35 | Jack Burnham, "Les Levine: Business as Usual," *Artforum* (April 1970). Reprinted in Burnham, *Great Western Salt Works*, 39.

36 | Bourdon, "The Plastic Arts' Biggest Bubble," 65.

From Boat to Bust: The Monsanto House Revisited

Theodore Prudon

In the decades after World War II, the American Dream seemed to be within reach. The real estate developer Abraham Levitt had made the attainment of a freestanding house on a small plot of land possible for (almost) everyone, and the auto designer Harley Earl had ushered into being the Corvette and the tailfin, both icons of speed and the future. The "Arsenal of Democracy" was to be turned into a machine for prosperity and consumption.[1] The first steps in this direction were to convert factories over to peacetime production, to apply wartime industrial planning techniques to new ends, and to find a purpose for the many new synthetic materials that had been discovered or developed during the war.[2]

One of these was fiberglass, which is moldable into almost any form, with the glass fibers taking on the role of rebar in concrete. Fiberglass products were found to be lightweight, able to resist high impacts, and able to take on myriad vibrant colors. They inspired a sense of unlimited opportunities and affordability. More than any other material, fiberglass became associated with futuristic aesthetics and connotations of social equality. These cultural associations—together with a long-standing tradition in architecture of designing and building "houses of the future"—prompted a number of companies to showcase futuristic, ideal homes whose living spaces, furniture, and décor were constructed entirely of plastic.[3] Some efforts along these lines had already begun in the 1930s and 1940s. Plastics got a boost in 1940, when *Fortune* magazine ran a series of articles highlighting the plastics industry and the Museum of Modern Art in New York hosted an exhibition of everyday domestic items, all made of plastic and all retailing for less than $10.

Plastics were concurrently being investigated for use in panelized systems in houses. The Vinylite House debuted at the Century of Progress International Exposition in Chicago in 1933; Vinylite, a copolymer of vinyl chloride and vinyl acetate, was used for all parts of the building. The plan had three rooms—living room, kitchen, and bath—enclosed by wall panels made of a Vinylite insulation core protected on either side by an aluminum sheet coated with Vinylite. The doors were constructed in a similar manner. The floor consisted of Vinylite mixed with slate powder. It did not have much success as a prototype, but it was an important precedent.[4]

In the boatbuilding industry, many had predicted that molded plywood would be the favored postwar material. The architect and designer Alvar Aalto had introduced plywood into furniture designs, and Charles and Ray Eames had further perfected the plywood molding process, building on their experience with plywood leg splints.[5] But in the years immediately preceding the war, the boat industry had begun to discover the potential of plastics: highly moldable, easy to fabricate, requiring little maintenance. Crosley Marine of Coral Gables, Florida, had made a few small plastic boats using ethylcellulose lacquer as early as 1936.[6]

The story of fiberglass is largely the story of the Owens Corning company. It was founded in 1938 and was immediately successful in manufacturing and selling efficient, low-cost glass-fiber insulation to replace the mineral wool that was then being used in houses and in the decks of navy ships. Initially, attempts were made to disperse the molten glass with compressed air, but steam was soon found to give better results. Individual glass filaments have tensile strengths ranging between 250,000 and 400,000 pounds per square inch (psi) and a stiffness of 10 million psi (in comparison, wood has a much lower stiffness of about 1.5 million psi).

Another revolutionary plastic was polystyrene, a hard, lightweight, inexpensive resin that is capable of flowing smoothly into sharply angled molds, thus appealing to inventive industrial designers. As molders became more confident with the material and manufacturers more convinced of its durability, it appeared in more and more places in a vast array of colors and opacities. Whereas the prewar material had been associated with broken toys, in the 1940s new high-impact polystyrene formulations were used to make a variety of household goods, such as Gillette razor blade dispensers, heavy Crystalon bathroom tumblers, wall tiles, suction-cup storage trays, lawn sprinklers, ice buckets, wastebaskets, and laundry hampers. An advertisement for Monsanto Chemical Company in 1941 illustrates a set of brightly hued eating utensils and explains: "Similar sets formed from sheet plastics had been best sellers in exclusive shops for two years at a premium price," whereas now they could be cheaply made by "one-shot" injection molding of polystyrene and were "selling like wildfire in chain stores at popular prices."[7]

Styrofoam was yet another revolutionary plastic material that offered unprecedented possibilities. Made by pressurizing liquid polystyrene resin into lightweight cellular foam, it was used experimentally during the war for rafts and life preservers. Promoters at Dow Chemical Company hoped that Styrofoam boards sliced from large blocks would eventually surpass fiberglass as the industry's preferred building insulation, a hope that was never fully realized. By the 1960s Styrofoam was commonplace in coolers, flowerpots, floatation devices, disposable coffee cups, and packing material.[8]

In the mid-1950s the major plastics manufacturing companies were making a deliberate effort to further popularize plastics, particularly in the domestic sphere.[9] Through research conducted under Ralph Hansen, Monsanto's director of market development in the plastics division, the company identified specific areas within the domestic economy that held the most promise for plastics. In 1955 Hansen generated a report recommending that the company give special attention to the home improvement market (both "do it yourself" and "please do it for me") specific to existing homes more than twenty years old, which accounted for more than $7 billion at the time and was projected to further climb in the 1960s. He wrote: "It is to this vast market, we should set our sights of advanced design." It would be necessary to develop "new ideas which will motivate the consumer desire into demand and finally into purchase." To that end, "the responsibility of the architects and designers was to create ideas based on the psychological desires of the consumer." As consumers do not always know "what they want and why they act," the

marketing department proposed the use of "intelligent experimental design, such as prototypes" to get their attention.[10]

Monsanto invested in two extensive efforts. It opened the Inorganic Research Building at Creve Coeur Suburban Campus in St. Louis, Missouri, which was designed not only to develop experiments with promising new synthetic materials but also to demonstrate the use of existing plastics in the building industry.[11] And it began developing the Monsanto House of the Future prototype, a completely new architectural typology.[12] Plastic furniture, toys, and auto interiors had proven to be so quickly accepted by consumers and manufacturers that Monsanto saw no reason why it wouldn't be possible to create similar consumer desires on a much larger scale through the development of a highly visible, widely publicized housing prototype. After all, plastics were already being used in almost every conceivable household application except structurally. And as a building type, the individual residential home—compact, with fewer structural constraints than public or commercial buildings—was an ideal laboratory for experimentation in design, materials, and construction.

In May 1954 Monsanto approached Pietro Belluschi, dean of architecture at MIT, to assist in its efforts. MIT was selected due to its close liaison with the plastics industry. For instance Albert Dietz, a professor there, was a specialist in housing construction and chair of the Society of Plastics Industry committee on plastics education. He had also worked on developing plastic armor suits during World War II.

Based in part on Dietz's earlier research in structural plastics, architects Marvin Goody and Richard Hamilton and plastics engineer Robert Whittier set to work on building an affordable and highly adaptable prototype. The Monsanto House of the Future would be the earliest full-scale use of molded fiberglass-reinforced plastics in a building application.[13] Dietz, Goody, and Hamilton settled on a structural solution that used a "unibody" or "monocoque" design concept—borrowed from the airplane and automobile industries—thereby taking utmost advantage of the characteristics of fiber-reinforced plastic shells.[14] For the Monsanto House, the shells were cantilevered from a square concrete wet core, six feet above grade and on all four sides. Each of the four wings of the standard plan, of which the tops and bottoms consisted of half-shells that were assembled on-site, contained one room with expansive full-height windows along the side. The bathroom unit located in the center core of this 1,280-square-foot house was similarly made from fully prefabricated units, with the two sections seamed together on-site.

The effect was convincingly futuristic. Completed in June 1957, the house was installed in Tomorrowland at Disneyland in Anaheim, California. | figs. 1 and 2 Tomorrowland, opened in 1955, was intended to represent the world as it would look in 1986. The Monsanto House remained open for ten years and had some twenty million visitors.[15] It was demolished in 1967, as it was no longer deemed futuristic enough.

Its construction was not without challenges. The half-shells, which resembled early fiberglass boats, were manufactured in hand lay-ups, meaning that the surface of a form or mold was covered with a layer of polyester and a glass-fiber mesh was placed over it. | figs. 3 and 4 New layers of polyester were placed over the existing layers and the mesh was thoroughly worked into the polyester matrix.[16] All this work was done by hand, making both quality control and dimensional accuracy an issue. As a result, the shells, while made from the same (or identical) molds, did not fit together precisely and needed to be trimmed and ground on-site with handheld saws and grinders.[17] Where pieces had to be connected structurally, the surfaces were roughened up to create better adhesion, and in photographs of the house, shadow lines are sometimes visible where the L-shaped shells come together. While its exterior fiberglass surface required no protective finish, joint lines were smoothed with polyester gunk and the entire surface was spray painted a uniform eggshell white to emphasize the pristine modernity of plastic.

The interior was as innovative as the exterior, with all surfaces, furniture, and fabrics made from plastic. The furniture represented the most modern designs as it was all available in the marketplace. | fig. 5 The house was equipped with a centrally controlled climate system, with vents running between the shells. The kitchen was fitted with all modern appliances, many of them projecting from concealed spaces. | fig. 6 Because of the unusual shape of the house, many of the elements were designed specifically for the house and their particular location. One of the major structural issues related to the rigidity of the material. Extensive calculations were conducted to assure the integrity of the L-shaped sections. Some of the most challenging problems were related to the connections between the various pieces, given the material's relatively large coefficient of expansion and contraction due to sun exposure. The upper shell was likely to expand significantly more than the lower one, placing considerable stress on a joint that was meant to be invisible.[18] Periodic on-site testing of the structural performance of the house demonstrated its potential. During its lifetime, it withstood several earthquakes with no evidence of structural weakness detected. Even the attempts at demolition in 1967 proved its material impact strength when a three thousand-pound wrecking ball simply bounced off, and a different technique had to be selected.

In spite of apparent popular interest, the Monsanto House of the Future did not bring about the building-industry revolution its designers had hoped for.[19] The cost of the building, estimated at $1 million, was prohibitive even for a prototype, and its fabrication and construction proved time-consuming. Many other designers also experimented with the possibilities of plastics in housing construction, but despite their innovative character and futuristic appearances, few of these prototype houses ever reached production. For instance, the Soviet Union erected a plastic house in Leningrad, which took the form of a ribbed twenty-by-twenty-foot module of polyester and fiberglass, while the Futuro House was produced for a limited time in Finland. | figs. 7 and 8 The latter, introduced in 1968 and looking even more futuristic than the Monsanto House, was advocated as an alternative to the geodesic domes popular at the time. In London in 1955, Alison

fig. 1 | Model of the Monsanto House of the Future being shown to Walt Disney, 1956

fig. 2 | The Monsanto House of the Future, by Monsanto, MIT, and Walt Disney Imagineering, Anaheim, California, 1956

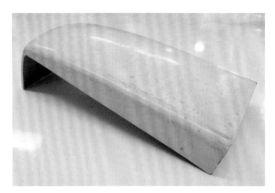

fig. 3 | Small-scale sample of fiberglass construction for field testing and structural calculations, Monsanto House, 1957

fig. 4 | Inside of the fiberglass sample, Monsanto House, 1957

fig. 5 | Dining area with furniture designed by Charles and Ray Eames and Russel Wright, Monsanto House, 1957

fig. 6 | Kitchen with futuristic-looking appliances, Monsanto House, 1957

From Boat to Bust: The Monsanto House Revisited
Theodore Prudon

fig. 7 | The Futuro House, by Matti Suuronen, Finland, 1968

fig. 8 | Interior of the Futuro House with fiberglass construction, Finland, 1968

and Peter Smithson designed the House of the Future for the *Daily Mail* Jubilee Ideal Home Exhibition. The structure of the building was described as molded in "plastic impregnated fibrous plaster." While the overall outside shape was square, all of the interior spaces, built-in furniture, and other furnishings had rounded shapes, corners, and edges. It is not surprising that it was described as cave-like. Many of the shapes resembled the now all-too-familiar premolded forms of built-in units such as showers and bathtubs.[20] The house was meant to be a statement about how technology was going to influence habitation in the imagined future of 1980. It was a prototype for living inspired by similar motivations as the Pavilion L'Esprit Nouveau by Le Corbusier some two decades earlier.[21]

The 1960s and 1970s saw plastics gain popularity in exterior panel or molded components assembled into larger units, taking advantage of their strength.[22] It was particularly popular in the United Kingdom; such panels showed up in the relay rooms for British Rail as well as Mondial House in London, designed by Hubbard Ford and Partners; the Olivetti Training Facility in Haslemere, designed by James Stirling; and the Herman Miller Facility in Bath, by Farrell and Grimshaw.[23] These molded panels resulted in distinctive exteriors because in general the panels were narrow and had rounded corners, edges, and flanges to give internal rigidity.[24]

Had the Monsanto House of the Future not been demolished, today it would be historic and worthy of preservation. It would also have presented an interesting case study as to what happens to plastic after some sixty years in the California sun, and perhaps initiated debates much sooner as to the recycling of aging plastics. Their long-term durability and preservation remains problematic, both physically and philosophically. Questions as to whether a material that was conceived as an affordable alternative with a limited economic and physical lifespan is to be preserved at all costs, or whether it can be replaced with a new "lookalike" of the same or more contemporary material while preserving the design, remain unresolved. A cohesive conservation policy for plastics—not just in historic buildings but also in

museum collections and so on—is one of the biggest challenges ahead.[25]

On a cost basis, an all-plastic structure in the 1950s could not compete with traditional techniques. But the impact of these experimental structures upon the architectural profession was very significant and now the Monsanto House of the Future is considered one of the most important architectural and material experiments of the twentieth century.

I am grateful to Katherine Malishewsky for sharing the information and images that she compiled as part of her master's thesis in Columbia University's Graduate Program for Historic Preservation. Her research help and insights were indispensable to the writing of this essay.

1 | At the end of 1940, the labor leader Walter Reuther wrote in a report titled "500 Planes a Day: A Program for the Utilization of the Auto Industry for Mass Production of Defense Planes": "England's battles, it used to be said, were won on the playing fields of Eton. This plan is put forward in the belief that America's can be won on the assembly lines of Detroit." President Roosevelt used the term in his radio address of December 29, 1940, when referring to Detroit and the production capabilities of the auto (and associated) industries. Anthony Carew, *Walter Reuther* (New York: Manchester University Press 1993): 34.

2 | A great deal has been published about the adaptation and use of materials and designs developed during the war and their marketing and application in the postwar decades. See, for instance, Beatriz Colomina, Annmarie Brennan, and Jeannie Kim, eds., *Cold War Hot Houses* (New York: Princeton Architectural Press, 2004) and Bill Stern, "War and Peace: Unexpected Dividends" in Wendy Kaplan, ed., *California Design 1930–1965: Living in a Modern Way* (Cambridge, MA: MIT Press, 2011): 178–201.

3 | Anthony Walker, "Plastics: The First Universal Building Material," in *Preserving Post-War Heritage: The Care and Conservation of Mid-Twentieth Century Architecture*, ed. Susan Macdonald (Shaftesbury: Donhead Publishing, 2001): 53–82.

4 | Albert Farwell Bemis, *The Evolving House*, vol. 3 (Cambridge, MA: The Technology Press, 1936), 572–73 and Jeffrey L. Meikle, *American Plastic: A Cultural History* (New Brunswick, NJ: Rutgers University Press, 1995): 84–85. The Vinylite system is identified as a panel type. The sponsor is identified as "anonymous." The drawings show only a simple plan, basic section, and detail, which is different from the description in Meikle, and is missing the aluminum sheet.

5 | The Eameses designed the plywood leg splints between 1941 and 1942, and they were manufactured from 1942 to 1945. See John R. Berry, *Herman Miller: The Purpose of Design* (New York: Rizzoli, 2004): 80–97.

6 | Daniel Spurr, *Heart of Glass: Fiberglass Boats and the Men Who Made Them* (New York: McGrawHill, 2004): 9.

7 | Ernest Brent, "Plastic House," *Popular Science Monthly* (April 1956): 144–47, 262.

8 | Meikle, *American Plastic: A Cultural History*, 189. The architect Alden B. Dow, a son of the founder of the Dow Chemical Company, created several buildings using Styrofoam shells and patented a sandwich panel using Styrofoam as insulation

between two plywood sheets. See Diane Maddex, *Alden B. Dow: Midwestern Modern* (New York: W. W. Norton and Alden B. Studio and Home, 2007): 84, 229.

9 | Stephen Phillips, "Plastics," in *Cold War Hot Houses*, 102.

10 | Ralph Hansen, "Plastics in the Design of Building Products and Their Markets," quoted in R. K. Mueller, "Confidential—first disclosure: the Plastics Division Presents the House of Tomorrow," October 3, 1955, 6–7. Box 3, series 9, Monsanto Historic Archive Collection, Washington University Library, St. Louis, Missouri.

11 | Phillips, "Plastics," 104.

12 | Ibid, 105.

13 | Irving Skeist, *Plastics in Buildings* (New York: Reinhold Publishing, 1966): 77.

14 | Albert G. H. Dietz, *Plastics for Architects and Builders* (Cambridge, MA: MIT Press, 1969): 16–17. In using the term monocoque "wings" to describe the structural principle of the house, he makes a clear reference to the design of aircraft wings. For a plan, see Quarnby, 50.

15 | Meikle, *American Plastic: A Cultural History*, 205–15.

16 | Dietz, *Plastics for Architects and Builders*, 102, gives a description of a hand layup. The hand layup is the opposite of a spray-up; in the latter chopped glass fibers and matrix are applied with a dual spray process.

17 | Meikle, *American Plastic: A Cultural History*, 210–11.

18 | A good and comprehensive analysis of the Monsanto House, its structure and its details, can be found in Elke Genzel and Pamela Voigt, *Kunststoffbauten: Teil 1—Die Pioniere* (Leipzig, Germany: Pöge-Druck, 2007): 40–71.

19 | In spite of the lack of success of the Monsanto House, Dietz continued his structural experiments with plastic in the design of a visitor shelter at the 1959 American National Exhibition in Moscow, which consisted of ninety "umbrellas" made from molded fiber-reinforced plastics, each twenty feet high and sixteen feet across.

20 | For a plan and photographs of the actual installation, see Peter and Alison Smithson, *The Charged Void: Architecture* (New York: Monacelli Press, 2001): 162–77 and Beatriz Colomina, "Plastic Atmospheres, 1956 and 2008," in this volume, 30–42.

21 | Helena Webster, *Modernism without Rhetoric* (London: Academy Editions, 1997): 39–41.

22 | The use of plastics in parabolic forms and other types of curved shapes and shells followed a trend in architecture and design in the 1950s and 1960s. Like concrete, plastics can be shaped into any form desired. While concrete is often applied in large-scale public spaces, such as airports or theaters, plastic materials were found at this time to serve well in smaller-scale settings or as molded panels, facilities, or goods. The fibers and the molding and forming techniques made it necessary to mass-produce products that were simple in design with clean lines, so that the fibers could be properly embedded and the components easily cast and molded.

23 | A. J. Brookes, *Cladding of Buildings* (London: Construction Press, 1983): 35–68. The fabrication, construction, detailing, and weathering of glass fiber–reinforced plastics is discussed here at great length and illustrated with examples.

24 | The Mondial House in London is a good case in point. Designed by Hubbard, Ford, and Partners as a telecommunications switching center, it was completed in 1978. To comply with a City Heights Policy that protects a particular view of St. Paul's Cathedral, the height was scaled back. In 2005 a planning application has been filed to allow for the demolition of the building and the construction of two new buildings using a third of the existing building. In the evaluation of the planning, the existing building is described as "a bold piece of architecture but unloved and [that] cannot be usefully put to another purpose without the kind of wholesale redevelopment envisaged." See *Mondial House, 90–94 Upper Thames Street*, Greater London Authority Planning Report PDU/1017/01, December 15, 2005. The building was demolished in 2006.

25 | Julie V. Iovine, "Museums Weep for Their Tupperware," *New York Times*, October 10, 1996: C1, C10. This article discusses the disintegration of many "fugitive" modern design objects, made of rubber, plastic, foam, et cetera.

The Plastic Line

Mark Wigley

We live in a plastic world. So much of what is around us is quietly plastic, from the thin layer of vinyl paint on the walls and polyurethane on the floors to all the fittings, pipes, wiring, fastenings, gaskets, furniture, panels, and packaging. There is plastic on and inside most of the objects we see, from the skins of our books to the cases of our equipment to the body of the latest aircraft. We even see our world through the plastic lens of eyeglasses or contacts and the films sandwiched between the layers of glass in our windows. We are ourselves increasingly plastic, with a wide range of polymers wrapping us and integrated into our bodies, from the fabrics of our clothes to the ever-expanding array of hearing aids, teeth, joints, arteries, and organs. We are almost always looking at, through, and from plastic, and yet we rarely see it. It is as if plastic is so ubiquitous, so integral to our environment, that it is not perceived.

This blind spot is remarkable in architectural discourse, where vast quantities of plastic are specified but rarely seen. The field simply doesn't want to see all the plastic that is such a major part of the substance and effect of buildings. The commitment to be faithful to the inner properties of materials falls away in the face of plastic. The very word *material* is reverently invoked by architects to capture a sense of authenticity, of "truth" to the intrinsic qualities of building elements, but plastic is simply not treated as a material. It is as if the plasticity of plastic—its ability to take any form, perform any role, and imitate any other material—renders it immaterial, lacking its own properties.

Think of all the architectural discourse devoted to the transformative properties of glass. Modern architecture is simply unthinkable without it. Glass is seen to liberate buildings and therefore the people who use them. No similar release is associated with plastic, despite the fact that it so often outperforms glass. Plastic is lighter, stronger, more resilient, and able to take any shape or degree of transparency, color, or texture. Glass is only able to perform today because of all the hidden films of plastic within it and the plastic gaskets and seals around it. Plastic is suspended inside glass and glass is suspended inside plastic. If the ability of glass to "dissolve" walls made the dream of modern architecture possible, then plastic is the most modern of materials. Its history coincides with that of modern architecture yet remains some kind of unacceptable presence within the field. It is as if it is still too modern today.

But what if plastic is never simply added to, coating, simulating, filling, insulating, or reinforcing architecture, but is architecture itself? What if this unmentionable material is carrying out the most fundamental of architectural responsibilities? After all, the main role played by plastic is to draw a line, defining a space by making a division between inside and outside, the most basic gesture of the architect. Think of the plastic coating on every wire that defines a space for the electricity, the plastic chamber that defines a space for the ink in a pen, the plumbing that defines the space for water, the layer of paint that defines an interior by keeping the weather out, the casing of an appliance, the seal on a joint, and so on. The role of plastic is always to draw and hold the line.

In the midsixties, architects explored the possibility that a building might be nothing more than the drawing of such a plastic line. Magazines were filled with curvaceous bubbles, capsules, and pods. Synthetic chemistry took over the role of providing the rustic hut, the basic shelter supporting human life. The solidity of traditional building gave way to the thinnest film defining the line between inside and outside. Buildings became all window. François Dallegret's "Environment Bubble" of 1965 is emblematic: a portable transparent double-skinned plastic dome inflated and serviced by a compact equipment package replaces the traditional house and all the social values associated with it. Likewise, Michael Webb's inflatable Cushicle of 1966, Haus-Rucker-Co's spherical Balloon for Two of 1967, Hans Hollein's cylindrical mobile office of 1969, Ant Farm's fifty-by-fifty-foot

Pillow of 1969, and so on. A new generation of experimental architects were no longer photographed earnestly at their drawing boards or on lecture podiums but look out at us from inside their plastic bubbles, capsules, pods suits, helmets, and glasses—a new kind of portrait of the architect, softly distorted by plastic. No special argument is made in favor of the material. Plastic is simply presented in its transformative transgression of the solidity of traditional architecture. The quivering plastic skin takes the modern architect's dream of lightness, movement, and transparency to its extreme. Buildings finally become modern in becoming portable, packable, flexible, instant, inexpensive, animate, responsive, expandable, and expendable.

This plastic wave was not only an experimental critique of traditional buildings by young radicals unlikely to build outside happenings, galleries, and the pages of magazines. It became the official representation of national cultural and technological pride. At Expo 67 in Montreal, the countless plastic objects displayed at previous world fairs gave way to plastic buildings. The United States was represented by the largest plastic building in history, Buckminster Fuller and Shoji Sadao's 250-foot-diameter sphere. Nineteen hundred plexiglass domes suspended within a steel net were linked together to form a single membrane between inside and outside, a huge plastic ball held together by a geodesic frame. The interior space was a vast twenty-story-high void with exhibits on a few floating platforms linked together by the longest escalators ever built. From the inside, the curves of the transparent acrylic only lightly distorted the view of the fair, city, and sky—dramatically realizing the dream of being all window, with visitors and exhibits seemingly hovering over the landscape. From the outside, the sunlight bounced off all the plastic faces to produce the effect of a huge translucent ball with mysterious shapes lurking within, a shimmering solid with an elevated monorail literally piercing through it. This image of a glowing ball vibrating with inner activity continued at night as the interior lights reflected off the inner faces and the moonlight off the outer faces. | fig. 1

The effect of the shiny plastic sphere echoed the plexiglass wraparound visor of the fiberglass helmet on the aluminized nylon spacesuit that was displayed on the highest platform inside the sphere, along with the capsules, satellites, lunar excursion vehicles, and parachutes of the forthcoming Apollo mission to the moon. The astronaut's spherical helmet and the geodesic bubble both demonstrated the extreme redefinition of enclosure made possible by the most advanced technological research programs. | fig. 2 A plastic sphere was offered for the species that now wrapped itself in plastic to survive in outer space. The building itself was thought of as a spacecraft, not so much built in Montreal as momentarily touching down there. Not by chance does a canonic image show it at night with its glowing surface seemingly echoing the moon seen floating above it. | fig. 3 Plastic was the launch pad to the future.

In the extensive coverage of the dome in architectural journals around the world, its 141,000 square feet of continuous plastic skin is always referred to but ultimately overlooked. The reports are captivated by the geodesic geometry of the steelwork, dwelling on the network of interlocked triangles on the outside and hexagons on the inside rather than the acrylic membrane suspended between the two. | fig. 4 *Architectural Design*, for example, describes the "clear spanning lacey filigree of metal, which will appear weightlessly poised against a background of cloud and sky."[1] Repeating an ancient bias, structure is privileged over surface, even if the only purpose of the structure is to hold up the surface, to hold the thin line between inside and outside in place, the "skybreak," as Fuller called it. The dimension of the hexagons was actually determined by the largest sheet of Plexiglas (ten feet by twelve feet) that was available at the time to mold each dome. Plastic drove the whole design. A few of the reports note that the Plexiglas was tinted green-bronze to reduce glare, but all the reports act as if the material does not affect them. There is usually a reference to the "transparent acrylic skin" at the beginning of each report and a few images in which the surface disappears, providing a clear

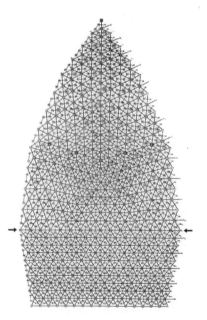

fig. 1 | Night view, Expo 67 U.S. Pavilion, by Buckminster Fuller, Montreal, Canada, 1967

fig. 2 | An astronaut's helmet reflects the dome, Expo 67 U.S. Pavilion, 1967

fig. 3 | Detail at night, Expo 67 U.S. Pavilion, 1967

fig. 4 | Geometry diagram of one fifth of the dome, Expo 67 U.S. Pavilion, 1967

window out from the inside. Yet there are always some other images from the outside that catch the reflections off the shiny plastic that render the interior mysterious and leave the sphere ambiguously poised between transparent, translucent, and opaque. These include closer views in which the surface of the curving array of hexagon-based plastic domes appears dark and shiny, yet with the pattern of the geometry of the web from the far side of the dome seemingly imprinted onto it. | fig. 5 Each hexagon seems to be filled with many smaller hexagons in a kind of multiplication of the pattern that seems to thicken the plastic surface. Likewise, views from a distance show a kind of eccentric mottled pattern inside the regular geometry of the surface. These more complex daytime and nighttime images tell a very different story than the accompanying analytical and technical text. The celebrated precision and clarity of the fixed geometry only serves to intensify the undefinable and ever-shifting sense of mystery.

Progressive Architecture is the only professional journal that finally succumbed to the sensuous effect of the plastic, and even this only happened after the main anonymous report had done the usual technical account of the space frame. A second essay of personal impressions of the fair by a writer happily loses sight of the metal:

> The first impression of the United States Pavilion depends on the light and the time of day. It might appear as thousands of reflective facets in direct sunlight, as a ghostly bubble on grey days, as a rosy diaphanous bloom at sunset, or as a glowing crystalline container of forms and colors after nightfall. Anyway, it is a beautiful object.[2]

Similar descriptions dominated the coverage in newspapers and popular magazines but this ever-changing effect is repressed in architectural publications, a major feat in the face of the largest plastic building in history and the sensation of the fair. Fuller's real architectural contribution is understood to be the geometric frame and even the passing references to

fig. 5 | Detail view, Expo 67 U.S. Pavilion, published in
Japan Architect, August 1967

fig. 6 | View of the 1976 fire, Expo 67 U.S. Pavilion, 1976

fig. 7 | Students demonstrate the lightness of the Necklace dome, Black Mountain College, North Carolina, 1949

fig. 8 | Exterior view of double skin with transparent polyethylene, Necklace Dome, by Buckminster Fuller, Black Mountain College, 1949

the plastic skin quickly fade away as the building is added to the list of major works of twentieth-century architecture. The surface was only momentarily acknowledged again when one of the acrylic domes caught fire during renovation work on the afternoon of May 20, 1976, dramatically engulfing all the others in a twenty-minute blaze. | **fig. 6** Plastic only became visible in its threat to the geodesic structure (which would symptomatically be restored twenty years later without the skin).

When architects think of Fuller, they don't think of plastic. The indelible image is the spidery geodesic web. Yet geodesics were inseparable from plastic. The first paragraph of Fuller's 1954 patent for the geodesic dome ends with "covering or lining this frame with a skin of plastic material."[3] The plastic covering is not an optional extra but the very reason for the lightweight structure. It is not by chance that the first geodesic dome that Fuller constructed was encased within a double skin of plastic. He did the project with students, as he would for decades with almost all the subsequent domes. In early 1949 his class at the Institute of Design in Chicago (his first appointment as a teacher) finished constructing a collapsible and packable fourteen-foot-diameter necklace dome in aluminum struts tensioned with aircraft cable. A few months later, the students folded up the structure and took it to Fuller's summer session at Black Mountain College in North Carolina. The main assignment there was to develop a double-skinned plastic membrane for the dome that would provide shelter and thermal insulation. The idea was to test the concept of the Skybreak House in which a plastic-skinned necklace dome would produce a new kind of domestic space without walls. Living inside a dome would be barely distinguishable from living outside. A tabletop plastic-covered model of such a radical house had been built by three of the Chicago students, complete with tree and bushes on the inside, and brought to Black Mountain, where Fuller had it photographed among the trees and bushes around the school to communicate the "Garden of Eden" effect of the most minimal enclosure. He insisted that paradoxically the latest technologies would so reduce the footprint of architecture that people would be returned to a direct experience of the pretechnological natural world. Architecture would no longer be an agent of disconnection. To live in a dome would be to reconnect oneself to the world. Architecture would finally be revolutionized by the lightest possible plastic membrane.

As the summer session began, the necklace dome from Chicago was quickly unfolded and reassembled. Three students held the rigid frame up above them on their fingertips to demonstrate its lightness before it was fixed about a meter off the ground on a ring of posts. | fig. 7 Fuller and eight of the students swung on it for the camera to demonstrate its surprising strength. A small wooden platform was then hung from it at a height that would place a standing person's head at the center of the enclosed space. As the double skin of transparent polyethylene was added to the inside and outside of the frame, Fuller sat on the platform, earnestly studying this "pneumatic" skin sealed in inflated hexagons and pentagons. | fig. 8 When it was finished, Fuller and the students lifted the dome above their heads—with three women sitting on the platform—to again demonstrate the combination of lightness and strength before it was set back on the posts, where it would remain for the rest of the summer. One of Merce Cunningham's students danced on the platform to demonstrate the new sense of freedom offered by the dome. She was photographed from below to show the lightly defined web of the plastic envelope surrounding her as she floated above the ground, dancing in a new kind of open space suspended against the backdrop of the natural world.

Fuller jumped up too and beamed proudly at the photographer looking down from the adjacent building as he stuck his head through the one hexagon uncovered for ventilation at the top of the dome, firmly grasping the geodesic frame with both hands. | figs. 9 and 10 More than simply being inside the structure, it is as if he is wearing it like a skirt, becoming part of the structure in this image, which was one of few images he would ever publish of this crucial first plastic dome.[4] In fact, he would publish three slightly

fig. 9 | Fuller sitting in the center of the dome

fig. 10 | Fuller wearing the dome

different versions of the same basic shot—the apparently spontaneous image being carefully staged like almost every image throughout his career. Yet this image may be the most important of all. Fuller later describes Black Mountain as the place where he had the pivotal idea that to be at the center of such a transparent dome allows one to understand one's place in the universe. The minimal plastic skin defines both an interior and a position in the world. The omnidirectional window floating above the ground turns architecture into a personal observatory, a panoptic platform that allows people to visualize the pattern of their world and thereby take responsibility for it.

The success of this first plastic-encased dome acted as the launching pad for decades of geodesic experimentation. The Fuller Research Foundation gathered a team of collaborators around him, mainly a set of his most committed students. His major innovation was not only the geodesic structure as an interconnected web of equal elements sharing all loads, but the idea of an interconnected web of researchers distributed across a series of nodes in different cities to work in parallel on domes—an interlaced network to study interlaced networks. Immediately after Black Mountain, one of the Chicago students at the heart of the Black Mountain experiments formed a key node in Montreal with a friend who had attended a Fuller lecture. Another was formed in Raleigh, North Carolina, by a group of teachers and students at a new school of design where Fuller was invited to teach on the basis of the Black Mountain work. When Fuller received the patent for the geodesic dome in 1954 and the first commissions for domes by the military, the Raleigh

group formed Geodesics Inc. to produce the designs, and a similar venture was set up in Cambridge, Massachusetts, by two students who had been inspired by the original Institute of Design experiments in Chicago. In the same year, Shoji Sadao, who had been yet another student of Fuller at Cornell in 1950, became the closest collaborator of all, working in all of the nodes and eventually forming an office with Fuller to carry out their shared design for Expo 67, assisted by many of the other former students operating in the network. The plastic sphere in Montreal emerges out of almost twenty years of research following the summer experiment with plastic at Black Mountain, a collaborative research program that was carried out in a distributed array of around twenty different schools where Fuller was a guest professor. Typically, Fuller would amaze a school with a lecture that would go for hours and would then be invited back to do a workshop with the students, which invariably involved building a geodesic dome or sphere. Each of the major questions he was asking, many of which involved experimenting with plastic, could then be investigated simultaneously in different places.

Already by December 1950, Jeffrey Lindsay, the key student at Chicago and Black Mountain who had a special interest in plastic (and set up the research node in Montreal with his friend Ted Pope), had erected a forty-nine-foot-diameter aluminum weatherbreak dome that was internally skinned with Orlon, a translucent acrylic fabric that had been introduced by Dupont that same year. A few months later, Lindsey built the first plastic glazed wooden dome as a possible commercial skybreak prototype. *Architectural Forum* devoted seven enthusiastic pages and the cover of its August

fig. 11 | Sequence of photographs showing the attachment of the plastic skin, Weatherbreak Dome, by Jeffrey Lindsay, Montreal, published in *Architectural Forum*, August 1951

1951 issue to these experiments with a "spidery new framing system."[5] It describes the plastic on each dome, even showing the attachment of the skin to the frame in Montreal in a cinematic sequence of seven photographs, and referring to a new project for a huge 411-foot-diameter dome with "a skin of a new type of plastic glass fiber reinforced polyester styrene." | fig. 11 The state of art in structure was seen to be inseparable from the state of art in plastic. Confirming the foundational role of the Black Mountain experiment, the final page shows the ecstatic Fuller wearing the first plastic dome at Black Mountain and the plastic Skybreak House model within the surrounding vegetation there alongside a listing of all the trustees and fellows of the Fuller Research Foundation.

Fuller had been relentlessly promoting the concept of the plastic-coated dome since early 1949, leading up to the Black Mountain test. After showing the necklace frame and first Skybreak House model to the Pentagon in February, he presented photographs of the model at an Ann Arbor conference in April showing that the skin could be adjusted from "omnidirectional clear" to "omnidirectional translucent" with some unspecified system of shutters between the inflated two layers of plastic.[6] The images and description were published in professional magazines like *Architectural Forum* and *Interiors* in the following months.[7] Fuller was still talking to newspapers about the concept using the same images more than two years later in the summer of 1951.[8] James Fitzgibbon, the young teacher who had seen the plastic-covered dome at Black Mountain and brought Fuller to North Carolina, had designed a house earlier in 1951 with an internal garden

using a version of Lindsay's aluminum Montreal dome with a fiberglass skin and lined with layers of Saran.[9] But Fuller himself only started to develop the concept further that fall with his students at MIT. They imagined a geodesic frame skinned in transparent Saran and expanded the role of plastic to include thin sheets of "polyester fiberglass laminate" for the demountable floor, ceiling, and wall panels. Their designs were presented at a January 1952 conference on housing at MIT and were referred to by newspapers and *Architectural Record* before being published in detail in the first issue of Yale's *Perspecta* magazine that summer. Fuller's introductory text again insists that an aluminum dome with an inflated "transparent plastic skin of double walled construction" could establish a new kind of space; a concept he now says could be expanded to a one-mile-diameter dome covering a whole city.[10] The architectural ambitions of plastic were growing exponentially.

Parallel to the hemisphere experiment at MIT, Fuller had been working with students at the Raleigh school on the design of a seven-story-high automated cotton mill housed in a three-quarter sphere. | fig. 12 Once again, a double-walled skin of plastic sheltered a dense package of equipment. For Fuller, plastic was quite literally the space of advanced technology. The design was finished in January 1952 and later published in *Architectural Forum*, which pointedly noted that the crucial "stretched plastic skin" is missing from the

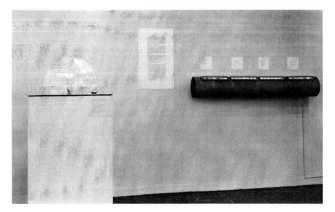

fig. 12 | Model of a geodesic cotton mill, assembled by Fuller's students, College of Design, North Carolina State University, Raleigh, 1952

fig. 13 | Model of a skybreak dome in *Two houses, new ways to build,* by Buckminster Fuller, Museum of Modern Art, New York, October 1952

fig. 14 | Interior view of the installation, Museum of Modern Art, October 1952

otherwise intricately detailed demountable model.[11] The project was also highlighted in the article "You May Live in Bubble House" that appeared in May in the Sunday supplement to the *Washington Post* and a number of newspapers around the country. The author interviewed Fuller's key collaborators in Raleigh and Montreal, concluding that the "biggest stumbling block" to dome houses is "the fact that FRF [Fuller Research Foundation] men have not yet found a suitable, light-weight transparent (or translucent) 'skin.'...But they're hoping that the right form of plastic will turn up any day."[12]

A few of Fuller's students from Raleigh worked with him that summer in the New York office of George Nelson (a founding trustee of the Fuller Research Foundation) to develop the plastic and metal model of the Skybreak House that was exhibited in August at the Museum of Modern Art, along with twenty-eight color slides of the earlier dome experiments.[13] The house would now be lifted off the ground on six posts to produce an even more minimal sense of shelter as the landscape flowed underneath, with a compact technical equipment package on the ground connected by umbilical tubes reaching up to the suspended living units. | **fig. 13** Once again, the plastic skin "ranges from transparent to opaque," as the wall text put it, but even the independent suspended floors were now transparent and, on Nelson's suggestion, all internal divisions could be temporarily made with colored plastic fabric stretched over aluminum poles. The nineteen-inch-diameter model was raised near eye level on a white pedestal alongside a huge blowup of the 1950 aluminum dome in Montreal, skinned in white Orlon and standing in the snow alongside trees without any other man-made objects in view. | **fig. 14** The wall text alongside the accompanying tubes of slides and the museum press release repeated the formula that geodesic frame plus plastic plus mechanical package equals nature: "a dome eighty feet in diameter, constructed with aluminum tubes and covered with a plastic skin that is weatherproof....Total mechanization, in Fuller's vision, would enable a return to man's earliest recorded home: The

Garden of Eden."[14] Fuller proudly appeared with the model in two television broadcasts just before the show opened.[15] Newspaper reviews were captivated with the idea of life in a plastic house and celebrated the "brilliantly engineered bubble" with its Orlon skin that transforms the traditional heavy house into a "transparent umbrella," as the MoMA curator Arthur Drexler put it.[16]

During the first months of 1953, students at Raleigh extended some of these ideas by building a thirty-six-foot-diameter experimental greenhouse—a wooden geodesic frame with a double-skinned bubble of transparent Saran suspended within it on nylon cords attached to hard plastic disks on each of the vertices and the doorway made of Orlon. Plastic was being asked to play an increasingly active role: the experiment tested the idea that the internal climate of the bubble could be controlled by raising and lowering the bubble so that valves would adjust the passage of air between the two layers of plastic. When the Saran skins lasted only long enough to be photographed, the students tried a single skin of polyethylene, which failed after eighteen hours, and finally Mylar was seen to show the greatest promise by surviving for ten days before the adhesives gave out.[17] A couple of months later, University of Oregon students built the first geodesic dome successfully covered with Mylar, which had only just been invented by Dupont.[18] The continuous refinement of the domes was again inseparable from the evolution in plastic. As Fuller recalled decades later:

> I would organize the students into aeronautical production.... The President of Dupont happened to be a friend, he had a student, son, up there at Cornell. He was interested. One reason and another there would be somebody you could get in touch with, and you said we are going, we are making an experiment, and we really, really there is no use in going through this without using the most advanced materials, and we understand you have a little better clear Plexi-Glass, or whatever it is, and these men would send you a special airplane of materials.[19]

Fuller pulled all his students into the evolving joint between geodesic frame and plastic skin. In the spring of 1953, for example, an experimental project at the University of Minnesota was the construction of a thirty-six-foot-diameter demountable dome with a very open wooden frame held in place by a diamond shaped web of cables of Dacron (a fiberglass neoprene cord again recently introduced by Dupont). The color-coded kit was packed up and trailered to the third Aspen Conference on Design that June, where Fuller was speaking, and was quickly assembled by the students then covered in the crucial layer of translucent polyethylene. Charles Eames, another founding trustee of the Fuller Research Foundation, promptly filmed Fuller inside the plastic space before students used it as their dormitory during the event.[20] | fig. 15 Daytime and nighttime photographs by Fuller himself captured the glowing bubble against the background of looming mountains and sky, with the structural frame and occupants turning into a mysterious ghostly trace. | fig. 16 The same dome was then trailered to Wood's Hole, Massachusetts, where it was temporarily reassembled and covered with a tightly fitting white skin to house twenty students from ten universities who had come to assemble a wooden dome designed, milled, and packed into a truck by a group of students at MIT. Fuller lectured the gathered students inside the first dome, was filmed during the construction of the second dome, and was photographed deliriously swinging from a rope hanging inside it on the night it was finished. The wooden frame was then covered in three layers of transparent Mylar to house a restaurant among the trees. Fuller later proudly recalled that the stretched plastic skin was so strong that it could be walked on and expressed disappointment that much of it was eventually replaced by opaque plastic.[21]

It is not by chance that this first permanent functioning building by Fuller is ultimately just a transparent plastic skin held in place by a geodesic frame that tries to do the most with the least. Likewise, it is not by chance that his first large-scale commercial project completed in the same

fig. 15 | Charles Eames filming Fuller inside University of Minnesota wooden frame dome, by Buckminster Fuller, Aspen, Colorado, 1952

fig. 16 | Exterior view at night, Wooden frame dome, photograph by Buckminster Fuller, Aspen, 1952

fig. 17 | Skin being installed, Ford Rotunda Dome, by Buckminster Fuller, Dearborn, Michigan, 1953

months was again a plastic line between inside and outside that had been modeled and even tested in plastic. For the ninety-three-foot-diameter Ford rotunda, a lightweight aluminum octet truss frame was covered with thin translucent polyester fiberglass panels tinted to produce a kind of kaleidoscopic effect from below that was celebrated in popular magazines like *Life*.[22] Fuller's plastic dream was becoming a reality and being magnified through the lens of the mass media. | fig. 17

Even in the iconic image of January 1954 in which Fuller stands with his back to us, watching a dome being carried aloft by a Marine helicopter—a scene covered by newspapers like the *New York Times* and repeated in most Fuller publications—the flying form is again plastic. | fig. 18 Its wooden lattice structure had been built in 1951 by Fitzgibbon, Stuart Duncan, and Manuel Bromberg (the founders of the Fuller Research Foundation in Raleigh) with their students and was later covered in chicken wire to support a rubber-plastic neoprene material.[23] The lightweight magnesium domes commissioned by the Marines on the basis of the successful flying test were prototyped by Geodesics Inc. in Raleigh a few months later in mid-1954, and were inevitably lined with a stretched plastic skin that was attached to the inside of the frame at each of the vertices. The pattern of this plastic tent was seemingly more complex than the geodesic structure holding it up.

Plastic was no longer seen as just skin. Already at the beginning of 1952, Fuller was actively pursuing the idea he had first modeled in 1949 of having the structure itself in plastic, with curved plastic panels simply attached to each other to form a self-supporting dome.[24] The hope was to build a full-scale translucent plastic Skybreak House in the garden of MoMA during the summer of 1953. In February 1952, George Nelson wrote to Arthur Drexler to follow up on their earlier conversations about the possibility of building a "plastic dome" house in the museum garden:

Discussions with Buckminster Fuller revealed on his part a special interest in a new kind of dome—a kind of plastic eggshell, without the wood or metal framework shown in earlier models, and much larger, 90' in diameter.... We therefore decided that if possible the house in the garden was to be a complete dwelling, constructed as a translucent plastic shell, designed as a quarter sphere with a 45' radius. A model of this structure is being built in my workshop.... At this point it seems advisable to concentrate on the technical problems posed by plastic shell, and to put aside consideration of the fascinating possibilities created by the space it would enclose.... A meeting of the Technical Council of Monsanto was set up, and consultation with it created more problems than were solved.[25]

The problems with construction, weatherproofing, and the unknown aging of plastic turned out to be overwhelming and the model exhibited at MoMA that August (still with the idea of raising funds to build at full scale in the museum garden the following year) was returned to the metal frame with plastic lining. But Fuller was dedicated to the possibility of an all-plastic dome, steadily increasing the structural role of plastic. With his first cardboard dome, erected by Yale students a few months later in November 1952, the structure itself was of a new type of cardboard made of thin layers of paper and plastic bonded together with resin. The outermost layer had a thin polyethylene film as the weather seal and any open triangles would be covered with clear plastic.[26] Likewise, the cardboard structure of Fuller's two domes at the Milan Triennale in February 1954 was covered by a tightly fitting Vinylite "bathing cap" that turned all the triangular openings in the geodesic web into sealed windows, and the cardboard itself was meant to have been impregnated with plastic for strength. | fig. 19 It was even labeled a "plastic dome" in "People in Plastic Homes," a *New York Times* magazine report on the "Plastic in Building" conference in Washington that year.[27] A month later, the cardboard struts of a dome, built

fig. 18 | Fuller watching a dome carried by a Marine helicopter, Raleigh, North Carolina, January 1954

fig. 19 | Installation of cardboard dome with Vinylite "bathing cap" at the Milan Triennale, by Buckminster Fuller, February 1954

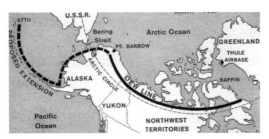

by students at the University of Tulane, to model a hanger for the military were treated with plastic; and with the same students, Fuller and Eames then developed the concept of a huge "Skyeye" radio telescope with the geodesic frame itself made of lightweight fiberglass-reinforced polyester resin struts—continuing the successful experiment to use such hollow plastic struts in the forty-foot-diameter "tensegrity" dome built by University of Minnesota students in December 1953. Plastic steadily migrated from skin to frame.

Almost inevitably, Fuller finally did away with the distinction between frame and skin with the fiberglass-reinforced resin panels of the "Radomes" to house the continental radar defense system.[28] The early versions at the beginning of 1954 were already the largest plastic buildings in the world. Only the bolts holding the plastic panels of the three-quarter spheres together were in metal. William Wainwright and Bernard Kirschenbaum, the partners of Geodesics Inc. in Cambridge who were in charge of the project, soon developed a way of making even those connections in plastic too. The definitive design of the fifty-five-foot-diameter Radome completed in early 1955 had 361 plastic components and was installed in 63 radar stations to form a 10,000-kilometer defensive line running across the arctic at the upper border of North America. | fig. 20 The plastic line no longer simply defined a domestic shelter but defined domestic security for a whole continent. The architectural responsibility of plastic had reached a whole new level.

In May of the same year, the surprising strength of the Radomes inspired the owner of the New York Dodgers baseball team to commission Fuller to design an enormous 750-foot-diameter translucent plastic dome to cover Ebbets field in New York. The idea was to make a dome more than twice as big as the largest previous clear span construction in the world. Fuller developed the design with Princeton students and their final large plastic model showed the translucent polyester resin skin reinforced with fiberglass and aluminum. A lot of media coverage was devoted to the three hundred-foot-tall plastic dome and the fact that many of New

fig. 20 | Map of the Dew line

fig. 21 | Model of a skybreak house for a "Home Style" theme park, by Buckminster Fuller, Grand Rapids, Michigan, March 1956

fig. 22 | Radome, Tensegrity Mast and Octet Truss Installation, Museum of Modern Art, New York, 1959

fig. 23 | Fuller presented the model of the Expo 67 U.S. pavilion to President Johnson, December 15, 1966

York's skyscrapers would fit within it. Plastic architecture was firmly in the public eye, redefining both private and public space.

By March of 1956, the most sophisticated version of the Skybreak House combined all of these evolving plastic techniques for an unrealized Homestyle theme park by the Home Research Foundation in Grand Rapids, Michigan, that was meant to feature fifty full-scale houses by leading designers like Paul Rudolph and Nelson. The design for the Fuller house by Geodesics Inc. in Raleigh started in late 1955 as a variation of the Radome, with domestic equipment rather than radar housed inside a polyester fiberglass three-quarter sphere, but ended up as a hemisphere raised off the ground like the version exhibited at MoMA in 1952. A translucent fiberglass paneled dome was to be hung from a lightweight magnesium geodesic frame and protected by a polyester fiberglass skin stretched between dome and frame. Environmental control was achieved by regulating air passage between the plastic layers and additional white plastic skins and movable translucent frames hanging within the space as sunshades. The detailed model shows domestic life suspended in the air and supported by a set of independent equipment packages resting on an elevated platform made of Fuller's octet truss. | fig. 21 With the whole scene glimpsed through three layers of plastic, the simple Black Mountain dome that positions its occupants in the cosmos has become a complex technical instrument with an equally complex aesthetic. As the centerpiece of the proposed theme park, the project was highlighted in numerous newspaper articles and images of the model were published in *Arts and Architecture*, *Interiors*, *House and Home*, and *Architectural Record*, even though Fuller himself would never refer to the project.[29]

Fuller's plastic buildings were not simply exhibited and publicized but were themselves a way of publicizing things, a communications device. His numerous exhibition domes designed by Geodesics Inc. in Raleigh for the United States Information Agency (USIA) were lightweight, easily assembled metal frames internally skinned with a stretched tent of translucent plastic-coated nylon, starting with the one-hundred-foot-diameter version assembled in Kabul in 1956 and culminating with the dome for the 1957 Milan Triennial that won the top prize that year (as had the vinyl-covered cardboard domes in the previous Triennale). The geodesic geometry is minimal on the outside with a very open web that almost disappears on the inside, where the geometric pattern of joints in the translucent plastic skin dominates the effect. The plastic glows on the inside during the day and on the outside at night. Once again, to enter the triangulated geodesic world is actually to enter the softened space of plastic. The heavily publicized exhibition of one of the original green-tinted Radomes within the garden of MoMA in 1959 (finally realizing Fuller's ambition of 1952), with its interior used for events and as an artist's studio, put on show the ability of a plastic bubble to put things on show. | fig. 22 More than a space to be occupied, plastic was understood as a way of seeing things.

The Expo 67 dome for the USIA fused all of this plastic research into a single spectacular monument to the new material. The design was first publicized in 1965 with a model that had the geodesic geometry of triangles and hexagons inscribed into the outer and inner surfaces of an acrylic sphere. The basic idea of a shimmering plastic architecture supported by a spidery web was emphatically established. Fuller repeatedly appeared alongside the model, from its press launch in June 1965 to its official presentation to President Johnson in December 1966 to an exhibition in New York just a few months before the building opened. | fig. 23 Echoing his original polemic at Black Mountain College in 1949, he once again describes it as a "geodesic skybreak bubble" that produces a "Garden of Eden" interior that allows one's position in the world to be grasped.

Now even the plastic surface is itself meant to be an intelligent organism, with an array of six motorized Mylar retractable shades inside each hexagon that respond to the angle and intensity of the sun through computer activation. The June 1966 issue of *Architectural Forum*, the magazine

fig. 24 | Working prototype of Mylar shades for the Expo 67
U.S. Pavilion, published in *Architectural Forum*, June 1966

fig. 25 | Buckminster Fuller displays the model of
the Dymaxion House with casein skin, Philadelphia,
December 8, 1932

that had so closely monitored each step in the evolution of the geodesic domes since the very first one at Black Mountain, devoted the most attention to the system of environmental control. After a full-page photo of the first plastic model, detailed technical drawings of the mechanism of the "animated surface" appear alongside a sequence of close-up photographs of the shimmering aluminized Mylar shades in operation on the first working prototype. | **fig. 24** The text even anticipates the sensuous effect of these overlapping mobile layers of technologically advanced plastic: "The effect should be little short of fantastic. For in the course of each day, as the rays of the sun light up the dome from different angles, the plastic skin will slowly change from complete transparency to polished 'chrome!'"[30] Jack Masey, who hired Fuller to do the Expo 67 building and had been commissioning the USIA domes for a decade had, not by chance, been working at *Architectural Forum* at the time that Fuller's first plastic domes were published in 1951. Each plastic step led to another in a relentless and increasingly global project.

It is as if the Expo 67 sphere was the seemingly inevitable result of a single obsessive trajectory of research, the product of almost twenty years of experimentation at the intersection of geodesic and plastic. The geodesic experiment literally took place inside plastic. If anything, it was the plastic line that remained constant while the geodesic props of the line evolved.

In fact, Fuller's entire career was encased in plastic. His Dymaxion house of 1927–1929 was already defined by plastic. The house is a 360-degree viewing platform hung on a central mast. Traditional outer walls have been replaced by triangles of double-skinned vacuum-sealed plastic suspended in a triangulated cable net, which is itself suspended in a larger net of cables. The continuous plastic wall flexes and can be adjusted by pulling up larger triangles of plastic behind it to block the light or provide privacy when necessary. The ceiling is likewise in plastic, evenly distributing the light from the plastic skylight above that has been reflected onto it by mirrors. The bathrooms are molded in plastic as single units. Fuller prescribes a wide range of plastics from transparent outer walls to translucent ceiling to opaque bathroom. Such plastics were not even available at the time. The only plastic in 1927 was casein, made from milk. It didn't have the properties Fuller wanted, but he specified it for the house in all his presentations and articles. His architecture aimed beyond the current performance of materials. Materials were used to reimagine their own future. In a 1975 lecture looking back on the design of the Dymaxion House half a century earlier, Fuller describes how it anticipates and "waits" for plastic to transform what is possible.

> But there were great indications of developments in the plastics, and so I made the working assumption that I would come eventually to clear material, that you could see through, that would not be glass, that would be lighter than glass, and would be almost as scratchproof as glass and so forth. I made really a lot of working assumptions like that, and tried to use the curves of already developed phenomena, to give me some idea of how fast I could expect the others. So when I was really designing a structure, a house, the Dymaxion house to have windows all around I was not planning the weight of glass. Glass is very heavy, and so I was waiting on a plastic, and finally a plastic that I would be able to have hermetically sealed.[31]

This "anticipatory" mode defined Fuller's work. Already in 1939 he argued that it was not a matter of waiting for "new" materials, like plastic, to be invented in the laboratory. Rather, materials are successively found by continuously and collectively exploring the existing world.[32] Fuller rejected any distinction between natural and artificial, seeing synthetic chemistry as the most natural space in which architecture could grow: "There is an unfortunate tendency to abhorency of the plastic. Our fingernails are plastic. Our eyes are plastic...."[33] Plastic is not a technological innovation but architecture's natural destiny on its inevitable path

toward invisibility. In 1942, Fuller confidently predicted that in the future dwelling industry "the synthetics (plastics) will predominate, in the end, product's visible surfaces."[34] Plastic is destined to be the barely visible surface of the invisible world. It takes architecture to the limit of materiality by drawing the thinnest possible line. This dissolving of the illusion of solidity started to be confirmed in 1953 when Fuller looked up through the mylar-covered web of the geodesic dome at Wood's Hole: "sitting inside it, you just didn't see any skin membrane at all. It began to seem that we were approaching a time when the construction would become entirely invisible."[35] Fuller had waited on plastic for a quarter of century to make such a palpable image of the invisible. In one of his last books in 1981, he recalled the moment in 1927 when the absence of the right plastic provoked both the desire and expectation for an imminent architectural transformation: "Quite clearly plastic materials of many kinds were desirable substances, as transparent and waterproof as glass but not easily breakable and of much lighter weight.... Wanting better materials and looking at one's own fingernails, one could say that such and such a material is ostensibly feasible, so it will be developed."[36] In Fuller's logic of continuous evolution, materials are always suspended between fact and desire. Each technical development stimulates the thought of yet another development and architectural projects appear within this kind of flow of material.

The display model of the Dymaxion House with which Fuller promoted the concept in department stores, galleries, magazines, and movies in mid-1929, and the larger version completed in early 1930, had the outer walls made of thin sheets of transparent casein, with the triangulated pattern of the cables etched into their surface. | fig. 25 Fuller stands alongside the model plastic interior, ready to enthuse about the urgent need to dissolve the solidity of conventional buildings. The dream of the plastic-skinned house as an omnidirectional window that was first tested with students at Black Mountain in 1949 was already in place twenty years earlier, as was even the basic mode of experimentation, since the design and models of the Dymaxion House were developed with a group of recently graduated students in an informal "designing school" that Fuller was running.[37] Fuller both waited for plastic to catch up to his designs and used available plastic to radicalize his designs, absorbing each new form of plastic into his redefinition of the house. His 1932 model of a ten-story version of the Dymaxion House encased the already plastic-skinned building in a rotating acrylic teardrop-shaped weather vane to reduce drag and when Plexiglas came to the market a year later, he immediately used it to form the wraparound window of the teardrop-shaped Dymaxion Car. He was proud of the fact that his Dymaxion Deployment Units of 1940 were the first houses to have Plexiglas windows and that his 1944–1946 built version of the Dymaxion House featured a 118-foot-long, 360-degree window made of two layers of Plexiglas. Plastic was therefore not added to a geodesic frame for the first time until a few years later in 1949 at Black Mountain. Rather the frame was simply the mechanism invented to allow plastic to take over the whole architecture.

Plastic was the dream material, the material with which to leave material behind. Its promise is to maximize connectivity and thereby to liberate thought. In every version of Fuller's architecture, which might in the end be but one extended project, it was the plastic line that defined both the interior space for modern life and the research space in which geodesic geometry was incubated. Fuller's architecture was made with and within plastic. His work alerts us to the possibility that we have gone from the dream of plastic houses to the reality of plastic housing architecture, which is precisely why we don't see it anymore.

1 | "US Pavilion," *Architectural Design*, July 1967, 333–37.

2 | James T. Burns, "How it is," *Progressive Architecture*, June 1967, 158.

3 | Buckminster Fuller, "Geodesic Dome (1954) U.S. Patent 2,682,235," in *Inventions: The Patented Works of R. Buckminster Fuller* (New York: St. Martins Press, 1983), 130.

4 | One of the rare exceptions, showing Fuller and a group of students holding up the plastic dome with three women on the platform to "show off strength, lightness of 50 pound, aircraft cable dome," appears in a survey article. See Ken Olsen

and Al Miller, "What do You Know About the Geodesic Dome?" *Better Homes and Gardens*, June 1957, 194; Fuller also showed the image as "testing the way earthquakes would affect such a structure" in his October 10, 1963 speech to UIA Congress in Mexico. See Buckminster Fuller "World Design Initiative," in John McHale (ed.), *World Design Science Decade 1965–1975, Phase I, Document 2: Inventory of World Resources, Human Trends and Needs*, (Carbondale: Southern Illinois University, 1965), 67.

5 | "Geodesic Dome: Bucky Fuller's Spidery New Framing System," *Architectural Forum*, August 1951, 144–51.

6 | "A transparent plastic skin of double wall construction is inflated to withstand hail, or hurricane impact loads. An interior shuttering mechanism provides one hundred percent variable optic control opaque to transparent." April 1, 1949 Ann Arbor talk, in Buckminster Fuller, "Preview of Building," in *Ideas and Integrities*, ed. Robert Marks (New York: Collier, 1963), 214; The concept was also highlighted in newspapers, as in Jeane Rockwell, "Fuller Describes Unusual Idea of Future Homes," *Ann Arbor News*, April 1949.

7 | "The top photograph shows Fuller's 'Autonomous Geodesic Structure' with its transparent shielding of plastic material set at 'omnidirectional clear' (by means as yet undisclosed)....Smaller photograph shows this package as seen from the inside. It is assumed here that controls are set at 'omnidirectional translucent' so there is privacy from prying as if the interior were 'surrounded by sunlit mist.'" "Fuller's New Super-Tent," *Architectural Forum*, May 1949. "The double walls of plastic are inflated to withstand rain, hail, snow, hurricane, and all other onslaughts, and allow '100 percent variable optic control...'" in "Everyday Eden," *Interiors*, June 1949.

8 | "Designer of Futuristic Buildings Shuns Conventional for 'Geodesic Pattern,'" *Christian Science Monitor*, June 15, 1951.

9 | Fitzgibbon's Brewer House design was published in Bruno Leon, "Tensile Integrity," *Student Publications of the School of Design, North Carolina State College* 1, no. 2 (1951): 30–39.

10 | Buckminster Fuller, "The Autonomous Dwelling Facility: The Geodesic Dome," *Perspecta* no. 1 (Summer 1952): 29–37.

11 | "Vertical Textile Mill," *Architectural Forum*, May 1952, 137–41.

12 | S. A. Schreiner, "You May Live in a Bubble House," *Parade (Washington Post Sunday Supplement)*, May 25, 1952, 6–7.

13 | Two Houses: New Ways to Build, Museum of Modern Art, New York, 1952.

14 | "Two Houses of the Future to be Exhibited," Museum of Modern Art, press release, August 22, 1952.

15 | Buckminster Fuller, interview by Durward Kirby, CBS, August 1, 1952; Also interview by Arthur Drexler, *Mike and Buff talk show*, CBS, February 10, 1952.

16 | Alice B. Louchheim, "New Ways of Building: Modern Museum shows Fuller and Kiesler," *New York Times*, August 31, 1952.

17 | Kenneth Goldfarb and John Nina, "The Architect and Agriculture—Two," *Student Publications of the School of Design, North Carolina State College* 4, no. 1 (1954): 12–15.

18 | The specifications for the dome call for 3,300 square feet of "Mylar Plastic Film" from Dupont and 120 square feet of "Saran Plastic Film." Buckminster Fuller, *The Artifacts of R. Buckminster Fuller, Vol. 3: The Geodesic Revolution, Part 1, 1947–1959* (New York: Garland, 1985), 175.

19 | Buckminster Fuller, "Everything I Know," session 8, part 3 (lecture, Buckminster Fuller Institute, January 1975).

20 | Eames had photographed Fuller's very first studio at the Institute of Design in 1947, see *Architectural Forum*, January–February 1972, 62–63; and would publish the first images of the Expo 67 dome under construction, see *Domus*, January 1967.

21 | Buckminster Fuller, "Everything I Know," session 11, part 6 (lecture, Buckminster Fuller Institute, January 1975).

22 | *Life*, June 8, 1953, 67–70.

23 | The teachers and students had built the thirty-foot wooden lattice dome in Fitzgibbon's backyard in 1951 as a test and had covered it with plastic in 1952, even if the genesis of the dome, along with its plastic skin, would never be mentioned by Fuller. An undated photograph of the dome under construction along with an interview of Fitzgibbon appeared in May 1952 in "You May Live in a Bubble House," *Parade (Washington Post Sunday Supplement)*, May 25, 1952, 6–7. It was also featured on the cover of *Student Publications of the School of Design, North Carolina State College* 3 no. 1 (1952): 12–15.

24 | In early 1949, Institute of Design students made a forty-inch dome of curved plastic "pan" elements attached to each other, and unsuccessfully tested the idea at a larger scale with molded fiberglass panels at Black Mountain College that summer. Likewise, in 1951 the students at MIT included a version of a hanger dome made of superimposed "diamonds of fiberglass laminate" alongside versions with metal frames.

25 | George Nelson, letter to Arthur Drexler, February 25, 1952, Exhibition #518 file, Museum of Modern Art Archives, New York. Nelson goes on to describe the technical challenges of "a plastic shell without supporting framework." In early 1952 Nelson developed a seventy-eight-foot-diameter version of the house for his own family using a model of Fuller's geodesic frame in which both the skin and the geodesic frame were in transparent plastic. His lecture on the design in Chicago in mid-June was covered by the *New York Times* the following day (Betty Pepis, "Architect Offers Bubble for House," *New York Times*, June 18, 1952) and formed the basis of a detailed illustrated article in the July 1952 issue of *Interiors* in which Nelson describes his hope for a plastic skin that could be adjusted from transparent through to opaque depending on mood or season and announces that his office will work with Fuller and some students on a new model "suitable for use as a scale prototype…a laboratory experiment at working scale." George Nelson, "After the Modern House," *Interiors*, July 1952, 80–89.

26 | "The Cardboard House," *Perspecta* no. 2 (1953): 28–35.

27 | Betty Pepis, "People in Plastic Houses," *New York Times Magazine*, November 28, 1954, 50.

28 | "Bucky Fuller Builds an All Plastic Dome," *Architectural record,* November 1, 1955, 235.

29 | The detailed drawings of the project were published for the first time in 1985 in *The Artifacts of R. Buckminster Fuller, Vol. 3: The Geodesic Revolution, Part 1, 1947–1959*. The design had been carried out by Geodesics Inc. in Raleigh, under Thomas C. Howard (one of Fuller's first students at the School of Design in North Carolina). Having worked on the Skybreak house model for MoMA in 1952, Howard played a key role in the evolution of the geodesic role of plastic. His 175-foot-diameter Climatron building in St. Louis of 1960, for example, featured 4,000 triangles of plexiglass. It took the original goal of the skybreak house to produce a Garden of Eden effect to a new level of sophistication by literally creating twelve different internal climates regulated by a central "brain." The public was offered its own low-tech version of climate control through plastic in 1966 when *Popular Science* made plans of a "sun dome" covered with transparent vinyl skin available, with 80,000 of the blueprints licensed to Fuller being sold within a few years. Charles E. Rhine, "Amazing Sun Dome," *Popular Science*, May 1966, 108–12.

30 | "Bucky's Biggest Bubble," *Architectural Forum*, June 1966, 74–79. This sensual effect was clearly part of Fuller's promotion of the advanced use of plastic, as, for example, in his presentation of the model two months before the fair opened. "The effect from the outside, according to the designers, will be of a many-hued dome, sometimes silvery and sometimes rainbow colored." Kathleen Teltsch, "A 20 Story Bubble by Fuller to Hold U.S. Expo 67 Display," *New York Times*, March 1, 1967. The newspaper reinforced the point in its preview a few days before the opening: "the skin is real, breathing if not living skin, composed of nearly 2,000 vari-proportioned acrylic hexagons that throb and change color…As a result of all of this, the bubble changes all day long and looks different from one angle to another—here clear, there silvery, elsewhere like a rainbow." David Jacobs, "An Expo Named Buckminster Fuller," *New York Times*, April 23, 1967.

31 | "But I also had to assume in 1927 the largest clear plastic we had was the watch crystal, and it was celluloid, and it was not a water-tight at all, and it got yellow very rapidly, and it scratched very badly. And this is simply what they made celluloid dolls and things like that, and it was highly inflammable. It was not until, well, in 1927 I started these things. That's all I really had to they had at that time poker chips which were opaque, made out of casein from milk." Buckminster Fuller, "Everything I Know," session 9, part 11 (lecture, Buckminster Fuller Institute, January 1975).

32 | "It is a careless viewpoint that construes objective manifestations of the new society such as a new plastic or a new alloy as constituting unique discoveries of the individual designer, as though he personally had made an original finding of a basic chemical element, whereas he has but naively encountered a compound of isolated elements only after years of operative effort by the army of anonymous laboratory workers has provided that latest status quo of materialization." Buckminster Fuller, "Architecture from the Scientific Viewpoint," (paper given at NYU on May 12, 1939), *Student Publications of the School of Design, North Carolina State College* 3, no. 3 (1953): 6.

33 | E. J. Applewhite, ed., *Synergetics Dictionary: The Mind of Buckminster Fuller* (New York: Garland, 1986), 296.

34 | Buckminster Fuller, "I Figure," in Fuller, *Ideas and Integrities*, 112.

35 | Buckminster Fuller "World Design Initiative," 68.

36 | Buckminster Fuller, *Critical Path* (New York: Macmillan, 1981), 267.

37 | Loretta Lorance, *Becoming Bucky Fuller* (Cambridge: MIT Press, 2009), 164.

fig. 1 | Polygal hollow-core plastic sheets in top floor renovation of Avery Hall, Columbia University, by Stan Allen, New York

Good-Bye Tectonics, Hello Composites

Greg Lynn

I would like to begin with a discussion of a fruitful, while slightly troublesome, alignment of digital media and plastics that emerged here at Columbia's Graduate School of Architecture, Planning, and Preservation almost two decades ago—an alignment initiated by the Paperless Studios, begun by then-dean Bernard Tschumi. At that time there was much excitement surrounding digital media for design, but it was still held at arm's length from questions of material and construction. Within a few years, however, the enthusiasm shifted from experiments with digital media to the question: "How do we get this stuff off the machine and into the world?" In looking to materialize these experiments, we—Allen, Hani Rashid, Jesse Reiser, Bernard Tschumi, and myself—didn't look to glass, steel, concrete, or wood. Rather, many of the faculty and students in these Paperless Studios began speculating about plastics. In fact, Stan Allen chose to renovate the top floor of Avery Hall using Polygal hollow-core plastic sheets. | **fig. 1**

Digitally produced surfaces first materialized as monolithic, materially uniform fiberglass, spanning in scale from the lofted interior of the Ost/Kuttner Apartment in New York by Bill McDonald and Sulan Kolatan of 1997 to the miniature models I built at the New Jersey Institute of Technology and exhibited at Artists Space in 1995. The latter were produced using stereolithography, or 3-D printing with plastics that are curable with ultraviolet light. Plastic was the default material by which these digital works became physical. Either due to an initial gravitation toward plastics or because the amateur digital renderings that were being made at the time suggested monolithic surfaces, journalists and other architects simply assumed that the ambition for digital technology in the physical world should be smooth, continuous, unarticulated, and materially homogeneous.

Soon the faculty and students began to ask, "When are we going to get a 3-D printer big enough to print out entire buildings?" With very little design insight or theoretical reflection, the material question was asked, answered, and deferred to engineers who needed to invent either a new material or a new machine. It was implicitly assumed by many at the time that the development of digitally designed buildings would plateau with giant 3-D printers of some plastic material resembling renderings. But the idea that a building needed to aspire to the look and feel of a rendering was not an ambition I shared. I was more interested in the surface geometry of Non-Uniform Rational B-Spline (NURBS) curve networks—a computer-based mathematical model for generating and representing curves and surfaces. My reactionary response to the mandate for seamless, monolithic surfaces was to back into what I then called "intricacy" and what today is the phenomenon of "parametricism"—a more complex rethinking of architecture's unique tectonic tradition using digital technology.[1]

The principles of composites are at odds with the principles of tectonics, and while neither has anything to do with the advent of the digital medium per se, composites, together with a design sensibility of composite construction, are rapidly gaining momentum and expanding across design fields. Architects, on the other hand, continue to revive what they believe has always made architecture unique from the other arts—that is, tectonics. Many of my friends from the worlds of composites have never heard the term *tectonics* and do not know what it means or else are perplexed as to why architects continue to cling to it against the material and constructive logic of composites. The title of this essay, "Good-Bye Tectonics, Hello Composites," claims that architecture need not retrench once again, as it did with International Style Modernism, into an antiquated paradigm freshened with contemporary spatial, material, and production techniques.

Tectonics connotes a particular design sensibility as to how things are put together. Specifically, it refers to discrete layers that are attached mechanically at certain points yet remain distinct in form, material, shape, and alignment. The meaning and implications of tectonics in architecture was redefined for the twentieth century by Kenneth Frampton; it has social and political dimensions when understood within Hannah Arendt's matrix of labor, work, and action. Ironically, more than curves and blobs, the single most pervasive indulgence that digital technology has facilitated in architecture is the fetishization and mindless proliferation of mechanical attachments. The digital has arguably reinforced the mechanical.

One symptom of my progressive allergy to a tectonic logic of design and construction is a disdain for bolts, nails, screws, and most other mechanical fasteners. This is not due to the labor involved in fastening, but rather to the redundancy and needless labor involved in multiplying layers, systems, and structures simply for the sake of complexity. Composites are not likely to involve mechanical, tectonic connections; if they have a detail, it is likely at the scale of fibers and probably involves chemical or adhesive bonds between surfaces and fabrics. In and of themselves they fuse different materials as one. Furthermore, composites are anything but labor-free and need not be understood against a tradition of craft-based assembly and production. In fact, they are presently the *most* artisanal method of construction, since the layers of cloth and fibers are often laid by hand rather than by machine. The process is executed in a workshop, not a factory, and requires the oversight of a skilled person with experience mixing glues, hardeners, and accelerants; in impregnating cloth and fibers; and in cooking and curing parts during production. Labor, work, and action are all deeply modified in the social sense.

In my own work I have a developed a new respect for glue. If I was pointing a recent design graduate toward the future with just one word, it would not be *plastics*, but *glue*.

Parametric Tectonics
A "detail" within a tectonic system is the celebration of two or more different materials, surfaces, or elements coming together at a point, line, or surface. In tectonic systems, details are understood to proliferate like jewels marking the masterful resolution of different things held together. The

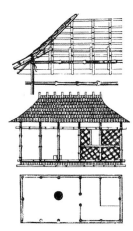

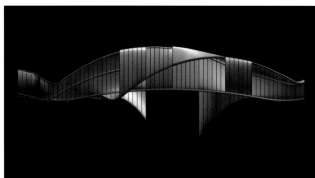

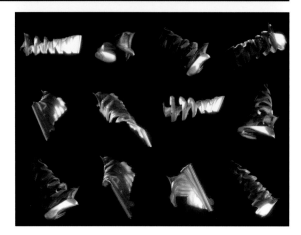

fig. 2 | Drawing of a Caribbean hut, by Gottfried Semper, 1851

fig. 3 | Elevation, Triple Bridge Gateway Competition for the Port Authority of New York, by Greg Lynn, 1994

fig. 4 | Hydrogen Pavilion for the OMV Corporation, by Greg Lynn FORM in partnership with Michael McInturf Architects and Martin Treberspurg & Partners, Vienna, 1996

epitome of the tectonic sensibility is best demonstrated in an 1851 drawing of a Caribbean hut by Gottfried Semper, where regulating geometric lineaments project through layers of structure and cladding connected by intricate details. | fig. 2 The tectonic details are the lashings, like those of a boat or tent. This particular example is one of my favorites, as it relies on a near-singular form of geometry and acknowledges differentials of force in the system and segregation of parts and materials where they bind. Disparate materials, surfaces, spaces, and the details that connect them are all organized by one geometry; the overall means are tectonic but they rely on the gradients of capacity in the materials and the binding itself. In contemporary architectural practice, digital technology—when directed toward parametricism—has often increased and enabled a proliferation of tectonics at ever-finer scales. The focus on details in any given whole assembly persists in a great deal of work today; the result is a celebration of even greater discreteness, not just between systems but within a system, requiring an exponential increase in connective details.

Perhaps the worst architecture of our recent history is that which has been based on a digital mode of parametrics without a conceptual or aesthetic foundation other than the complication, conflagration, and mindless variety of unique elements, which are present seemingly for no other reason than the fact that they are possible. These works effectively trumpet variety for variety's sake. When applied to broadly tectonic issues of structure and cladding, they have essentially been used to superficially complicate and entrench a corporate language that I believe is now exhausted. Championing undiscerning variation, often argued for on the basis of structural expressionism, contextualism, or both, these works have become standard practice among corporate firms.

What the Germanic and Scandinavian late Modernists elevated as a tectonic art form, and what the British high-tech generation made popular, is now being repackaged as a bland digital blend, where pseudomodular iterations deliver an artificially complex version of tectonics. Any ethical impetus latent in the original focus on work or labor of assembly is lost. Where previously the tectonic detail resolved a transition by celebrating it with a figure of assembly and construction, digital tectonic details now form a kind of nebulous cloud. This cloud represents the aforementioned "intricacy" when deployed in the service of spatial and volumetric definitions. When they are used to add character to an off-the-shelf curtain wall or brise soleil, I personally become numb to the reanimation of deadening familiarity. My interest in composites is in part a reaction to a conceptually vapid use of new digital mediums underpinned by habitual tectonics.

Animate/Animation

More than twenty years ago I acquired my first Silicon Graphics Incorporated (SGI) workstation and a Wavefront animation software license, enabling me to model using techniques such as force fields and particle animation. For several years, I had been using Bentley's Microstation, which I believe was the first commercial NURBS modeler. I knew that Alias, Wavefront, and Softimage had spline modeling tools as well, but most important to me were the particle, Binary Large OBject (BLOB), and force field deformer tools. I was interested in designing forms and spaces from the perspective of vectors and forces, rather than static points in space.

The Triple Bridge Gateway Competition (1994) was the first time I used these tools as a design medium. I was simultaneously learning and designing with the software. The competition, sponsored by the Port Authority of New York, called for a "triple bridge" over Ninth Avenue. The design of the project and its basis in animation software (using NURBS) is based on the lofting of catenoidal arcs as structural tubes connected by a series of surfaces forming an enclosing envelope. | fig. 3 This was done using animated paths that crisscrossed three-dimensionally.

Almost every preoccupation I have had with surface modeling as well as every architectural feature I've invented related to digital media all emerged as problems in this project. These included the reversal of surface normals from inside to outside along their length; "blebs," which are self-intersecting loops resulting from the offsetting of splines for material thickness; the need for profiles that deform along parallel and multiple nonparallel paths; and the lofting between two or more slightly offset surfaces to produce flanges and louvers. When first using this technology, my initial reflex was to translate the controlling geometric system into a tectonic construction of primary and secondary structure, fenestration, interior room subdivisions, and building systems. When friends and collaborators in the fields of transportation, aerospace, and racing sailboats saw the complex geometry of my building designs, they laughed at how the same surface was incorporating so many elements while defining the overall structure.

In 1996 I was commissioned to design the Hydrogen Pavilion for the OMV Corporation in Vienna. | fig. 4 The design concept was similar to that of the Triple Bridge Gateway, but without the self-intersecting and braided geometry of the twisting tubes. An envelope of laminated, curved wooden beams and ruled surfaces was designed with constraints supplied by an "inverse kinematic" (IK) skeleton in order to avoid self-intersecting curves. An IK skeleton is a series of adjacent lines connected with joints of rotation that can be limited in degree as well as stiffness. By moving any element along the skeleton, the entire linkage is adjusted within the preset constraints. The proportioning IK chain of limited flexure was aligned to solar data on the south facade and views from the autobahn on the north facade.

It was a simpler formal language than the previous project, with a different method of form generation via urban and solar context. Nonetheless, it employed a similarly conventional tectonic principle that was subtly adapted using the digital medium so that each and every part of the building was unique in order to produce a flowing, differentiated pattern connected with the site on the autobahn. All of the projects I was designing were intricate digital redeployments of tectonic systems with complex singularities. This holds true as well for the flowing syncopated interior and

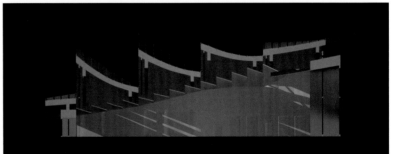

fig. 5 | Rendering, Hydrogen Pavilion for the OMV
Corporation, 1996

fig. 6 | Section, Hydrogen Pavilion, 1996

fig. 7 | Korean Presbyterian Church, by Greg Lynn FORM,
New York, 1999

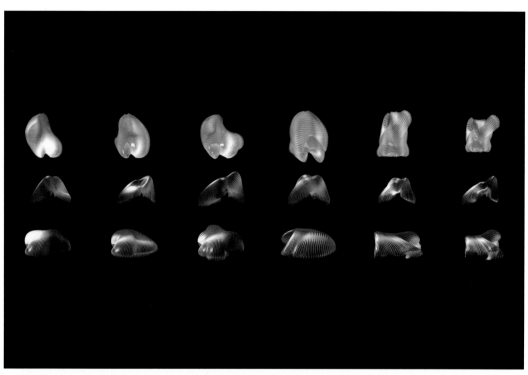

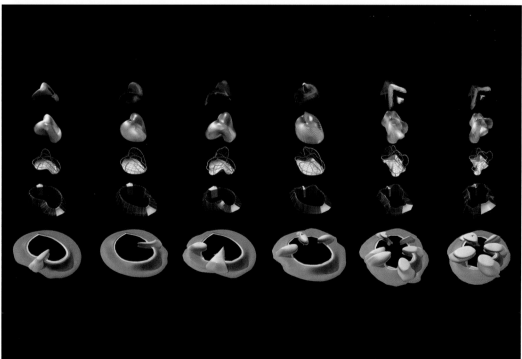

figs. 8 and 9 | Embryological House, by Greg Lynn
FORM 2000

exterior panels of the Korean Presbyterian Church (1999), where each one of the linear structural elements and ruled surfaces is different in both dimension and angle; there are typical details, but every location and size is unique. | figs. 5–7

At the 2000 ANY Conference at the Guggenheim Museum in New York I presented the Embryological House— a conceptual project in which I designed tens of thousands of houses all at once using a parametric logic of articulation and construction controlled by variable geometry and site constraints of sun angles. | figs. 8 and 9 A family of controlling curves determined the parameters from which unfolded the tectonic development of the exterior envelope with lozenge-shaped fenestrations, a secondary skin of louvered shading, and a primary and secondary structure modulated with the controlling geometry. There, Peter Eisenman questioned how design decisions are to be made when one is faced with the variation of a set of primitive forms with an internal tectonic logic: How can one determine the "best" house? To me the series was a single house that happened to have fifty thousand variations, all equally desirable.

The term *primitive* was a key concept for comprehending the project. Coined by William Bateson in the 1890s and central to his critique of Charles Darwin's theory of random mutation, "primitives in variation" explained the persistence of typologies or species within environments that continuously invoked a regulatory internal logic while simultaneously mutating.[2] Like an architect, Bateson located this internal regulation not in body plan but in growth by symmetry, where similar things evolve differently. What came to be called "Bateson's Rule" persists in developmental biology today.

More than the Embryological House, the design for a set of flatware for Alessi best epitomizes my antitectonic protosensibility. | fig. 10 It began with Alberto Alessi saying to me, "Greg, you should begin the design with a spoon, as all great flatware begins with the spoon. Bring a spoon back to us, and we will turn it into the fork and the knives and all the serving sets." From this origin, approximately forty-two different elements—from cake servers to fruit spoons to oyster

forks—were to be derived. I realized that they were going to have all the fun and that Alessi didn't really know me if he was asking me to design the perfect thing and then let him adapt it.

On the flight back to Los Angeles I made a primitive diagram showing the form and articulation needed to make either a spoon, a fork, or a knife (a sharp edge, tines, and webbing) that could be unfolded and articulated differently. | fig. 11 I designed this primitive in an animation package and targeted each point of control of the geometry with sliders, like those used to mix sound. By mixing some spoon with some fork with some knife, I could come up with the classic flatware typologies. There was no "original thing" being modified to make the others; it was a family. Each element came from the same source, but none of them came from the same typology. When you see them, you can tell they belong to the same family, but there is no single instance that can be identified as the typological ideal. By reading Emily Post, among others, I learned about the forms of flatware in relationship to their functions. New elements such as the cheese knife—which is both a knife and a single fork tine for cutting, stabbing, and serving cheese—were invented precisely in this way. Now, whenever I look at flatware, all I see are bad versions of spoons.

The implications of such an approach when considering a building system of components—cladding, for example, or structure—lend themselves very easily to variations within one layer of the building. We used such an approach with Robert Aish and Bentley for the design of a new cladding and structural frame for the Kleiburg Block (2007) in the Bijlmermeer district of Amsterdam. | fig. 12 But this parametric approach using variation and primitives is very difficult to think of in terms of composites. Composite construction and the design methods associated with it do not result in exponential variations of elements; they are fiber-based, and therefore the variations are too microscopic to lend themselves to expression in the conventional architectural sense. Although Bateson invented the concept of primitives in 1890, I could not have conceived of design primitives without the

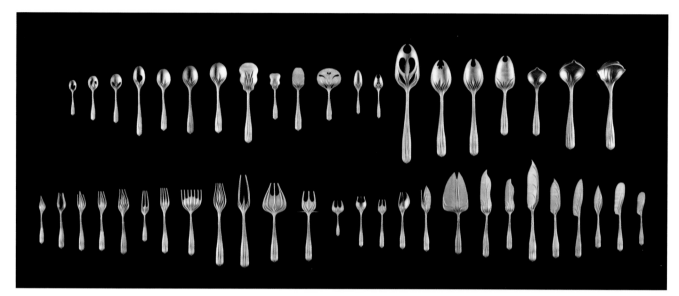

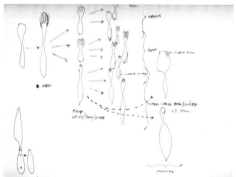

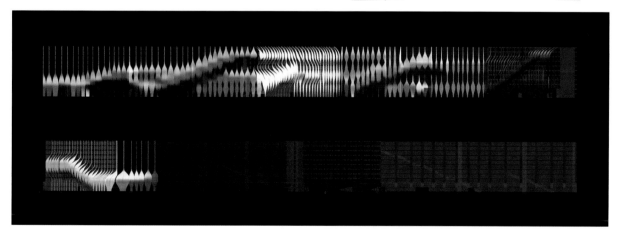

fig. 10 | Set of flatware for Alessi, by Greg Lynn, 2007

fig. 11 | Sketch for flatware for Alessi

fig. 12 | North and south elevations, Kleiburg Block, by
Greg Lynn FORM, Amsterdam, 2007

fig. 13 | *Tingler*, by Greg Lynn and Fabian Marcaccio,
Wexner Center for the Arts, Columbus, Ohio, 1999

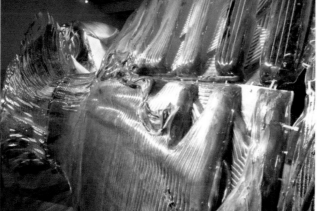

figs. 14 and 15 | *The Predator*, by Greg Lynn and Fabian Marcaccio, Columbus, 2001

digital medium. The flatware—as a transition from tectonics to composites—would have been unimaginable without digital tools; the collection is somewhere between monolithic objects defined by fiber-scale variations and a collection of varied elements and tectonic components. Perhaps the same concept holds for composites, as there certainly have been many composite materials over the last fifty years, including of course the oldest composite material, concrete.

Carbon fiber panels bolted to a steel frame do not adhere to a composite design sensibility, but rather fetishize it through tectonic applications. More than twenty years after the first response to computer software with variegated, "nonmodular" tectonic assemblies, this approach is still understood as the vanguard of the architecture field. There is a crisis in tectonics that can be seen by the presence of two different conferences on the subject of digital tectonics within a few weeks of this "plastics" conference. Two of the most talented designers and intelligent thinkers using digital tools today, Patrik Schumacher, who advocates for parametricism, and Ali Rahim, who advocates for elegance, are theorizing the need for the persistence of tectonics within, and due to, the digital medium.

Plastics and Composites

My first foray into plastics, the gateway material to hardcore composites, began with thermoforming sheets, in a collaboration with the painter Fabian Marcaccio. We started with a building-scale installation at the Secession Museum in Vienna called the *Tingler* (1999), which we were asked to reinstall at the Wexner Center for the Arts in Columbus, Ohio, for the exhibition Suite Fantastique (2001), curated by Jeffrey Kipnis and Sheri Gelden. | fig. 13 Marcaccio and I were both disappointed with the work's tortured tectonic quality and wanted to fix it with a new design, which became the *Predator*. | figs. 14 and 15 I was using plastics as a construction material for the first time, and also beginning to think plastically in terms of figure and ornament. The texture of Marcaccio's "paintants" was translated onto

the plastics—there was both the image on the material and a relief texture that was partially correlated with the image. It was built in my studio, and it technically ramped me up for this new mentality, as I bought a very large CNC router in order to produce it myself. In the Embryological House models I had started using the CNC tool paths as a decorative and structural pattern on the surface instead of making it smooth, as is the convention with a router. In the *Predator* the corrugations did stiffen the panels, but they were mostly ornamental. Later, the idea of integrating elements into rippled surfaces as well as disguising joints in panels by sweeping across them like icing on a cake became a technique that I used in a variety of interior projects such as the PrettyGoodLife Showroom in Stockholm (2001) and Uniserve's Headquarters in Los Angeles (2011). | figs. 16 and 17 In many of these cases, the material was a formed plastic sheet whose skin started to act like a relief, taking on a kind of two and a half dimensional quality, as in the earlier surfaces developed with Marcaccio.

This leads to my first principle of composites: surface minimalism. This simply means using surfaces to do what was previously done by one or more components. It is a fast technique to eliminate tectonic frames and cladding. This idea of coincident surfacing is not geometric, but rather uses surfaces to organize and swallow up what might otherwise involve several discrete building components. This leads to my second and third principles of composites: load paths and dynamic ergonomics. My interest in developing a sensibility of composites, rather than advancing what I see as an antiquated tectonic sensibility, is thanks to my collaboration with, and education by, designers and builders in other fields. It may also be because my intuition suggests that composites are somehow friendlier to the digital tools into which the field of architecture is currently migrating. The following case studies are all driven by industrial design constraints rather than building constraints. They are digitally designed forms—from the first concept and sketch—and they are all ergonomically intimate with the body.

The benefits of surface minimalism became clear with chair design, as I realized that tectonics weren't going to have much currency here. As was and still is common in the building industry, where we deal with tens of thousands of elements at a minimum, we might say, "I have the computational power and digital vision to make ten thousand pieces that are all different, and they're all going to come together." In the building industry people get excited about that. When you go to Vitra and you say, "This chair is currently made out of eight pieces. I'm going to make a new chair out of a thousand pieces and they're all going to be different, and they're all going to come together," they look at you like you're an idiot. They don't think you're being innovative. They think you're being *retarditaire*.

In furniture design, innovation lies in reducing the number of components, like Verner Panton's Panton chair (1960), which is made in one shot of molded plastic. I tried to respond to that situation. I studied the integration of elements on a surface by looking at late baroque architecture, for example Bernardo Vittone's brick chapels, which include Santa Chiara in Bra, Italy (1742), where discrete components are modeled across a single surface. The Vitra Ravioli chair has a soft top made with a computerized knitting machine that modulates the number of knots on the surface to produce a three-dimensional fabric that can conform to a complex three-dimensional surface. | fig. 18 The dimension across the arms is more than twice the dimension along the front of the chair; there are twice as many knots across the bucket seat as there are across the back. The painted fiber-reinforced plastic base acts like the legs of a conventional chair and the bucket serves as the arms, seat, and back in a single surface. The idea was to make a chair from two surfaces: one hard, one soft.

An earlier, and more mechanical, example of surface minimalism is a magazine case that I designed for *Visionaire* magazine. Greg Foley, the designer and editor at *Visionaire*, paired me with Hedi Slimane (who was running Dior Homme). *Visionaire* sells each issue for about five hundred dollars, a price justified by the exotic cases. On our initial

fig. 16 | PrettyGoodLife Showroom, by Greg Lynn FORM, Stockholm, 2001

fig. 17 | Universe Headquarters, by Greg Lynn FORM, Los Angeles, 2011

fig. 18 | Vitra Ravioli, by Greg Lynn FORM, 2005

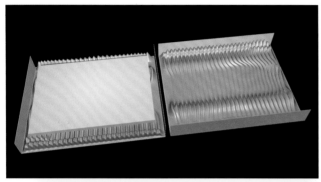

fig. 19 | Case for *Visionaire* magazine, by Greg Lynn, 2001

fig. 20 | Alessi Coffee and Tea Towers, by Greg Lynn, 2003

conference call, Slimane said, "I love your work, and I want you to have total freedom. There's only a few constraints. Make it a rectangle of an exact dimension in Cool Grey Number Three, and there can be no visible signs of attachment, such as hinges or clasps." I got off that call wondering what to do, as there was so little room to maneuver. I decided to make the supporting cradle as well as the hinge and clasp hardware with a floating surface inside a folded, powder-coated, aluminum Cool Grey Number Three case. Inside, there is a plastic vacuum-formed insert that bites together in only one way: vertically. | fig. 19 When you close the case and hold it in any way other than precisely vertically, it stays closed. We eliminated the hinges and the clasps by modifying the contours of the surface, so the magazine floats on similar smaller ripples inside the case. This was the first instance in which I eliminated hardware by employing surfaces to do the work of what had previously been a mechanical solution.

I applied the rippled texture of the CNC tool path at a much smaller scale to the superformed titanium Alessi Coffee and Tea Towers (2003). Along with a dozen other architects, I was asked to revisit the design of coffee and tea services on the twenty-fifth anniversary of the first such project, which had included sets designed by Michael Graves, Robert Venturi, Hans Hollein, Richard Meier, and others. I was told that the problem with architects designing coffee pots is that they hate handles, and was asked to include handles in my design. I responded by making the entire surface one giant handle. | fig. 20 An inner flask holding the hot liquid is sandwiched between two textured skins bonded to the flask with silicon, allowing the containers to be held anywhere without burning your hand. The texture invites the shapes to be held. There is a double-orientation to each element: the tray can support the vessels vertically when they have liquid in them, and their shapes are also imprinted on the tray so that the four vessels can be flipped on their backs and locked into the tray for display, like an open flower, when they're empty and sitting on your coffee table (or in most cases, in a museum). | fig. 21

For the fabrication process, I was asked to supply a digital design for 3-D printing, which would then be given to artisans at the Alessi factory and produced in sterling silver. Given the budget, I realized that I might be able to tool them myself and have them made in titanium using superforming. I found High Tech Welding in Orange County, California, and we built prototype molds in my office, then vacuum-formed plastic into them to test the concept. They then rebuilt these molds in a graphite material, welded together two titanium skins along their edges, and heated the skins inside the molds in a roughly one-thousand-degree oven in a zero-oxygen atmosphere. Pumping in argon gas inflated the heated titanium into the molds. Finally, some oxygen was pumped into the molds and ignited, driving the soft titanium into the tool paths and giving the sheets their final shape and detail. The concept of a textured exterior shell separated from the interior hot liquid flask was commercialized in the Alessi Supple Cups (2005). | fig. 22 These have no tray but are designed with mating curves so that they can nest together. Each one has 120 adjacent handles, forming a rippled surface.

These projects manufactured in woven cloth, fiberglass, titanium, and ceramic are all plastic in their conception. Common to all of them are the principles that 1) the surfaces work as structure, usually as shells, 2) the surfaces are ergonomic, and 3) what might have been multiple tectonic elements are integrated into a single or reduced number of surfaces. These three principles were, for me, the beginning of a composite sensibility. They all required the production of a mold rather than the mere measurement and fabrication of a material, by 3-D printing or other means. The requirement of a mold is a particular constraint of plastic materiality. Poured concrete is a plastic material in this sense, as it is cast into a mold or formwork. And just like formed concrete, a plastic matrix that flows into a formwork can, while liquid, have integrated reinforcements added into it, oriented along load paths. Composite builders have adopted this sensibility by replacing steel reinforcements

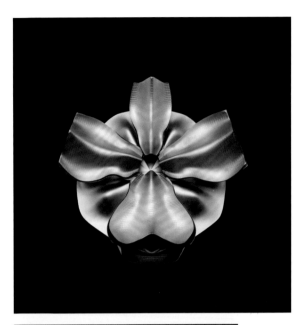

fig. 21 | Alessi Coffee and Tea Towers, by Greg Lynn, 2003

fig. 22 | Alessi Supple Cups, by Greg Lynn, 2005

with woven fabrics or unidirectional fibers or tapes, which are then cooked together and consolidated. The important principle at work here is that unlike a mechanically assembled structural frame, these fibrous materials can have all of their different layers in oblique orientations relative to one another and to the form they are making. This is the most powerful idea regarding composites: the patterns and geometry of structure can be completely separate from the geometry of form, aperture, interior, or spatial subdivision. This is true plasticity.

And it is a provocative concept for architects in particular, because in our discipline, despite digital technology, we maintain the idea that a singular geometry should govern and control all systems of construction, enclosure, articulation, and decoration as if projected via Xray through the building. Despite the shift from platonic geometry to splines, polygons, and subdivision surfaces, there is still a received notion of using the geometry to define a spatial envelope as the centerline or lineament location for building components and details. Despite the proliferation of the digital medium, geometry is still regulating tectonics by defining form and pseudomodularity at the same time. What has taken me nearly twenty years to realize is that the geometry that defines a space or volume need not be the same geometry that defines its construction by parts. In fact, in composite structures as well as the Finite Element Analysis (FEA) that often accompanies their design and engineering, the geometry of shape and the geometry of construction are completely different. The former logic is of shape, and the latter is of load paths. The dissociation between the envelope's geometry and its structure can apply to the location, arrangement, or geometry of interior room subdivisions, circulation, fenestration, and mechanical building systems. There is no geometric hierarchy.

The contemporary racing sailboat is an example of a building-scale object built with the plastic sensibility of multiple geometries. The global form of the deck and hull follows a geometry of hydrodynamics, deck functions, and accommodation, whereas the structure and details follow a logic of load paths and reinforcement regions defined by layers and orientation of woven cloth and unidirectional fibers. Increasingly, functional, aesthetic, and structural components are integrated into fewer and fewer surfaces. There are very few pieces of metal—which has a low strength-to-weight ratio in comparison to fibers—on a racing sailboat. Nor is metal used much anymore in high-performance automobiles; Formula 1 racecars are now built almost entirely out epoxy resin and carbon-fiber-reinforced plastics.

In the world of plastics, everything needs a tool to be formed against and therefore each object is built at least twice. But a mold, tool, or plug can be used more than once. Even when building only one part, tools can be used for more than one material, as when Bill Kreysler used one mold to fabricate the three-by-two-meter Sciarra Chandelier (2010) in translucent-fiber cloth and fiber-reinforced cement. Unrolled stainless steel rings are used to separate the mold into regions, and, once molded, the individual parts mate along grooves and are connected together into a monolithic shell.

Another solution is the invention of a flexible tooling system for plastics such as that developed by Bill Pearson at the North Sails factory in Minden, Nevada. We used their load path sails, which are one of the lightest and strongest materials on Earth, for the Swarovski Crystal Palace at Design Miami (2009). | fig. 23 The surfaces are constructed in layers, beginning with Mylar, miles of pre-impregnated (pre-preg) natural and red dyed aramid fiber and carbon fiber, Swarovski crystals, and a final layer of Mylar. | figs. 24 and 25 The glue that holds this together is already impregnated on the surface of the fibers, and at room temperature it is tacky. The whole construction is sealed in a vacuum bag and cooked under pressure to heat the pre-preg fibers and consolidate the materials together into a monolithic sheet. What is unique about this North Sails process is that it is happening on a deformable mold in the flying shape of the sail so that the membrane is already in a complex curved shape as it is laid up and cooked. The fibers are drawn by a robotic arm on a gantry in sweeping curves across this three-dimensional dynamic mold.

fig. 23 | Swarovski Crystal Palace, by Greg Lynn and North Sails, Miami, 2009

figs. 24 and 25 | Swarovski Crystal Palace during fabrication with the flexible tooling system, developed by Bill Pearson, Minden, Nevada, 2009

fig. 26 | Tape material made of parallel strands of carbon and Dyneema

fig. 27 | 3Di chair prototype, by Greg Lynn and North Sails, Art Institute of Chicago, 2011

fig. 28 | 3Di chair during fabrication, 2011

Pearson is now producing a new tape material made of parallel, unidirectional strands of carbon and Dyneema—a lightweight and high-strength polyethylene—laid side by side. | fig. 26 As a single layer it is fragile, but when laid in patterns and cooked together it makes a membrane that does not need the Mylar layers to hold the fibers in place. We worked with this material for two chair prototypes commissioned by the Art Institute of Chicago. They are the lightest chairs ever made, weighing just a few ounces. | fig. 27 Like the Panton chair, they are monolithic and seamlessly change from rigid to flexible. These chairs are a new form of structure never before seen in architecture—or any other field, for that matter. Each one is a compression shell under its own weight, taking the shape of the mold on which it was formed. | fig. 28 Once someone sits in it and overcomes its compressive strength, however, the carbon tapes get loaded into a tension material that behaves like a fabric. We had roughly eight hundred pounds loaded onto it (three adults and a child) and it didn't fatigue. Thin strands of Spectra fiber are glued between layers of tapes to provide support; it is all fiber, without any metal hardware. I have always disliked purely tensile materials; no matter how exotic the methods—whether the chain models of Antoni Gaudi, the soap bubbles of Frei Otto, or the rolling ball and relaxed point clouds of digital methods—what is being calculated is an optimal gravity-derived shape; it is called "form finding" rather than "design." Engineers love it, as it is a situation in which form and structure are identical, which they call "optimized." I apologize to the engineers out there who love tensile fabrics, but those fabrics are only ever one shape, and what they call optimized, I find to be sagging.

To the great concern of my friends and family, I've recently become obsessed with boats. Apart from my fascination with the ocean and harnessing the energy of the wind, I am passionate about sailing because of the material innovation present in that industry. Of course the design sensibility of yachts is burdened by the habit of ensconcing wealthy owners in a cocoon of brass and wood. There is also the "cabin"

that sits like a primitive hut on the deck of the boat. But when it comes to the rig and sails that move the boat through the air, and the hull and foil forms that move the boat through the water, I've discovered that naval architecture is now indistinguishable in its technical sophistication and intelligence from aerospace engineering, while being much less costly. For better or worse, I'm now getting into this world and trying to make some trouble via a few small projects, transforming the styling and interiors while learning from designers about Computational Fluid Dynamic (CFD) modeling of surfaces and FEA design of structural shells. I now have all the tools required to make composite prototypes in my studio so we can laminate and even cook them in-house and learn more about the materials we are designing.

I was recently asked by the Tourism Development & Investment Company in Abu Dhabi to design two boats for an island resort: one a catamaran for day sailing and transport to dive locations, and the other a fast, fuel-efficient luxury power shuttle from the mainland to the island, as currently people arrive on the island via a small jet. These were designed in collaboration with the yacht designer Fred Courouble. The SunCat disposes of the traditional cabin in favor of a "flying carpet" of carbon that rests on six points, floating above the deck to provide shade. | figs. 29–31 It incorporates a cockpit for one person to operate the boat. I had the opportunity to meet with one of the largest commercial boatbuilders in the world and was told a story about the time they worked with Philippe Starck. When Starck started his design process he asked if they would lend him a boat for the summer and requested it to be delivered to his garden. They set it up, and then not long after got a call asking if they could come back and move it. When they arrived with a crane, Starck said something like, "I thought these things were always sideways," so they made a special cradle to hold it at a twenty-degree angle. He lived in this sideways boat in a garden in southern France for a summer while he designed. That's why he is brilliant: he had the intelligence to think about how you live in a boat differently than you do in a house. It's an opportunity to live on

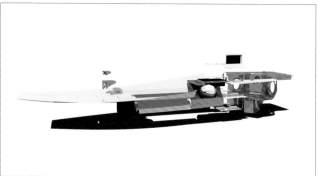

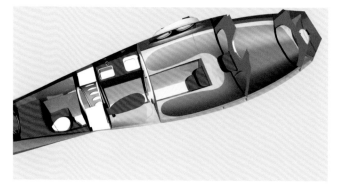

fig. 29 | Fifty-six-foot SunCat catamaran, by Greg Lynn and
Fred Courouble, 2009

figs. 30 and 31 | Composite boat surface with integrated
equipment and functions

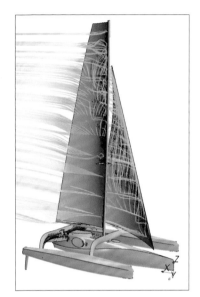

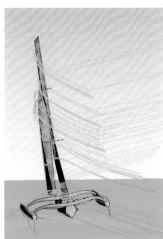

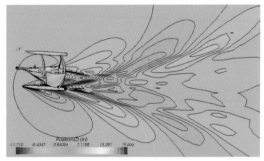

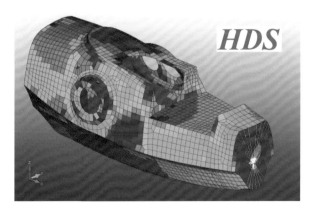

figs. 32–36 | CFD performance analysis and FEA structural
analysis, by Fred Courouble

fig. 37 | Molded benches, Woodland Cemetery, by Erik Gunnar Asplund, Stockholm, 1940

the walls for a little while. Similarly, I've been looking at how the ergonomics of a boat are constantly moving and nonhorizontal, and this is affecting how I think about architecture. Now, when I see a wall, I start thinking about either rolling it over or leaning against it.

I am designing a boat for myself as a way of exploring the language of composites, as well as how to live intensively in an interior where you occupy the walls as well as the floors. Like in a space capsule, all of the equipment and functions are intensely integrated into the surfaces to save weight and space, as well as to produce an ergonomic interior landscape without redundancy but also with curvilinear comfort and the multipositioning of functions. In addition to the interiors, I am generating the styling cues and then Courouble analyzes and engineers them with the full power of state-of-the-art CFD performance analysis and FEA structural analysis from Americas Cup consultants. | **figs. 32–36** Strange forms and surfaces created primarily for style can have performance consequences, and thus the design-and-optimization loop begins. It is important to understand that there is no one optimal shape, but instead a cycle of design, analysis, and engineering. Usually this cycle begins with a precedent and is driven by common sense and experience. In this case, many assumptions and precedents were tabled in favor of an alien initiation of surface language for the hulls that was then tweaked into high performance. This project is now designed and engineered, and, amazingly, the entire carbon construction weighs less than two tons, supports loads of tens of tons, and will move under wind power at close to thirty miles an hour at one and a half times the speed of the wind. This project, as well as my passion for sailing, has affected the way I think about more conventional architecture and design problems: making things lighter and stronger, designing things that move and rotate, and taking a new approach to ergonomics.

Composite ergonomics are not really about the materials or method of manufacture as much as they are about using surfaces for multiple purposes. The Ravioli chair was designed to be occupied facing forward, for instance, but you can also throw an arm and a leg diagonally over the back. In the same way, floors, walls, and built-in elements can be used for a multitude of purposes, all of which are integrated into surfaces. A precedent that I have returned to continuously in this respect are the molded benches attached to the plywood veneered walls in the chapel waiting rooms at Woodland Cemetery in Stockholm by Erik Gunnar Asplund. | fig. 37 Perhaps no surface is as multifunctional as a flat floor, but from the flat there is a multitude of ergonomic surface possibilities. Composite ergonomics can range in scale from the details of absorbing equipment into plastically deforming surfaces to the scale of subdividing spaces with curved, folded surfaces.

The Bloom House in Los Angeles is inspired by this approach to molding walls in curves, at the scale of both rooms and furniture. All of the mechanical equipment that was not custom made, including the fireplace, cabinets, lighting, kitchen appliances, and bathroom fixtures, is integrated into custom-shaped surfaces. | figs. 38 and 39 Inside the bathrooms, the vanities, sinks, mirrors, and linen closets are swallowed into surfaces that are sliced and thermoformed in Corian. Much research and development was invested in this house to make the bathrooms and kitchen affordable using inexpensive molds. All the equipment, door handles, and mirrors are absorbed into these molded composite surfaces. Most important is the spatial quality that emerges from this plastic approach to molding walls and ceilings. The ground-level living space is one room, but it is subdivided, modulated, and made comfy by curved walls that fold out from the long, lateral party walls. The home office, breakfast nook, powder room, pantry, dining room, and living room are all defined within this single continuous space by curved plaster walls. The floor is modulated and stepped to define different spatial zones. In order to bring the height of the living and dining rooms into a comfortable scale, the ceiling is modulated in height and shape by a large, luminous lantern built out of fiber-reinforced composites by Bill Kreysler.

figs. 38 and 39 | Bloom House, by Greg Lynn FORM, Los Angeles, 2010

figs. 40 and 41 | Traveling pavilion for the Index Awards, by Greg Lynn FORM, 2011

Ironically, plastics often prove to be more sustainable and economical than natural materials such as timber and brick. I am presently trying to use plastics in a nondisposable—daresay collectible—manner. I was commissioned to design traveling pavilions for the Index Awards (2011), which feature "Design to Improve Life" in five categories. More than eighty objects are displayed outdoors in a variety of climates at international design festivals over a two-year period. | **figs. 40 and 41** The Index Awards celebrate sustainable design, and they are Danish, so there was an initial presumption that renewable wood construction would be the most desirable approach. Instead, carbon-reinforced plastic was the clear winner in terms of energy use, durability, and ease of transport. We were able to fit all nine pavilions and the display vitrines into a single shipping container, saving hundreds of thousands of Euros and energy over two years. The pavilions were so durable that there was zero maintenance. The whole approach to the design was to be sustainable not just in material, but in transportation, operation, and life cycle. It made me realize that plastic almost always wins when it comes to material efficiency and sustainability. Plastics are so efficient that we throw them away, and this becomes the entire problem with them. If there is a way to encourage permanent, and not disposable, use of plastics, then they will become a long-term sustainable solution due to their ease in forming, efficiency, strength-to-weight ratio, and recyclability.

This brings me to one final expression of plastics: the plastic brick. I have two kids who are now too old for big plastic toys, but there was a time when my wife, Sylvia Lavin, and I would get attached to their cute, colorful, large, hollow, roto-molded, plastic toys and were heartbroken when they would grow out of them. We live in Southern California, where many kids go to schools where plastic toys and television are forbidden in favor of wooden toys and books, which we find very silly. In fact, we have never had a sentimental attachment to a wooden toy our kids have owned, only the plastic ones. Nonetheless, we would dutifully take the outgrown plastic toys to the secondhand shop.

At the time, I was fascinated with Matthias Kohler's work of stacking bricks in complex bonding patterns from a seminar at the ETH Zürich; I was also following Office dA's work with manually stacked masonry using digital tools for design and documentation. Out of this confluence I had the idea to build a wall in our house out of the recycled hollow plastic toys. I would use them as bricks and stack them together by interlocking them intricately. I started by scanning them at high resolution and composing them in the computer. | figs. 42 and 43 My plan was to find their intersections with one another, cut them with a robot, and weld them together; the development and manufacture of this was all done by Andreas Froech's company Machineous. We made several furniture elements using these recycled, or upcycled, toys, including a Duck Table, Eggplant Dining Table, Eggplant Side Table, Shark Table, Dog Shelf, and Whale End Table. | figs. 44 and 45 We have a website where we will buy these toys for more than their original retail price, and we have eBay alerts for whenever they come on the market. We only manage to get less than a dozen of each model per year, and we need thousands to make walls and enclosures out of them. Because we couldn't find enough toys, we designed a custom, hollow, roto-molded brick and launched an interior wall system called Blobwall that was marketed by Panelite and manufactured by Machineous. We have built several of these walls commercially and a giant Blobwall Brick Dome at SCI-Arc. | fig. 46

My wife kept telling me that she thought the right scale for the Blobwalls and the Toy Furniture was a fountain. On a visit to Rome I spent several hours visiting most of Bernini's fountains and realized why her intuition made so much sense. A building, as I have mentioned, is composed of tens or hundreds of thousands of similar parts. Fountains are a very strange typology that piles together disparate figures. For example, Triton's Fountain by Bernini has four dolphins with four scrolls, two keys to the city, beehives with bees, large shells, and Triton, holding another shell from which he drinks. So the fountain typology has more figures than

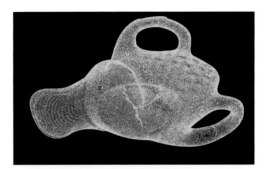

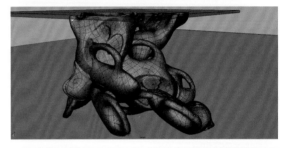

figs. 42 and 43 | Scanned hollow plastic toy recomposed digitally

fig. 44 | Duck Table, by Greg Lynn FORM, 2008

fig. 45 | Eggplant Side Table, by Greg Lynn FORM, 2008

sculpture and fewer than architecture. In 2010 I made a site-specific fountain for the courtyard of the Hammer Museum in Los Angeles. Whales make the pool, Blobwall bricks are the rusticated base, and sharks have water streaming out of them. | fig. 47 The *Fountain* traveled on the top of a container ship across the Atlantic and is now in Vienna at Thyssen-Bornemisza Art Contemporary. I designed and built *Fountain 2* (2011) as two counter-spiraling sequences of Blobwall Bricks and sharks. | fig. 48 This larger-than-furniture, smaller-than-architecture use of plastics is about upcycling existing quasi-disposable objects into permanent objects of use.

In closing, I will note that plastics are more about chemistry than geometry. My friend was an assistant director on a 2007 Zak Penn film called *The Grand*. He asked me if I had any models they could borrow that might work for a scene in which Woody Harrelson presents a series of tragically failed casinos. They ended up using the very first model of a Blobwall brick. The actors are asked to improvise during a poker competition, and there is a funny moment when Harrelson explains one casino. He totally gets the plastic sensibility and the fact that it is all about chemistry:

> I like this one, too. It's called Hector's Frozen Cart. Now, I'm going to be candid with you and let you know that I don't know what I was thinking when I came up with this particular design. But I was under the influence of cocaine and heroin and marijuana and LSD and mushrooms and some ecstasy…and you know how sometimes you get that cocktail just right and then there's just a boom!

1 | See Patrik Schumacher, *The Autopoiesis of Architecture, Volume 1: A New Framework for Architecture* (Chichester: J. Wiley, 2010) and Patrik Schumacher, *The Autopoiesis of Architecture, Volume 2: A New Agenda for Architecture* (Chichester: J. Wiley, 2012).

2 | See William Bateson, *Materials for the Study of Variation, treated with especial regard to discontinuity in the origin of species* (London: Macmillan & Company, 1894).

fig. 46 | Blobwall dome, by Greg Lynn FORM, SCI-Arc, Los Angeles, 2005

fig. 47 | *Fountain*, by Greg Lynn FORM and Andreas Fröch, courtyard of the Hammer Museum, Los Angeles, 2010

fig. 48 | *Fountain 2*, by Greg Lynn FORM, Los Angeles, 2011

Projects

Blobwall and Bloom House

Greg Lynn

The design of the Blobwall (2005) begins with the redefinition of architecture's most basic building unit, the brick, in lightweight colorful plastic. The wall system is built of a low-density, recyclable, impact-resistant polymer. Each wall is assembled from individual robotically trimmed hollow bricks that interlock with exacting precision, eliminating the need for glue or mortar. The brick elements are modular but each component is specifically trimmed to a unique shape based on how it intersects with its neighboring bricks. The complex interlocking between bricks is defined geometrically in 3-D; then intersecting curves are extracted and used to program a CNC-robotic arm with a cutting head that custom trims each element. The discarded scrap material is then ground up and reused to make more bricks. The use of plastics for construction might seem counterintuitive to preconceptions of sustainable materials but here plastics are not disposable but permanent. The energy required to fire a traditional brick and the energy used to transport and assemble it is saved through the use of lightweight and minimal material in the rigid, hollow plastic brick. Blobwall domes, partition walls, and fountains are freestanding, indoor-outdoor constructions. The blob unit, or "brick," is a trilobed hollow shape that is mass-produced through rotational molding. Each assembly uses one of six color schemes that are composed of a gradient blend of seven different brick colors. In the Renaissance, palaces were designed to mix the opulent and the base, the elegant and the rustic. Stones were hewn so planar faces could stack and bond, but the outward faces of the stones formed cloven and rustic facades. The Blobwall recovers the voluptuous shapes, chiaroscuro, and grotto-like masonry textures of baroque and Renaissance architecture in pixelated gradients of vivid color. It is both product—like a child's toy—and building.

The Bloom House (2010) is situated on a 35-by-90 foot lot adjacent to a beach in Southern California. The volume maximizes the allowable mass on-site; what once was a series of bungalows is now a dense neighborhood of row houses. The infill house was designed with a complex section of interlocking spaces and voluptuous interior wall and ceiling surfaces that emerge through a rectangular volume to frame ocean views and allow for sea breezes. In order to capitalize on the facade and views to the beach, the house has large operable doors and windows to create an indoor-outdoor living room. The other three sides of the boxlike volume are fenestrated with curved, eyelet-shaped windows that pinch to align to a continuous stainless steel reglet that wraps around the house. The structure of the house is eliminated at the corners, eroding the volume and giving diagonal views to the Pacific Ocean. The interior of the house is based on a new type of space that is neither "free plan," like so many beach lofts, nor raumplan of interlocking volumes. The paradoxical mandate from the owners was to design an open continuous space that was intimate and cozy. The internal volume is modulated with curvilinear surfaces that emerge from ceilings and walls to define enclosures, furniture, and light. By curving, folding, puckering, and looping surfaces it was possible to make an open space that also had discrete pockets. Views are controlled with undulating walls and ceiling as well as modulating floor heights. Across the length of this open space is a self-supporting luminous fiberglass lantern attached to the ceiling. The lantern is panelized into twenty-two parts, each joined at flanges. Two curvilinear enclosures at one end of the lantern contain the powder room and office and in the living room a wall bulges to define the fireplace. Within this one vast folded room is a living room, dining room, powder room, kitchen, breakfast nook, and office. The house is divided vertically into two and a half stories with the garage, maid's room, and utility rooms located on the level below the living space, with three bedrooms and two baths above and a large roof terrace with unobstructed views of the Pacific Ocean.

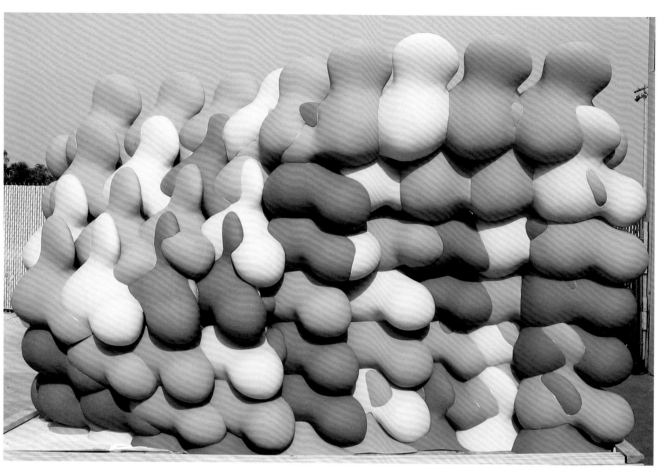

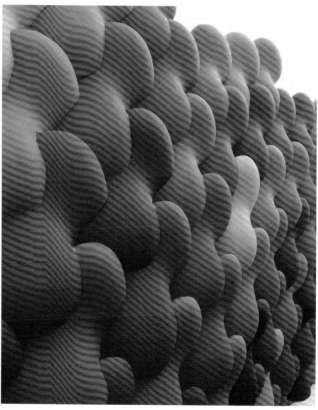

Full-scale mock-up, Blobwall, 2005

Detail

Blobwall and Bloom House
Greg Lynn

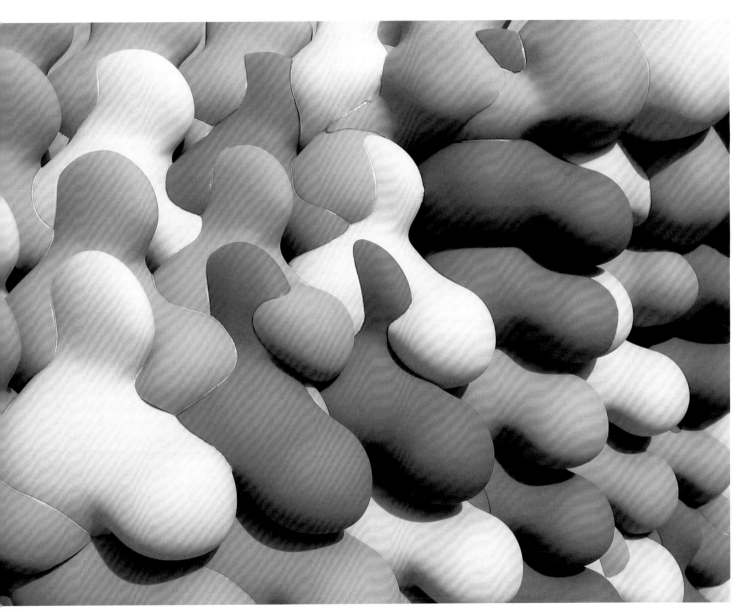

Detail

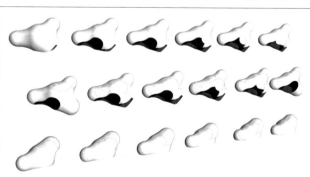

Blobwall pavilion

Schematic design for bricks

Blobwall and Bloom House

Greg Lynn

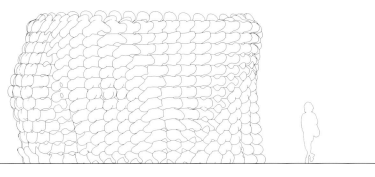

O Wall

40 x 13 = 520 bricks

scale 1' = 1/4"

O Wall plan and O Wall section

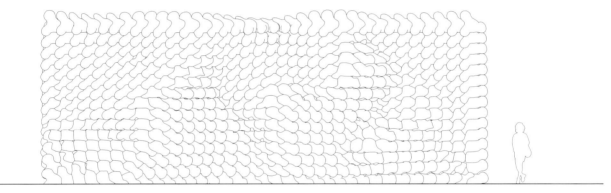

I Wall

35 x 15 = 525 bricks

scale 1' = 1/4"

I Wall plan and I Wall elevation

Blobwall and Bloom House

Greg Lynn

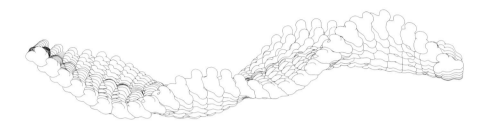

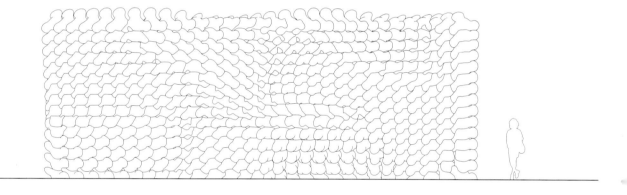

S Wall

40 x 13 = 520 bricks

scale 1' = 1/4"

S Wall plan and S Wall section

Fireplace and living room, Bloom House, 2010

opposite:

Interior view with kitchen beyond

Sculptural light fixture by Bill Kreysler

Living room

opposite:
Roof plan

Second-floor plan

First-floor plan

Basement-level plan

Kitchen and island

Kitchen cabinets

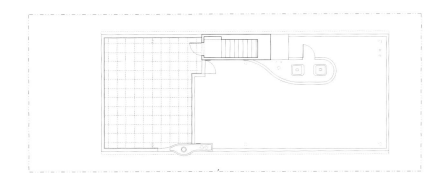

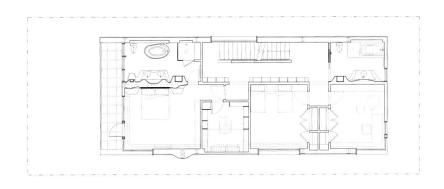

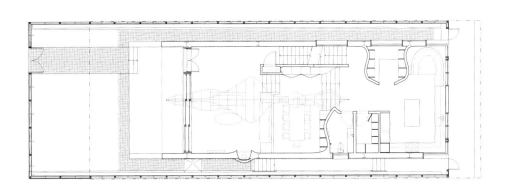

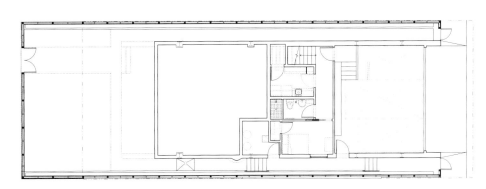

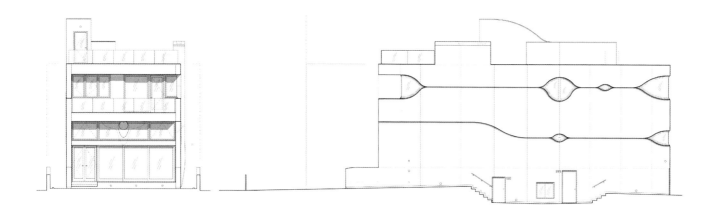

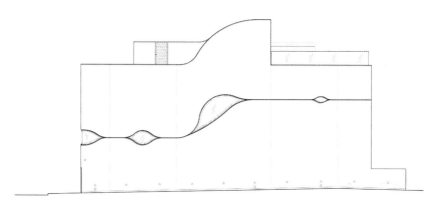

Elevations

Plastic Man Goes to Market

Michael Graves

The superhero Plastic Man was one of my idols as a teenager growing up in Indiana in the 1940s and early 1950s. My friends and I looked forward to the adventures of this comic book character who represented not only the morality of a bad guy turned good, but also the public's fascination with plastic as a material. As the story goes, during the course of a robbery, a burglar named Eel O'Brian was shot and doused with a vat of acid. He fled the crime scene and lost consciousness. Upon awakening, he found himself in a monastery, where kindhearted monks converted him from a dastardly criminal into a daring law enforcer much like Superman. During his rehabilitation, O'Brian discovered that the acid had transformed his physiology so that he could now stretch to any length and contort himself into any shape. He thereafter became known as Plastic Man. On the cover of the May 1949 edition of the comic book—which cost all of ten cents at the time—Plastic Man is featured wildly outstretched, like a rubber band, speeding into space and rescuing the so-called last man on Earth. The subliminal message was that plastic was a savior as well as a symbol of the future. | fig. 1

With his chemical transformation and his malleability, I think of Plastic Man as a paradigm for the material itself, and its applications in product design and manufacturing. In addition to being able to assume various shapes, one of Plastic Man's chief attributes was his durability. Typical of plastics of his time, he had limited abilities to alter his color. His red and yellow striped uniform resembled many examples of Bakelite flatware. This association is so compelling to me that I am going to focus not on the use of plastics in architecture, but rather on the other side of our design practice: consumer products.

In designing products for retailers such as Target and manufacturers such as Alessi, I often find myself thinking back to the Bakelite objects of my youth, and their predecessors made of the thermoplastic called celluloid. These are the types of objects that used to make going to the flea market so interesting. Because three-dimensional design and the specific materials used for it are so integral to each other, a brief history of products that use plastics is relevant here.

All the chemistry, manufacturing techniques, and nomenclature associated with the plastics used in products are mind-boggling. In the beginning, plastics incorporated ingredients of biological origin, such as cellulose, but they became completely synthetic by the early twentieth century. There are many permutations, each with different properties. Products over the decades have incorporated dozens of types of plastics and a wide variety of manufacturing techniques.

In the mid-nineteenth century, cellulosic plastics, including celluloid, were utilized to make objects of daily use such as boxes, shoehorns, serving utensils, buttons, trinkets, and the like. | fig. 2 The colors and translucency of the material are quite intriguing. It could be molded easily and, early on, was often used in place of ivory, which was becoming scarce. Cast-plastic serving utensil handles replicated ornate carved ones made of ivory. Even as utensil styles evolved and Bakelite and other plastics became prevalent, one still commonly found the handles of flatware and other tabletop utensils imitating ivory, principally by their color and their feel to touch. Many of these were made in England. I remember being invited to the home of the architect Jim Stirling and eating dinner with silverware that had mock-ivory handles. Over time the handles had acquired slight variations in color, which gave them charm and an even greater resemblance to well-worn ivory.

Bakelite was invented in the early twentieth century by a Belgian chemist named Leo Baekeland. He too was looking for a substitute material, in his case, for shellac. Shellac, like cellulose, is of biologic origin and can be considered a "natural" plastic. The by-product of the lac beetle, shellac would eventually have limitations in its availability, unlike mass-produced synthetic plastics. It also was susceptible to scratching, and marring when exposed to water or acids.

Bakelite, a trade name, was the first fully synthetic plastic and was more durable than biologic plastics. (It is generically referred to as a phenolic because it uses the compound phenol, along with other ingredients, such as formaldehyde.)

Over the following decades, the American market saw a proliferation of kitchenware, desk accessories, game pieces, jewelry, and other objects made of Bakelite, many of which featured jolly, fetching colors and witty designs. | fig. 3 In flatware of the Art Deco era and shortly thereafter, we see terrific combinations and patterns that juxtapose different colors of plastic, or combinations of translucent and opaque plastic. There are also wonderful examples of celluloid and phenolic plastics that imitate the mottled look of tortoise-shell—like ivory, a scarce material that fell out of favor for conservation and environmental reasons.

As plastics became more prevalent, the designs became more complex, as did their assembly. This is especially true with Art Deco radios and clocks, which came in a fascinating variety of shapes and colors. One of my picture books featuring Deco clock radios shows one design that was available in twelve color combinations. I cannot imagine that all of these could have been brought to market; generally, retailers try to limit such variations for cost reasons. | figs. 4 and 5 I bought a similar radio at a flea market in the 1960s for about $10. It has a little handle for your convenience in carrying it from room to room. This represented real progress. The old RCAs were very big, like pieces of furniture. Now you could transport your music.

These radios were generally made of phenolic plastic, but they included celluloid and acetate components—the buttons and the faces—since those materials were very easy to mold. The radio faces have curious, anachronistic graphics that are almost Victorian, a stark contrast to their modern, curvilinear bodies. Looking at the clock without its back, you see that the cylinder where the front is attached to the back is simply cast as part of the mold. This required fewer parts and less labor, streamlining not only the appearance, but also the production.

In 1948 designers such as Charles and Ray Eames were creating molded fiberglass chairs that emphasized the plasticity of the material. These were clearly conscious aesthetic decisions that reinforced their interest in mass production. Ten years later I was working in New York for the architect George Nelson, who was also the furniture designer for Herman Miller. Eames also worked for Herman Miller, and he and Nelson were friends. Nelson's molded fiberglass Swag chair had a very tenuous connection between the arms and the back. I thought it seemed unstable, but what he wanted was to allow the back to give a little with the sitter's body weight. It works, principally because of the plasticity of the material. Later, in the 1960s, numerous molded, mass-produced chairs were designed in Milan—Joe Colombo's stacking chairs of 1968 and other versions by Vico Magistretti—and could often be seen in cafes throughout Italy and France. These were made of acrylonitrile butadiene styrene (ABS) and sometimes of fiberglass-reinforced polyester. Personally, I am charmed by the Dahlia chairs by Gaetano Pesce. Made of polyurethane foam, they are not quite symmetrical and rather lumpy, like comfortable cushions with folds of fabric. | figs. 6–10

Italian design has long fascinated me. I am an Italophile at heart after spending two years as a Fellow of the American Academy in Rome in the early 1960s. I admired how good design in Italy was essential to the quality of life, a lesson that I applied to the design of furniture and consumer products as our product design practice became commercially successful in the late 1970s and early 1980s. Italian design remained a source of inspiration, so it was probably no accident that my design career was launched through my association with Alessi, whose factory is in Crusinallo, just north of Milan.

I was sitting at a fancy dinner with Alberto Alessi in Milan one evening in the 1980s and the woman sitting next to me was the chairwoman of Italtel, Italy's version of AT&T. She said, "I'd like you to design a telephone for me and my company." I replied, "I'd love to design a phone for you, but

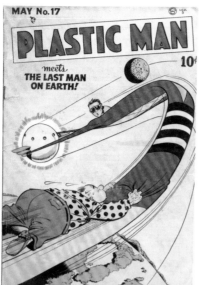

Plastic Man Goes to Market
Michael Graves

figs. 4 and 5 | Art Deco clock radio, front and back without the cover, circa 1960s

fig. 1 | *Plastic Man* cover, May 1949

fig. 2 | Objects of daily use made from cellulosic plastics from the mid-nineteenth century

fig. 3 | Kitchenware made of Bakelite in the mid-twentieth century

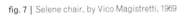

fig. 6 | "Sedia Universale" plastic stacking chairs, by Joe Colombo, 1968

fig. 7 | Selene chair, by Vico Magistretti, 1969

fig. 8 | Molded plastic armchair, by Charles and Ray Eames, 1948

fig. 9 | Swag chair, by George Nelson, 1958

fig. 10 | Gaudi chair, by Vico Magistretti, 1970

let's leave the so-called designer phone to the fashion folks and I will design an everyday phone." What was everyday in Italy at that time was not bad, but I thought I could improve upon it. I went about designing a simple black phone, but unfortunately soon received word that the client had passed away and the project was off. I later convinced Target to take it, and it had a very good run there. Since we tend to work in categories for Target, we designed other phones too, including a white wall phone, which I now use in my own kitchen. | figs. 11 and 12 These phones were made of ABS plastic and manufactured in China. (It seems odd today to discuss phones that actually attach to the wall. Nowadays we walk around with our little waferlike phones that fit in our pockets.)

One day we received a message from the factory saying that they could not continue making the wall phone. They told us, "The white phone, the one that looks like a ghost, is signed by someone called Graves, and our workers refuse to make it. If we are to continue to make it, we won't put the word *Graves* on it." We replied, "All right, you make it and we'll arrange for someone else to put the name on it." And that's what we did. You just never know what you will encounter in this business.

Of the many clocks we have designed, the earliest one was for Alessi, made out of ABS plastic and metal. | figs. 13–15 It featured a bird, like the whistle on our teakettle, a reference to the phrase "time flies." This was the first time I took something to Alberto Alessi unsolicited. Normally he would call and ask me to design some new widget. I had bought a nautical clock at a flea market, and it had a front face that opened like a door, making it easy to change the time. It was also very deep in section, which I liked. We based a new design on this clock, made a model, and gave it to Alessi in a box. When he opened the box, he just smiled and said, "No changes. I love it the way it is." That was the only time that ever happened to us.

The combination of plastic with other materials became a significant factor in the clock radios we designed for Target, which were manufactured by the Dutch company

Philips and in a toaster, also for Target, which was manufactured by Black and Decker. | fig. 16 This cobranding of the products was intended to give the consumer the confidence, given my name, that they would be well designed and, given the manufacturer, that they would function well. Both of these are made of ABS and are "shell-overs" of existing working parts. Thus, the interface of plastic and metal materials became a consideration in the design process. For example, with the toaster, the plastic would melt if placed too close to the metal heating element, so the shape of the top opening was fashioned to avoid that.

In designing a Brita water pitcher and ice bucket for Target, we experimented with combinations of materials and different manufacturing techniques. The bodies are double-walled SAN (styrene acrylonitrile), a hard plastic. These products, to me, demonstrate how beautiful plastic can be as a material; their translucency evokes a sense of water and ice. The knobs are polypropylene and the handles are polypropylene that has been "over-molded" with TPE (thermoplastic elastomer), which provides a soft touch where you grasp it. While they are all plastics, the specific materials were selected for their particular performance. | figs. 17 and 18

In a set of cook's tools for Target, we could beat the price of metal by making them out of PA (polyamide), which is sometimes referred to as nylon. The business end and shank are made of PA and the handle has been over-molded with a TPE sleeve to create a comfortable grip. | fig. 19 As with the ice bucket and pitcher, we were able to use various molding techniques in the design. The so-called stick goods—mops and brooms mostly—that we have designed for Target similarly use a combination of materials and molding techniques, each chosen to fulfill a certain function. | fig. 20

We also used over-molding in several of our toilet bowl brushes for Target. These have been huge sellers. We get weekly sales reports from Target that tell us how our products are doing. Early on, I thought there must be a mistake, since they reported selling six thousand toilet bowl brushes. I did not say anything, but just waited. The next week there

fig. 11 | Wall phone for Target, by Michael Graves

fig. 12 | Telephone designed for Italtel, by Michael Graves

fig. 13 | ABS wall clock designed for Alessi, by Michael Graves

fig. 14 | Wall clock designed for Target, by Michael Graves

fig. 15 | Desk clock designed for Target, by Michael Graves

fig. 16 | Clock radios for Target, by Michael Graves

were seven thousand sales. Who knew there were so many dirty toilets in America! These were offered only at Target at the time, not in hardware stores or other places you would expect to find such an object. My brother, who was a banker, called me up and said, "It's a good thing your mother doesn't know about this." Suddenly she was *my* mother, not ours. The next week the toilet bowl brush was featured as a design object in *Time* magazine. My brother called and apologized.

The products we designed in the early 1990s for Alessi were made of ABS and represented technological innovations in the manufacturing of plastic consumer products. The legs and handle were attached to the body using an ultrasonic welding technique, which is more common today but at that time had principally been used in hardware, tools, and plastic stemware. | fig. 21

With Alessi, however, we started out on the luxury end of the market with the Coffee and Tea Piazza. | fig. 22 Alberto Alessi's grand marketing scheme involved asking a dozen architects to create little scenes with a coffeepot, teapot, sugar, creamer, and spoon arranged on a tray. He planned to exhibit the drawings, the prototypes, and the final products at Max Protetch Gallery in New York and at museums throughout the country. If they were bought, it would be by major institutions such as the Metropolitan Museum of Art. Because of this exclusivity, Alessi did not care what they cost. Mine cost $25,000. It combined phenolic plastic mock-ivory handles with sterling silver bodies, demonstrating that plastic is perfectly acceptable at the high end of the market and can hold its own with semiprecious materials.

After we designed the tea service, Alessi came back to us and said, "Yours sold the best, so we're going to reward you with a contract to design a stainless steel kettle for everyday use, since that is why we're bringing our business to America." He wanted the kettle to boil water faster than any other kettle on the market, and we discussed how a broad base and conical shape could accomplish that. He had previously made another kettle, designed by Richard Sapper, which had a handle that overheated since it overlapped the

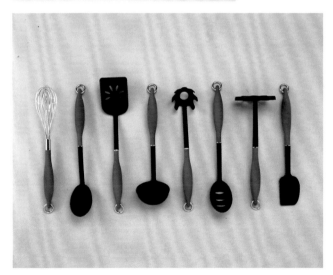

fig. 17 | Brita water pitcher, by Michael Graves

fig. 18 | Ice bucket for Target, by Michael Graves

fig. 19 | Set of cook's tools for Target, by Michael Graves

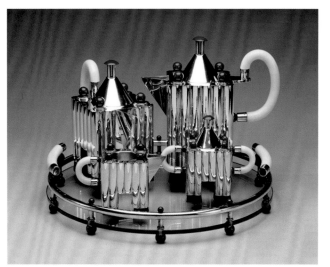

fig. 20 | Stick goods for Target, by Michael Graves

fig. 21 | Thermos jug for Alessi, by Michael Graves

fig. 22 | The luxury Coffee and Tea Piazza for Alessi, by Michael Graves

burner, and it required lifting with an oven mitt. So I placed the handle on the top, where it would not be exposed to heat, and made it out of a material called polyamide, which also kept the heat in the metal from transferring to the hand. I colored the handle blue, which signaled that it would be cool to the touch, whereas the whistling bird is red, so you instinctively know to use a mitt there. Besides, by the time the water is boiling, the bird is also making a lot of noise. | figs. 23 and 24 The Alessi collection grew, and we continued to use the language of red, blue, and black polyamide handles and knobs combined with stainless steel. That kettle continues to outsell all Alessi products.

When we started working for Target, they wanted a kettle as well. The vice president who hired me wanted the water to boil as fast as it did in Alessi's, so the shape was similar. | fig. 25 We placed a little whirligig at the spout so that when the water boils, it spins like a tornado, a kinetic effect that amplifies the effect of the steam coming out. We wanted to call the kettle Dorothy, but the buyer did not have a sufficient sense of humor. So it is called Spinning Whistle Teakettle. Since the whistle is a double helix, it would have been virtually impossible to make it out of any material other than plastic.

When we first started working for Target, one of the products that I most wanted to design was a chess set. Josef Hartwig had designed a marvelous chess set for the Bauhaus. He hinged the four quadrants of the chessboard and it folded square, to fit inside a box, along with his geometrically composed pieces. You can now have a remake of his design for $400, or you can have mine for $49.95. I made a wooden box the dimension of half the chessboard, which hinges open. There are polyester-resin chess pieces inside, and checkers for the less smart. | fig. 26 The weight of our pieces is substantial, giving them a very solid and high-quality feel. They are made of cast polyester with the addition of talc and resin to increase the weight.

I will end with two examples of brilliant promotion, both involving innovative uses of plastic materials. One is

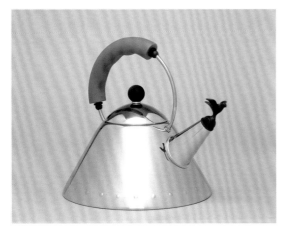

fig. 23 | Teakettle for Alessi, by Michael Graves

fig. 24 | Alessi collection, by Michael Graves

fig. 25 | Kettle for Target, by Michael Graves

fig. 26 | Chess set for Target, by Michael Graves

fig. 27 | Washington Monument Restoration Project, by
Michael Graves, 1998

the Washington Monument Restoration Project funded by Target, and the other is the original launch of our Target collection. We first met Target when its PR agency called and said, "We would like you to design the scaffolding for the Washington Monument. Target is going to pay for the restoration and it doesn't want just ordinary scaffolding. They want an architect to make it special." In designing the scaffolding, we made two major decisions. The first was to make the scaffolding follow the contours of the monument rather than stepping in and out, which would have been typical. The platforms for performing the repointing and other masonry repairs were inside. Then, to the outside, we attached a fabric that had been dipped in a plasticizer, basically the kind of material used for construction fencing. It was laid in a running bond pattern that mimicked the mortar pattern of the monument, the very material that was being repaired. | fig. 27 General Electric, one of Target's partners in the donation, devised a lighting system to illuminate the monument from within, so it glowed at night. The mortar pattern allowed us to tell at a giant scale the story of the building restoration, which we also did through children's books, exhibits, and a film.

While we have designed around 2,500 products for Target over the last dozen years, the initial launch in 1999 was a brilliant PR move that set us on a path to success. The Target PR folks wanted to know what Alessi had done for its launch, and when I told them about the galleries and museums that displayed the Coffee and Tea Piazzas, they wanted to do something similar. They rented out the Whitney Museum of American Art in New York one night,and hosted a gala press party showcasing our new products. Following the party, Target unrolled an extensive ad campaign in print, on TV, on billboards, and even on buses. I was especially amused by a friend's snapshot of the back of a bus driving down Nassau Street in Princeton. The bus, wrapped in plastic, became a giant advertisement for our ABS plastic toaster, which was cleverly tagged "Pop Art."

I was recently interviewed in the Home section of the *New York Times* for an article called "A Question and an Answer." The interviewer asked me if my colleagues gave me a hard time when we started to design products that would be produced at these enormous scales, as we have been able to do. I said, "Oh yes, of course, but you know they're all racing to Target for an interview." Certainly other architects besides me participated in the early, very exclusive programs by Alessi and Swid Powell. But the mass market was a place I wanted to be. From Josef Hoffmann and the Wiener Werkstätte, to the Bauhaus or even Charles and Ray Eames—none of them had a chance to produce products except in a craft manner, which made their prices out of reach for the average consumer. Even though Alessi has been able to mass-produce our teakettle, the price is still high. It is the tremendous buying power of Target and other mass retailers that makes their prices so affordable. It is no coincidence that our ongoing quest to increase access to good design for the greatest number of people has been profoundly influenced by the use of plastics and the inventiveness that comes with its malleability and many possible manufacturing techniques. This has been a dream since the days of Plastic Man, and I am proud to be part of the movement that made it come true. I am sure he would be proud as well.

LAMBDA + PlayBox

Juan Herreros

2000

The possibilities and contributions of plastics to architecture—beyond the materials associated with installation and insulation—was a natural interest of mine, one that arose after years of constructive design proposals made with Iñaki Ábalos at the end of the 1990s and the beginning of the 2000s. Texts such as "A Fragile Skin" or slogans like "System Versus Detail" explain our interest in establishing construction rules to make not only technical decisions but also conceptual or spatial ones.[1] Similar to our explorations in the volume *Tower and Office: From Modernist Theory to Contemporary Practice*, these construction rules established the relation between technique and architecture; between the disposal of technical resources and architectural ideals.[2] These explorations drove us to accept a generation of polycarbonates—sufficiently stable from a chromatic point of view, with acceptable thermal conditions and viable programs of assembly and attachment—and incorporate them into our repertoire of dry construction systems with important spatial and conceptual consequences relating to the construction of a translucent, fragile, simple, and light architecture. Early use of these products can be seen in the Gymnasium Building in the Retiro Park, the Valdemingómez and Pinto Waste Processing Plants, the studio of the painter Luis Gordillo, and the Colmenarejo Public Hall, all built surrounding Madrid, and in the EcoMuseum, which was a part of the Forum master plan in Barcelona.

2009

The design for the Munch Museum in Oslo was a competition submission, and the facade was subsequently developed as a combination of polycarbonate and methacrylate panels. The intent was to build a reactive mechanism capable of responding to the tenuous phenomenological stimuli of the long Norwegian winter so that the building would take on a constantly changing appearance with activation from sun, clouds, or mist. This dynamic state, which we sought to emphasize with the slogan LAMBDA and for which the design is widely recognized, is achieved with a double facade with a flat interior polycarbonate skin and an external methacrylate skin. The latter bends into three different ripples, thus creating a ventilated chamber capable of regulating heat exchange between interior and exterior. The sustainability aims for the Munch Museum are high: the building seeks to lead in energy performance, reduce carbon dioxide emissions, and meet passive energy requirements. The exterior actively contributes to this aim with a well-insulated facade system that further reduces unwanted heat loss and the need for extensive mechanical heating and cooling. The design process for the facade focused on high insulation values, impermeability, minimization of thermal bridges, and the use of solar protection and shading. New materials available on the market will allow us to ambitiously meet certain parameters of heat exchange, natural light, and dazzling visual effect as well as to fulfill passive energy requirements, creating a visually permeable structure that connects the collective experience inside the museum with the fjords of Oslo. The building becomes a distinctive feature of the landscape.

2012

It is virtually impossible to list the diverse plastic materials employed in the PlayBox project. PlayBox is a space for invention and productivity. The intent is to stimulate creativity via a building that allows work, encounters, conversations, and presentations by enabling its occupants to constantly invent new ways of using it. In reality it is an "office" where individuals can take over the space instantly and define it in a variety of ways through their own creative processes. The client is a small film producer wishing to use stage techniques to activate an illusory and malleable area that would encourage experimentation and provoke new forms of communication, innovation, and teamwork. The choice of materials takes into account factors such as ecological footprint, recyclability, and the absence of polluting materials. The floors are made from recycled tires; partition walls are heat-toughened resin panels with an 85 percent recyclability level due to the absence of heavy metals, halogens, or biocides; recycled CD cases are used in the partition walls; a "spaghetti" curtain with strips of programmable LED lights reacts to sounds and movement; a seamless, reflecting synthetic-resin sphere floats weightlessly and insinuates that we dwell in a constantly changing atmosphere; three lenticular compartments etched in vinyl are used as a meeting room, a kitchen, and a quiet room, respectively; and there is a large table of irregular geometry, the occupation and sharing of which its users have to improvise. All the ingredients in this experimental project are reminders that while we first learned about plastic from objects, today it is a powerful instrument for spatial and perceptive manipulation.

1 | Iñaki Ábalos, "A Fragile Skin," in *Areas of Impunity* (Barcelona: Actar, 1997); "Detalles Constructivos y otros Fetiches Perversos," in *Arquitectura al Detalle*, eds. Fernando Aranda and Amparo Tarín (Valencia: EAUPV, 1997).

2 | Iñaki Ábalos and Juan Herreros, *Tower and Office. From Modernist Theory to Contemporary Practice*. (Cambridge: MIT Press, 2003). Revised edition from the original: *Técnica y Arquitectura en la Ciudad Contemporánea. 1950-1990* (Madrid: Editorial Nerea, 1992).

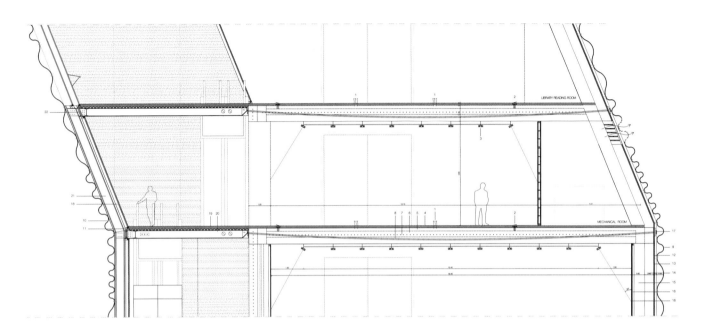

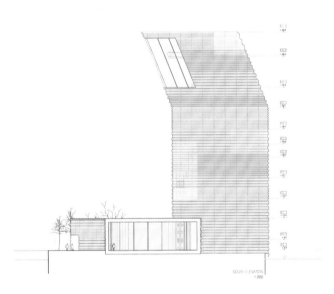

Section detail, Munch Museum, by Juan Herreros
Arquitectos, Oslo, 2009

South elevation

Sectional perspective

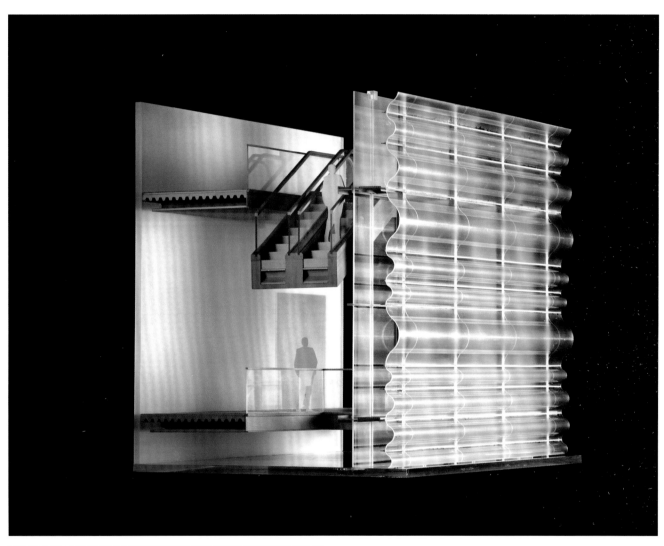

First-stage competition model

Concept model

Interior view, Playbox Film Headquarters, by Juan
Herreros Arquitectos, Madrid, 2011

Programmable LED light curtain

Partition walls

Reflective resin sphere

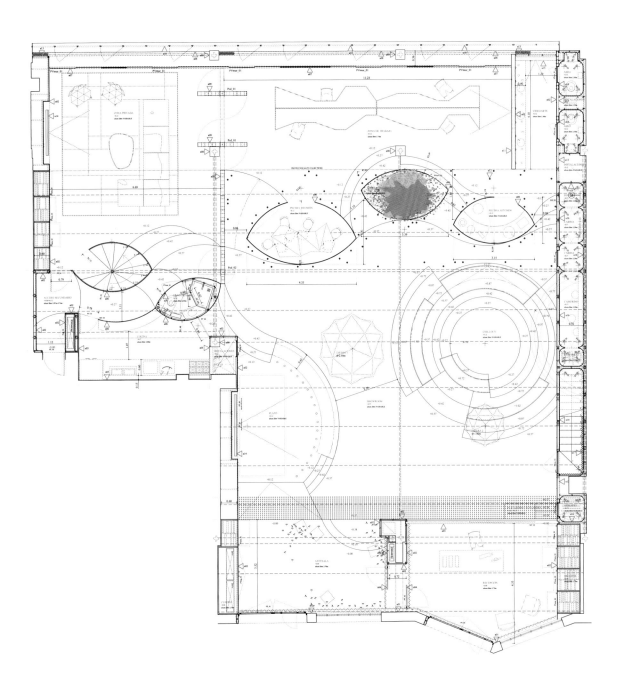

Floor plan

LAMBDA + PlayBox
Juan Herreros

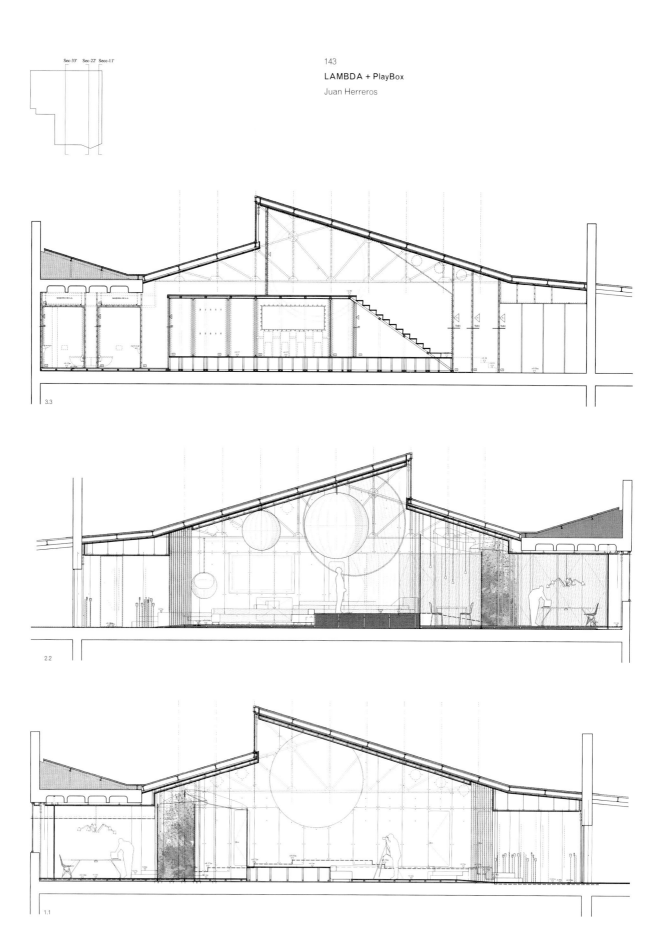

Sections

The Song of the S(t)yrene[1]

François Roche

Syren = Sirène (French) = Mermaid
Styrene = vinyl benzene, an organic compound with the chemical formula $C_6H_5CH=CH_2$. This derivative of benzene is a colorless oily liquid that evaporates easily and has a sweet smell and high toxicity.[2]

Once upon a time… A fairy tale seems like the perfect way to start a "plasticology," to unfold a historical dispute between the fossil and living nature, between what is decomposed and has laid deep within the earth for millions of years, and what is seasonally cultivated in real time on the surface of the planet. The opposition between the organic and the inorganic could be posed instead in terms of the secondary effect of each substance by asking *what kind of smoke do we want to breathe*? Would we prefer psychedelic travel enabled by plants, in the pursuit of William Burroughs and Carlos Castaneda, choosing to intoxicate our minds; or would we prefer the floating, invisible particle residue of the petrochemical industry, choosing to pollute our lungs by breathing what's left of the BP, Exxon, and Total oil by-products, consubstantial with the ideology of progress, mass-industrialization, proto- and crypto-capitalism, and mainly dedicated to the comforts of a Western standard of living.

The reader might legitimately feel confused by the introduction of these alternative pathologies—smoking the postindustrial effluences from plastic industries or smoking weeds associated with various shamanistic practices, but in 1937 the debate was precisely on this point. Through the Marihuana Tax Act, the Roosevelt administration taxed the entire hemp production chain, from farmers to resellers and consumers, to directly support its direct competitor and synthetic clone, the patented DuPont material Nylon.[3] The most relevant detail is not that prohibition by taxation was a puritan adaptation of the earlier prohibition of alcohol; rather it is the manner in which industrial companies such as DuPont defined a lobbying strategy of an "innovation by substitution,"

using the synthesis of fossilized nature to produce similar by-products, an industrial echo of the first Neolithic plants "tamed" by humans.[4]

There is a simultaneous analogy and dissymmetry between oil extracted from decomposed nature and hemp from a cultivated one in terms of potential of transformation, physical behavior, strength, resistance, and the characteristics of manufactured products. More effectively, the main dissymmetry arises from concentrating power and economy, which is at the base of production and social organization. It should be ridiculous to compare the world empire of petrochemistry—born from the capitalist economic system and disseminated agriculture—with a multitude of owners and different local implications.

Synthetic nature appears to be in diametric opposition to the natural: economically, politically, ecologically, and capitalistically. In the twentieth century, the oil versus hemp battle resulted in a complete eradication of hemp and a domination of oil, including the control of the means of extraction, of the science at the base of the transformation, and of the global market, with the infrastructure of the United States serving as a vector of dissemination and massification.[5] The animated nature of the multitude of ingredients and the handmade knowledge of various expressions, anomalies, and singularities at the base of various crafts, in turn, is antithetical to the fossilized, transformed nature of industry, used for spreading needs and desires through a massive, repetitive, standardized, and advertised production dedicated to an ideology of progress directed by branding.[6] This factual transition seems simple but the irony of history, due to unexpected reasons like price and rarefication of oil, war on black gold shadows, consciousness of the collateral effect, mutation of capitalism, and more, hemp has returned to the United States. Beginning in California as a key site for agricultural production, and invading many other states—this time just for drugs—a medical alibi with pseudoprescription by pseudodoctor concealed the original reason for its prohibition: voracious industrial competition.

Now we have a choice—what kind of smoking, or nonsmoking, pollution do we prefer to affect our lungs and minds: monoxide smog or the smoker's arabesque?

In this global *malentendu* full of logical stuttering, pure nonsense, and absurdity, can we define a trajectory that reveals this antagonism without falling into cynical reductionism or political naivete?[7] Can we simultaneously develop a resistance and a resilience through positive criticism, which can rearticulate the relationship between commodities and their *raison d'être*, between singularities and technologies? What potential is there in the historical and intrinsic conflict between these two natures? In their whispering, might they tell us something else?

Some apparatuses and scenarios reveal some of these antagonisms and formulate a hypothesis of political non–master planning. These projects navigate from the recognition of pollution, shifting from an aesthetic that could be called "petroplasticology"—a controlled and accurate technology— toward some potential substitution by "bioplastic"—plastic that has a specific life span—which could be described as a chemical advantage for self-organized, undetermined structures. It boils down to the following questions.

Can we use petroplastic in an endogenous-exogenous strategy? Extracted from the recesses of the earth, petroplastic can be a paradoxical agent of territorialization. A house for classes and siestas—a computational, yet handmade, local production—is driven by a local mammal, a generating station whose gears are attached to a two-ton steel counterweight powering the pneumatic movement of the elastomer membrane, aerating the hot and sweaty climate. | figs. 1–4

Can we use petroplastic for organizing a simulacrum of its own impermanency and apparent fragility? Unfolding in the countryside, an authorized, nonbiodegradable petrochemical fabric is used for the whole envelope, an envelope that is spread out and disseminated amid the surrounding nature to preserve newly planted trees from destruction at the hands of rabbits, creating domesticity out of an agro-industrial logic? | figs. 5–10

Can we use petroplastic as a filter for collecting other types of plastics, where a voluntary, domesticated pollution will attract "wild" pollution, taking on an ambiguous status and an aesthetic of visible decomposition? Project Filtration is a simple ten thousand square-meter development of Baïse riverbank in France, which carries nitrate and insecticide plastic bag residues abandoned by farmers in their fields, as if awaiting a natural depolluting service that will erase the traces of their chemical addiction. And paradoxically they return to the visible spectrum when the river is down again, hanging from the branches as if floating above the river. | figs. 11–13

This structural calligraphy of such systems might work as mechanized stereotomies, composed of successive geometries according to a strategy of permanent production of anomalies with no standardization or repetition, except for the procedures and protocols that lie at the base of these technoid slums' emergence and research.

1 | *Le Chant du Styrene* (1959), 19 mins., color. Directed by Alain Resnais, text by Raymond Queneau.

2 | "Styrene," *Wikipedia, The Free Encyclopedia*, http://en.wikipedia.org/wiki/Styrene.

3 | A small shortcut history: 8000 B.C.: woven fabric from hemp; 1619: Jamestown Colony, Virginia, passes law requiring farmers to grow hemp; 1666: in France Colbert built the "Corderie Royale" to assume the quality and quantity of production of ropes and sails; 1794: George Washington advised, "Make the most of the Indian hemp seed and sow it everywhere"; 1840: 176,000 hectares of hemp was grown in France; 1919: 18th Amendment to the U.S. Constitution for alcohol prohibition; 1933: 21st Amendment for the end of alcohol prohibition; 1937: Marijuana Tax Act from Harry J. Anslinger; 1941: *Hemp for Victory*, propaganda movie of U.S. army to relaunch hemp production for the war effort, and simultaneously Henry Ford's hemp car for the farmer to relaunch hemp production and the U.S. economy.

4 | By-products included: fiber, fabric, oil, rope, celluloid, paper, bensin, molded processes, and even the Henry Ford hemp car. Hemp has been prohibited in Japan since 1948. The prohibition in European countries was one of the conditions for the application of the Marshall Plan, for the launching of the economy of reconstruction after the World War II cataclysm. Both refer to the Marihuana Tax Act of 1937.

5 | We have to recognize that plastic was good for capitalist processes. We could even argue that they have the same genome, the same DNA: the parallel between one mold amortized by millions of similar repetitive prints and clones and the pyramidal managerial schema which underlie both production and profit fit to perfection, as an ideal scientific, political, and economical business plan.

6 | See John Ruskin, *Stones of Venice* (New York: Wiley, 1860), and Walter Benjamin, "The Work of Art in the Age of Mechanical Reproduction," in *Illuminations*, ed. Hannah Arendt (New York: Schocken Books, 1968).

7 | Conventionally translated as *misunderstanding*, it is literally *mishearing*.

fig. 1 | Animal "engine" driven by the muscle power of an
albino buffalo, Hybrid Muscle, by R&Sie(n), Chang Mai,
Thailand, 2003

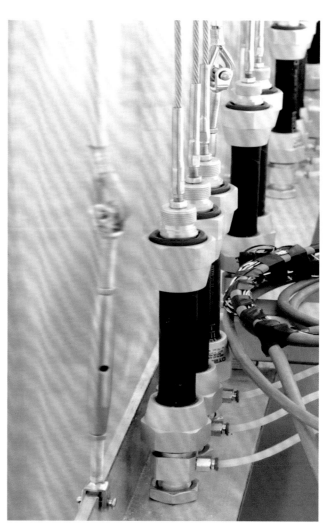

fig. 4 | Mechanical energy is transformed into electrical energy

fig. 2 | The natural ventilation through silicon facade leaves works in the same way as the teak leaves of temporary shelters

fig. 3 | Mechanical energy is stored through the lifting of a two-ton steel counterweight

fig. 5 | House for Judith and Ami Barak, Shearing, by R&Sie(n), Sommières, France, 2001

figs. 6 and 7 | The tent construction provides protection from the weather

fig.8 | Interior living space

figs. 9 and 10 | The tent material camouflages the house into the landscape

fig. 11 | Prototype of plastic roof along the riverbank,
Filtration, by R&Sie(n), River Baïse, France, 1997

fig. 12 | Metaphorical and literal filter of pollution

fig. 13 | River at low tide

The Light Pavilion

Lebbeus Woods and Christoph a. Kumpusch

I wake and moonbeams play around my bed,
Glittering like hoar frost to my wondering eyes.
Up towards the glorious moon I raise my head,
Then lay me down and thoughts of home arise.

"Night Thoughts," Li Bai (701–762 CE)

This project was an extension of drawing—a condensation and material manifestation of thoughts. Poring over construction documents with Lebbeus again and again, I can safely say that the ideas did not stop when the building process began. Rather, the demands of the "real project" triggered further conceptualization. Located within an innovative mixed-use complex of towers designed by Steven Holl Architects, the Light Pavilion offers visitors the opportunity to explore a prototypical space of the future. They walk up and through a complex network of luminous spaces that are ephemeral, evocative, and changing.

The Light Pavilion is designed to be experimental, giving us the opportunity to experience a type of space we haven't experienced before. Whether it will be pleasant or unpleasant, exciting or dull, uplifting or frightening, inspiring or depressing, worthwhile or a waste of time is not determined by the fulfillment of any familiar expectations, as we have never encountered such a space before. We shall simply have to go into it and pass through it. That is the most crucial aspect of its experimental nature, and it makes us—its transient inhabitants—into experimentalists.

The elements defining it do not always follow the rectilinear geometry of its architectural setting, but instead obey a geometry defined by dynamic movement. Their deviation from the rectilinear grid releases the spaces from static stability and sets them in motion. Translucent plastic-sheathed columns articulating the pavilion's interior are illuminated from within and visibly glow at night, creating a luminous arena into which the solid architectural elements appear to merge. Glass stair treads pick up the sheen of the columns and reflect their colors. One ascends by several possible paths to balconies overlooking pools and landscaped gardens in the plaza below, all while enjoying a succession of framed views of the Chinese city of Chengdu beyond. Steel works throughout to sustain the illusion of weightlessness.

Other senses of the word *plastic*—giving shape to something, modeling form, having sculptural qualities—also play out in the pavilion. It is a shaped environment, a carefully authored series of spaces that play out in time and direction. Modeling form in light, as light, was central to our creative process. There is an undeniable link to sculpture and architecture's interrelationship with that discipline. From distances across the city, the pavilion is a beacon of light. It radiates subtly changing colors for different holidays and times of day, the months and years. It is designed to expand the scope and depth of our experiences into new dimensions. That is its sole purpose, its only function.

opposite:

Illuminated balconies, paths, and stairs, the Light Pavilion by Lebbeus Woods with Christoph a. Kumpusch, in the Raffles City complex by Steven Holl Architects, Chengdu, China, 2012

Elements deviating from rectilinear grid

Colored lights in illuminated columns

Plastic columns

The Light Pavilion
Lebbeus Woods and Christoph a. Kumpusch

Pavilion as a beacon of light

overleaf:
View of pavilion from the street

Reflection of illuminated columns on ground

Merging architectural elements

Illuminated plastic columns

overleaf:

Interior space

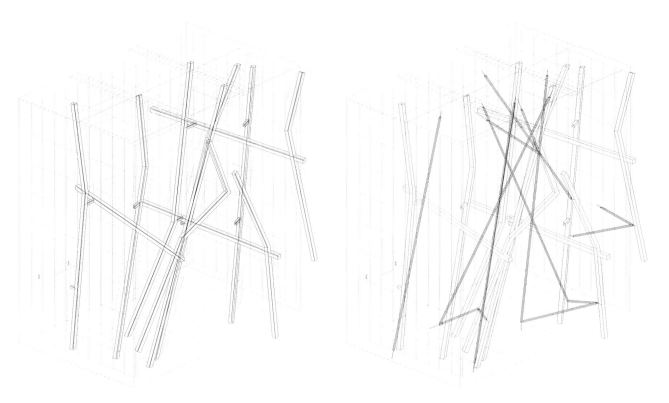

Axonometric drawings

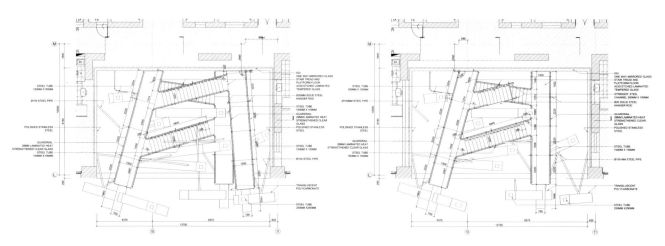

Plans

The Light Pavilion

Lebbeus Woods and Christoph a. Kumpusch

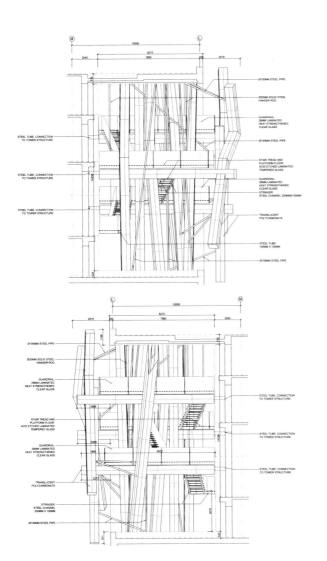

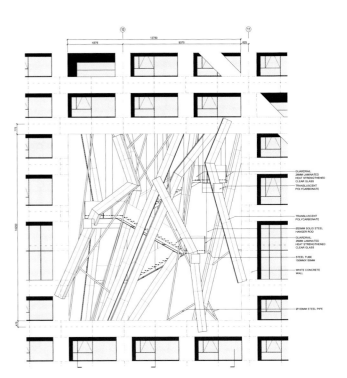

Sections

Elevation

LightShowers

Yoshiko Sato and Michael Morris

LightShowers (1996–ongoing), a collaborative and interactive traveling installation, recapitulates temporal themes in the studio's body of work that explore and celebrate light and water as concepts and as sustainable resources. Syncopated lighting and video, and a deep attention to form and space, define this multimedia construction, which was digitally fabricated and hand tooled out of the DuPont Company's acrylic-based composite material known as Corian. Over the course of five international presentations, more than 70,000 visitors have experienced the work's physical and temporal dimensions.

The work was inspired by medical research on biofeedback healing techniques employed in the Center for Complementary and Alternative Medicine at New York-Presbyterian Hospital/Columbia University Medical Center. It is conceptually grounded in nonsectarian practices of meditation, in which the mind and body are serially scanned for sensation and focused awareness. The modular pavilion integrally houses a platform in which seven people can rest. Sensors inside the "stone/egg" seats respond to the visitors' presence by activating delicate arrays of one hundred gently pulsing blue light-emitting diodes (LEDs) concealed underneath the platform's surface. The seven-second LED interval is synchronized to the rhythm of the breath of a human at rest, while the luminous, flowing oceanic video images by Paul Ryan promote universal reflection and repose, fostering an overall ambiance of equanimity and well-being.

Originally conceived as an ideal material for future medical environments, Glacier White Corian was selected not only for its antimicrobial benefits and durability, but also for its crisp white color and ethereal luminosity, which enables light to resonate from and reflect upon its surfaces. The distinctive constructive possibilities that the material permits are articulated in the balanced composition of two expressive forms: the seamless laminations of the monolithic seating and the geometric panel configuration of the platform. The material was CNC-milled and routed according to extensive drawings and models. The surfaces were then hand tooled and sanded to accommodate our desire for human touch in the final fabrication.

LightShowers extended these luminous, aquatic, and meditative themes from the museum gallery into the trade show hall environment through the design of a freestanding pavilion to envelope the interior platform installation. The forms, shapes, and colors of the pavilion design were inspired by studies of water in various states—from solid ice to liquid to vapor. After extensive light and material studies, a CNC-routed mold was created to thermoform individual sheets of stock-size Corian Illumination Series to their maximum physical limits as wall panels. The wall of identical, cojoined panels is meticulously detailed to provide interior seating and views while modulating the lighting cast upon and from within its surfaces. Pulsing flat-sheet phosphorous lighting and silica glass fiber optics further animate and illuminate the undulating material, synchronizing the visitor's presence with its temporal setting.

LightShowers
Yoshiko Sato and Michael Morris

View of installation, LightShowers, by Morris Sato Studio,
Wilmington, Delaware, 2006

Elevation

overleaf:
View of the "stone/egg" seats

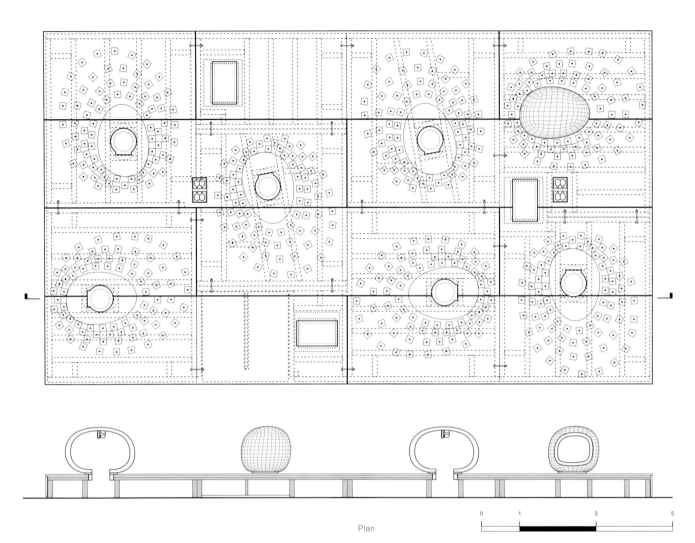

Plan

Elevation

0   1   3   5

LightShowers
Yoshiko Sato and Michael Morris

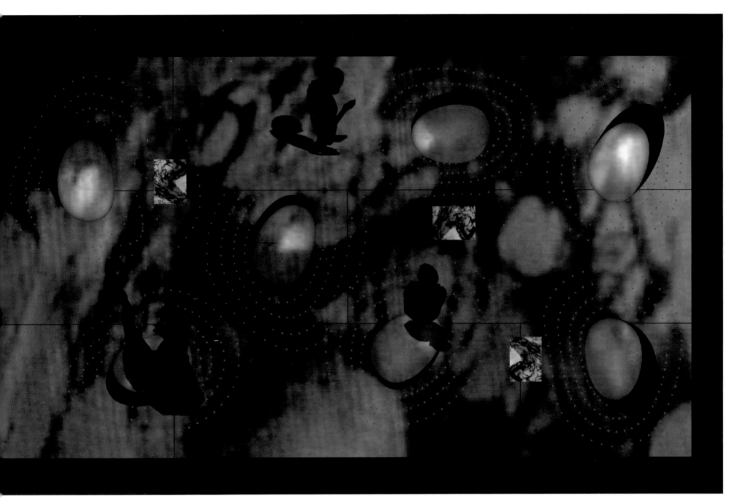

Rendering of platform

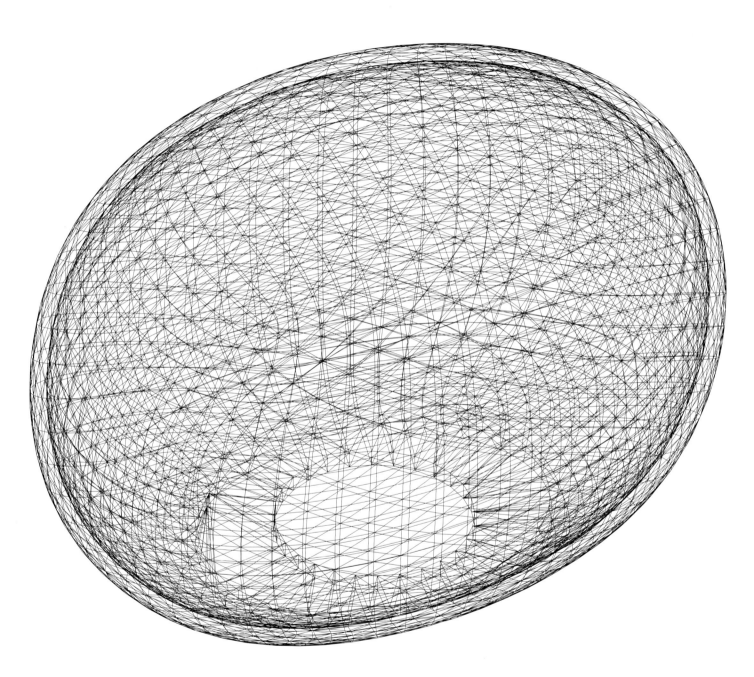

Wireframe rendering of a "stone/egg" seat

opposite:

Detail of the seats

Structure and Energy

Structuring Plastic Flow

Johan Bettum

Plastics are the quintessential twentieth-century industrial material and come in either a liquid or a molten form. Roland Barthes thought that plastics were so transmutable that they, paradoxically, were entirely dependent on their context and yet at the same time able to dissolve it. For him, plastic substances represented "the total transmutation of matter" and could become anything. "The whole world can be plasticized."[1]

Barthes's view of industrial polymers reflected their postwar emergence in virtually every area of industrially produced artifacts for human consumption. Their ubiquity was accompanied by a plethora of possible forms, and countless characteristics produced by their modifiable chemical backbone of carbon-carbon links. His view of the whole world as "plasticized" anticipated how composites present us with the twenty-first-century material paradigm par excellence. Reinforced polymer composites are plastics' structural companion, in which the industrial polymer serves as a material matrix that embeds the reinforcement system and other possible additives and fillers to create an entirely new material system with novel performance characteristics. | fig. 1

Contemporary polymers and their reinforced composite counterparts present architecture with an entirely new material realm that is radically different from what architectural theory and practice previously relied upon. With a specific history spanning little more than fifty years, plastics and reinforced polymer composites are difficult to place within the annals of architectural thinking and making. At the end of his book on reinforced concrete and thirty years prior to Barthes, Sigfried Giedion looked forward to these latter-day composites without actually having knowledge of them: "It is hoped that our age will form a new building material that comes closer to its demands....Just as the nineteenth century—at a given moment—developed iron and ferroconcrete for its needs, so we can assume that our age, too, will find the material that responds to its demands."[2]

Since their emergence in the mid-1950s for structural and semistructural applications in architecture, reinforced composites have largely been understood as highly moldable, based on their polymer component. Echoing Barthes, the typical view is that these material systems can take on any form and provide absolute freedom in design. It is a truth, with modifications. Firstly, consisting of two or more material components, the variable and modifiable viscosity of the polymer or resin is only one part of the equation. The embedded reinforcement that compensates for the typical brittle and low-strength polymer has its own characteristics and performance criteria. Secondly, architectural forms, whether constructed from subelements or not, result from a series of processing and manufacturing steps to produce a usable surface, and these steps contribute to the definition of what is possible; they structure the plastic flow of polymers and therefore the possible architectural forms as well. Two models, one accounting for internal material conditions and the other for external manufacturing conditions, explain how the plastic flow of resins is channeled and modified.

Architectural Design and the Composite Paradigm

A composite surface constitutes an organic whole and, depending on its components, it may perform multifunctionally in a smooth and integrated fashion, but it must be understood in terms of the components and their relations to one another. For this reason, industrial polymers for structural applications are, without exception, one element in a "composite system," where "system" stresses the heterogeneous nature of the material composition and the primacy of relations between parts. Thus, composites are the antithesis of hybrids, which blend their constitutive elements into a new entity that maintains no internal relations by assimilating its discrete parts through transformational processes.

The profound penetration of digitally controlled and computational processes into virtually every realm of human production sets our era radically apart from the pioneering days of structural plastics in architecture. For composites

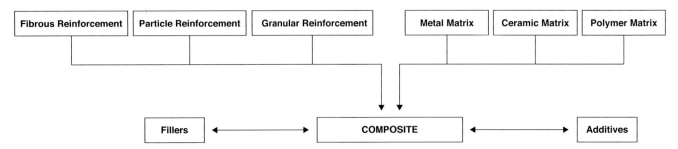

fig. 1 | A material matrix of reinforced polymer composites

with advanced textile reinforcement systems, the effect of this is exhaustive, and it presents architecture with an unprecedented opportunity to access material variables and modify them for architectural ends. Current research interests in the field include establishing a multiscale computational design framework that encompasses how the material systems are designed, analyzed, and manufactured for construction. Aspects of such integrative processes are already in use in enclaves of large-scale building enterprise but largely tend to practical concerns, such as rationalization and systematization of the construction process.[3] Questions of design and the role of architecture are less central, and architecture is faced with the challenge of comprehending the paradigmatic changes it awaits and taking advantage of the opportunities these changes offer for self-reinvention and formal development. In this context, the relationship between material and manufacturing variables and how they structure plastic flow in load-bearing composites must be understood for the possibility that they could contribute to a radical rewriting of selected theoretical and practical models in architecture.

Theoretically, the variables and tools that go into this vast complex of considerations all have to do with relations that comprise material, geometric, technological, and methodological conditions. These must be understood through models of integration across differences between components, their constitutive geometry, technological procedures, and professional cultures. In this respect a hybrid model fails, since the key is to maintain inherent differences for their generative potential within a totality that relies on discrete modalities, relations, and integration. The material model of such a totality is the composite model, which is one reason why these material systems constitute the material paradigm of our time with the promise to deliver on how architecture can be informed and rethought through contemporary material conditions in ways Giedion hoped for.

Gilles Deleuze and Felix Guattari's philosophical model of synthesis, which runs like Ariadne's thread through much of their work, sheds a clear, albeit convoluted light on this. Their model is not the opposite of analysis nor the resolution of oppositional terms. Rather, it presents production through difference, with elements maintained across relational interfaces.[4] In short, it is a composite condition that in turn is entirely reliant on design. The centrality of design for the material systems is due to the principal fact that the systems do not exist prior to being composed and are manufactured for a specific purpose. Vistasp Karbhari, a structural engineer and composite specialist, states, "Composite design...is not just the design of an artifact or structure, but essentially the design of the material of which the artifact is to be fabricated, and the design of the fabrication process, in addition to that of the structure itself."[5] Hence, with composites, design is the overall strategy that makes materials, technology, tools, and people active in a coordinated, productive setting where the beginning of the work process must include considerations of desired end results in a hitherto unprecedented manner.[6]

This means that material characteristics are connected to desired effects early on in the architectural design process, and that knowledge and methods practiced by various disciplines must be systematically integrated with one another.[7] A composite paradigm invites the marriage of bottom-up and top-down approaches. It brings about a deep, vertical integration of technology with a wide, horizontal integration of protagonists and their methods in the design process.[8] Finally, it composes the synthesis of scalar geometric paradigms at every level of material formation, from the smallest to the largest: the geometric definition of the reinforcement system, the design of the composite elements in which the reinforcement is embedded, and the design of the composite building elements and architectural form.

Structural plastics in architecture must be understood within the totality of this composite paradigm that centers on design. The issue at hand is as much about comprehending possible restrictions and limitations in the work process as it is about mapping the infinite spectrum of opportunities that the material systems offer.

The External or Processual Mode of Structuring Plastic Flow Prior to 1973, during the pioneering days of structural plastic applications in architecture, the work of Renzo Piano's Studio Piano was extraordinary.[9] Exploring serially produced modular elements, lightweight structures, space frames, and the unique lighting conditions that reinforced plastics can provide, this work composes a largely forgotten but ingenious oeuvre that eclipses many latter-day efforts by other architects.[10] One example is the design of the Italian Industry Pavilion at the Osaka Expo in 1969—a large, rectangular shed built from prestressed steel frames featuring double glass-fiber-reinforced polyester panels with an interstitial air chamber in between, giving an ambient daylight effect inside. The design pretensioned the envelope based on wind and seismic criteria and produced a modular, easily transportable structure with a reduced number and weight of components. | figs. 2 and 3 The reinforced polymer skin, reports Massimo Dini, was chosen for its "low coefficient of elasticity [and thus capacity for] deformation."[11] Molded with a central, protruding apex, each panel had a joint between the composite skin and a

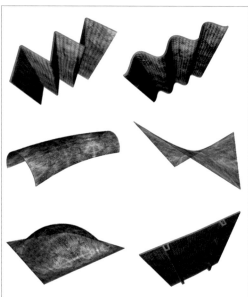

fig. 2 | Double glass-fiber-reinforced polyester panels and prestressed steel frames, Italian Industry Pavilion, by Renzo Piano, Osaka Expo, Japan, 1969

fig. 3 | Diagram of polyester panel, Italian Industry Pavilion, 1969

fig. 4 | Albert Dietz's six geometrical typologies as alternative strategies for achieving "maximum efficiency and utility"

tensioning pin that pierced the panel at the apex. At these points, the panels were incised with stiffening folds flowing to their perimeter in a star-like pattern. The geometric articulation and detailing of the panels was specific to the choice of reinforced polymer composites and rendered a frozen image of the plastic flow of the polyester resin.

The proclivity for articulated geometry with reinforced plastics represents both the specific design freedom it offers and the necessity to compensate for the material systems' weaknesses. In 1969 the Massachusetts Institute of Technology engineer Albert Dietz, who was central to the construction of the Monsanto House of the Future in Disneyland (1957–68), listed six geometrical typologies as alternative strategies for achieving what he called "maximum efficiency and utility."[12] These typologies were the conoid section, hyperparabolic, domed, folded, corrugated, and ribbed surfaces. Dietz argued that maximum efficiency and utility must be understood primarily as a means to compensate for the material systems' inherent low coefficient of elasticity, while providing the elements with sufficient stiffness for a given structural purpose. He also cited the capability of these geometric forms to alleviate stress in the material systems due to their thermal behavior. "Corrugated and other folded surfaces will take up the movement," he wrote, as "repeated stresses caused by temperature changes (and expansion and contraction in the surface) can lead to fatigue, cracking, and failure. [Moreover, a] double zigzag fold has been found effective in absorbing expansion and contraction in both directions without motion along the edges."[13] | fig. 4

Studio Piano's Osaka Pavilion showed both curved and folded articulation at work. And the studio's proposal for the Italian Pavilion for the Milano XIV Triennial two years earlier was an even more radical demonstration of how material systems bring technology and design to the fore in planning and manufacture. This unrealized project proposed a self-supporting, undulating shell covering an open plan, foreshadowing the logic of the single-surface architecture of the 1990s and after.[14] | fig. 5 The project included extensive

research "to overcome the structural limitations of shells as simple forms divided into identical subcomponents and to provide a virtually unlimited range of forms free of the constraints of size and shape imposed by the current mass production techniques."[15] A number of tests were built using double glass-fiber-reinforced polyester skins with expanded polyurethane cores. The significance of this project lies partly in its scalar shift in geometric articulation from details to also include a heterogeneous global geometry of the composite parts and the architectural form. With its continuously differentiated envelope, divided into a set of prefabricated surface components with "no mediating hierarchy of intermediately scaled parts," the project anticipated a future that is yet to come.[16] The prefabricated elements measured two meters by two meters and were to be chemically welded together on site. The research and design process revolved around surface studies in which plaster models were used to make vacuum-formed polymer membranes. The resulting scale shells were tested for deformation as tension membranes and for compression by inverting them. | fig. 6

In order to translate these models to full scale, Studio Piano devised a flexible mold where the surface geometry of each component could be varied according to input that was read from the plaster models at the scale of 1:10. The real-time geometric translation was accomplished with a pantograph controlling the hydraulic pistons without the aid of the numerical computer controls that are readily available today. The method made a significant break from the standardization and homogenization of elements that characterized serial prefabrication at the time.[17] | fig. 7

Studio Piano's studies for this pavilion exemplify how the formability of reinforced composites can be approached to make strategic use of the polymer component's plastic flow. Meanwhile, Dietz's typologies for design offer a corresponding shorthand systematization of the possible geometric variation at hand. Yet the integration and use of technology, not least in manufacture, continues to present the most pressing challenge for tapping into the vast resource that reinforced

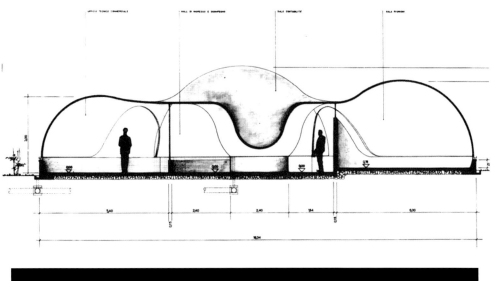

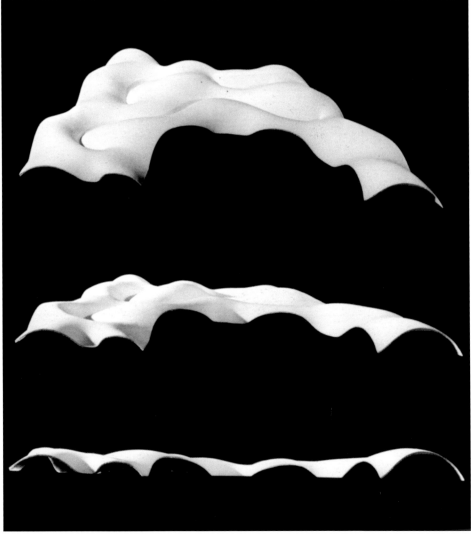

fig. 5 | Section drawing of unrealized proposal, Italian
Pavilion at the Milano XIV Triennial, by Studio Piano, Milan,
1967

fig. 6 | Plaster models used to make vacuum-formed
polymer membranes for the unrealized proposal, Italian
Pavilion at the Milano XIV Triennial, 1967

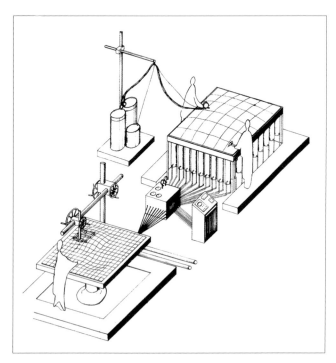

fig. 7 | A flexible mold designed to translate the scaled
models to full scale, by Studio Piano, 1967

composites present for architecture. This is precisely why Studio Piano's studies and flexible mold manufacture for the Italian Pavilion in 1967 are unique in the short history of reinforced plastics in architecture. The experimental design anticipated an engagement with the opportunities offered to architects by innovative methodologies as well as new material and processing technologies. This has profound implications with respect to the use and control of material systems in structural and architectural design. Piano was fully aware of this, and he was explicit about the need for architects to reseize control in the design and production processes. "Once, when architecture really was a craft," he said, "the architect used to design his work instruments before he designed the actual buildings. Nowadays, in order to express oneself, it is absolutely necessary to 'edify' these instruments, which are at present in the hands of 'uncultivated' and corporative operators. Form, if it ever is to emerge, must also emerge from this reappropriation of the 'cultural' and material instruments of building."[18]

The Internal or Systemic Mode of Structuring Plastic Flow
While the case of Piano's Italian Pavilion presents a processual mode of structuring plastic flow, the material systems themselves, together with newer computational technologies, give a systemic mode that regulates the same. The systemic mode is given by relational, geometric conditions in the given material organization across small distances and interfaces between the fibrous elements in the reinforcement. Since Piano's pioneering projects, massive developments in the textile industry have shifted the main focus from reinforcement systems made of shorter strands of glass-fiber bundles to advanced industrial textiles made from various continuous and fibrous yarns. The simple fabrics of the former come with stochastic geometry and display isotropic behavior, whereas the latter are characterized by anisotropic behavior and a highly modifiable fibrous geometry.[19] | fig. 8

When a composite is formed, the polymer matrix flows into and fills the interstices or voids that are part of

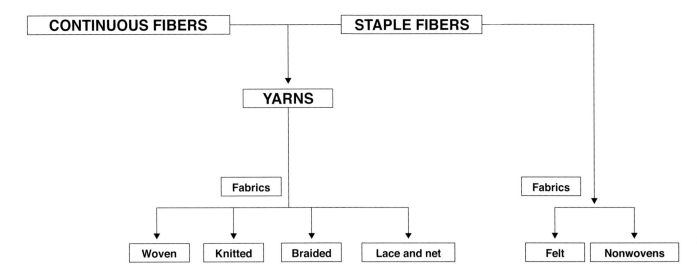

fig. 8 | Diagram showing the shift of material usage in the
textile industry to obtain highly modifiable geometries

the reinforcement system. Saturating these tiny spaces between the textile elements with resin is crucial to achieving an optimal result, and the stiffness and strength of a fiber-reinforced system increases proportionally with the amount of fiber present.[20] The main factors that influence the mechanical properties of the composite system pertaining to the specific fiber product and its assembly are the basic mechanical properties of the fiber itself, the surface interaction of fiber and resin (the "interface" bonding), and the amount and orientation of fibers in the composite. In the composite system, the load distribution is absorbed by its "low-modulus matrix reinforced with high-strength, high-modulus fibers, [where] the plastic flow of the matrix under stress transfers the load to the fiber."[21] Through the transition of stress induced by a load from the matrix to the fibrous reinforcement, there results a transfer of material dynamics from one scale of geometry to another larger scale, which in turn anticipates further scalar shifts in material dynamics toward the scale of the architectural object.
| figs. 9 and 10

The fibrous condition is geometrically defined and, as such, is independent of the material in question. As industrial products, whether organic or synthetic, fibers are produced in continuous form and defined geometrically as linear filaments of material with a more or less uniform crosssection less than 100 micrometers and an aspect ratio (length to diameter) greater than 100 to 1.[22] From these "building blocks," yarns and other fiber products are manufactured by geometrically bundling or gluing the fiber filaments together.[23] Textiles are thus material systems of a high order with complex internal relations. Depending on the manufacturing technique, these internal relations consist of a discrete distribution of interlacing (weaving and braiding) or interlooping (knitting and stitching) of the yarn elements, based on their continuity.[24] Hence, a textile is essentially a dynamic material system that consists of a vast collection of discrete, virtual joints in a continuous material field. In textile and composite science and engineering, the challenge is to model, simulate, and analyze these systems so that they can be embedded in layers within a polymer matrix that will exhibit predictable behavior for a particular, desired end result in the composite application.[25]

The design geometry at stake is usually categorized on three scalar levels that are integrated with one another.

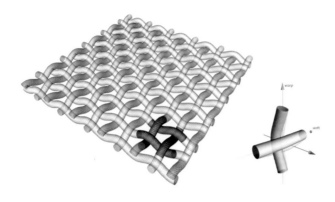

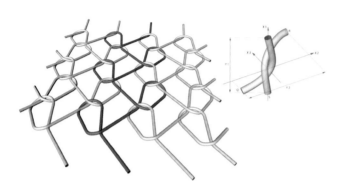

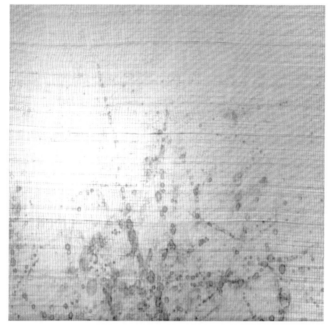

	Geometry	Cell Model (≈ cell unit)		
Braided			Composition:	- yarn
			Formation:	- intertwine
			Cell link:	- orientation: trellis
				- length: short
				- continuity: continous
				- mobility: limited
				- entanglement: flexible
Knitted			Composition:	- yarn
			Formation:	- interloop
			Cell link:	- orientation: oblique
				- length: long
				- continuity: discontinous
				- mobility: tremendous
				- entanglement: mobile
Nonwoven			Composition:	- fiber
			Formation:	- bond
			Cell link:	- orientation: random
				- length: very short
				- continuity: either
				- mobility: very slight
				- entanglement: rigid
Woven			Composition:	- yarn
			Formation:	- interlace
			Cell link:	- orientation: orthogonal
				- length: short
				- continuity: continous
				- mobility: limited
				- entanglement: flexible

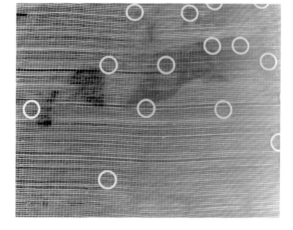

figs. 12 and 13 | Interconnectedness and relational
condition of the elements make one locality contingent on
its neighboring area and other local, virtual hinges.

figs. 9 and 10 | Diagram showing a variation of the
orientation of fibers in a composite and the "interface"
bonding between the fiber and the resin

fig. 11 | Diagram showing different textile design
geometries

First, there is the microgeometry of the fibers and yarns. Second, there is the meso-level, constituted by the geometry of the fiber and yarn entanglement in the reinforcement system; this is described as the "geometric unit cell," which is the smallest repeated unit in the overall geometric composition of the textile. The third level pertains to the total form of the fiber assembly, with its various degrees of deformability and structural behavior. This last level defines a macroscale geometry given by the specific textile preform and determines the resin flow in the mold and the integration with the resin at the yarn interfaces.[26] | fig. 11

The relationship between the continuous and the discrete in fibrous textile forms cannot be overemphasized. Textiles present continuity of linear fibrous and yarn elements. Geometrically, the cohesion of the textile form rests with the interlacing and interlooping of the same elements. The local zone of these geometric events defines a large set of virtual hinges, each of which potentially contributes to the dynamic character of the material system. In other words, the space of the textile is made up of continuous material elements and discrete geometric events decussated by voids. The material system embodies a hyperarticulated, finely tuned heterogeneous space within which the constituent elements define a fluent whole. The status and performance of any one locality within this space relies on the ambiguous relation between these three variables: the continuity of the yarns, the geometric singularities that give the system its cohesion, and their minute interstices. A given locality cannot be isolated and reduced to an ideal singularity. The interconnectedness and relational condition of the elements always make one locality contingent on its neighboring area and other local, virtual hinges.[27] | figs. 12 and 13

The sum of these integrated, geometric relations and how they pertain to the use of reinforced polymer composites in architecture constitutes the systemic mode of regulating plastic flow.[28] At every level of design, whether carried out by textile or composite engineers, in structural or architectural design, the challenge of saturating the voids in the reinforcement with resin has a bearing on the structural and aesthetic results. Whereas this only makes up one of many research areas in composite science, it clearly reflects how industrial polymers or plastics are part of reinforced and structural composite applications in architecture. The role of plastics revolves around questions of integration across a wide scope of considerations that facilitate the flow of their systemic processes. For architecture, the same integration presents a new synthetic design model that relies on relational, material, geometric, technological, and methodological conditions for architectural ends. Ironically, tectonic theory—which is unique in addressing the materiality of architecture—has always been concerned with the coordination of structural, constructional, and aesthetic considerations, yet it has proven largely ineffective in accounting for plastics and their structural composites.

A Last Word on Integration: Tectonic Theory

In abridged form, traditional tectonic theory employs autonomy and homogeneity to lend the material basis for architectural design to a supposed one-to-one, predictable relationship between idea and object. The theory engages the material geometry of architectural forms to assess the load-bearing capacity of constructive elements in aesthetic terms and presents its classical distinction between structure and surface to relate architectural forms to a transcendental regime of representation and "truth." | figs. 14 and 15

Barthes's transmutable plastics obviously fit poorly with the tenets of traditional tectonic theory. But plastics and reinforced polymer composites do not replace tectonics; the latter remains a theoretical site for thinking and rethinking architecture through its materiality.[29] Yet, precisely due to plastics' inability to conform to traditional tectonics, this immense group of transmutable materials presents the most evident symptom of why the theory must be reconsidered.[30] Through the centrality of design with reinforced composites, the focus of coordination shifts from exclusively prioritizing the architectural object and its critical context in aesthetic

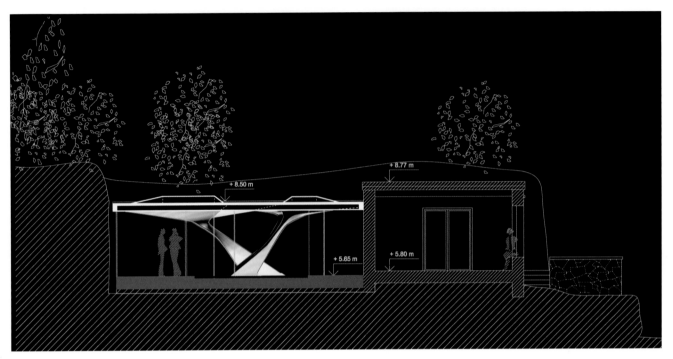

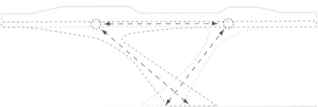

fig. 14 | The material geometry allows architectural forms to be structure and surface.

fig. 15 | The architectural forms of composites represent the structural function.

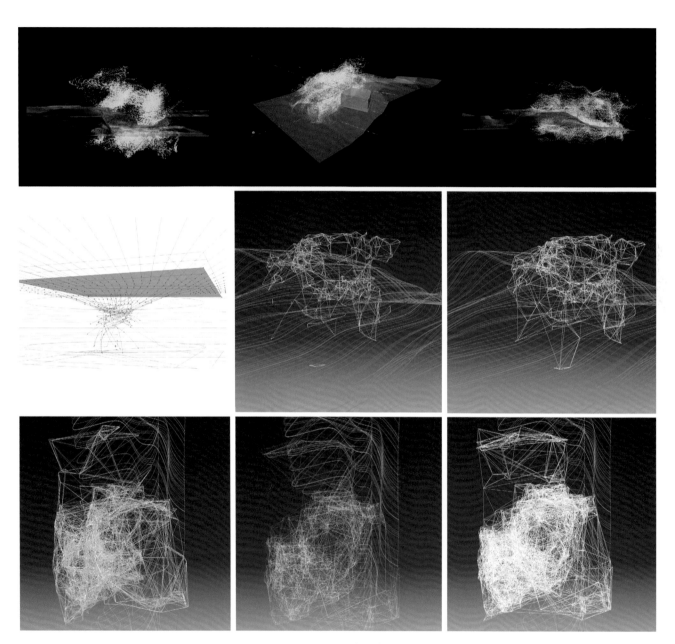

fig. 16 | Geometry as an organizational tool for
architectural form

terms, to distribution across the gamut of design concerns. This includes the coordination of material and structural variables with spatial, temporal, and aesthetic effects across the various scales of the material's fibrous geometry. Design ideas and incentives then become linked to architectural goals through the flow of material information in the work process.

The relationship between reinforced composites and architecture suggests that traditional theory and practice have reached a critical moment when they no longer suffice to account for advanced, contemporary instances of material technology and their potential for architecture. If this is the case, then architecture must face the challenge to reformulate its theoretical and practical foundations. It can do so through its reliance on geometry as a key organizational tool, echoing the reliance of traditional tectonics on architectural form and components for meaning. | fig. 16

Tectonics, considered through the composite paradigm, is not restricted to the customary manner in which architects fit parts together, segregate between horizontally composed massing and vertically spaced columns, or apply surfaces and envelopes to a load-bearing structure.[31] Rather, it presents integration beyond the question of physical form and reissues geometry as the chief means for unfolding architecture across scales, various disciplinary contributions to the work process, the manufacturing process, and, last but not least, plastic flow.

1 | Roland Barthes, "Plastic," in *Mythologies* (London: Vintage, 1993).

2 | Siegfried Giedion, Building in France, Building in Iron, Building in Ferroconcrete, trans. J. Duncan Berry, Texts and Documents (Santa Monica: The Getty Center Publication Programs, The Getty Center for the History of Art and the Humanities, 1995). First published as *Bauen in Frankreich, Bauen in Eisen, Bauen in Eisenbeton,* (Leipzig: Klinkhardt & Biermann, 1928).

3 | For example, the use of building information modeling (BIM), or software-centered processes for producing and managing information pertaining to construction.

4 | Their idea of synthesis takes on various forms, but is described in detail in Gilles Deleuze and Félix Guattari, "Anti-Oedipus: Capitalism and Schizophrenia," trans. Robert Hurley et al. (Minneapolis: University of Minnesota Press, 1983), 68–113. Synthesis as the opposite of analysis and the resolution of opposing terms composes a classical model of negotiating difference by eliminating it.

5 | V. M. Karbhari, "The Role of Expert and Decision Support Systems in Composites Design and Manufacturing," in *Computer Aided Design in Composite Material Technology III*, ed. S. G. Advani et al., Third International Conference on Computer Aided Design in Composite Material Technology (Cadcomp 92) (London: Elsevier Applied Sciences, 1992).

6 | Deleuze and Guattari call this "the connective synthesis of production." Their description of it moves through detailed considerations of the Oedipus complex and engages Freudian phenomena. Emerging in the discussion is an economy of triangulation, in which things come together and are defined, ("Anti-Oedipus," 68–70). However, the automated computational processes pursued in advanced design studios and corporate settings often conflate these nuances of production. These processes tend to replace the efficacy of the computational that could include the sensuous performance of material systems with a superficial and rationalizing efficiency.

7 | Just like composites are the antithesis of hybrids, this approach is the antithesis to "form finding," a process in which the architectural form is principally predetermined by the interaction of compositional material formation in response to one or more criteria without the agency of design intuition and architectural criteria. This typically involves material formation in response to gravitation (Gaudi) or with a material medium such as a liquid (Frei Otto and Lars Spuybroek's experiments with threads or yarns embedded in a liquid).

8 | This is equivalent to a bi-directional model of methodological integration that Scott Marble presented at the Columbia Building Intelligence Project (C BIP) in Stuttgart, June 1, 2011.

9 | Between 1965 and 1970, some of this research was carried out in close collaboration with the structural engineer Z. S. Makowsky in London.

10 | The work composed various projects for industrial buildings and pavilions, some of which became the basis for designs well into the 1980s, such as the IBM Pavilion (1985). The initial research was conducted to explore physical applications of construction materials and their characteristics with the recognition that "the first work involved in a project is not, strictly speaking, necessarily architectural."

11 | Massimo Dini, "Renzo Piano: Projects and Buildings 1964–1983," *Architectural Documents* (Milano/New York: Electa Editrice/Rizzoli International, 1984), 32.

12 | Albert G. H. Dietz, *Plastics for Architects and Builders* (Cambridge: MIT Press, 1969).

13 | Ibid., 66–7.

14 | The project was all surface, rendering a continuously differentiated space given by heterogeneous geometric articulation of the composite envelope.

15 | Toshio Nakamaru, ed. *Renzo Piano Building Workshop, 1964–1988*, A+U Extra Edition 3 (Tokyo: Yoshida Yoshio / a+u Publishing, 1989), 163.

16 | Reyner Banham, "Making Architecture: The High Craft of Renzo Piano," in *Renzo Piano Building Workshop, 1964–1988*, 151–58. Banham suggested that the work of Piano's studio could have branched off with this project, instead it was a one-off in his oeuvre.

17 | Piano, downplaying the radical step that this involved, has said: "Once the conceptual problems of optimization of the shell had been solved, production of the casting itself was relatively simple. This led us to devise a strange instrument: a sort of pantograph that drove a set of pistons over a rubber membrane. When the shape looked satisfactory to us, the membrane was used as a mould to produce the final casting." He was fully aware of the radical steps they were making. Piano has referred to this project as the most interesting of the studio's projects in this

period. He states: "The research into shell-shaped structures was partly motivated by the curiosity that led us to investigate the properties of shells, which allowed great rigidity to be achieved with very thin materials. There was, however, a desire to imagine new worlds as well....From the viewpoint of structural calculation, the project's interest lay in the great versatility of forms that could be obtained by the same process of design, calculation, and construction....The shell structures did not involve just a quest for a vaguely organic elegance, but the adoption of a model of space in continuum, developed through compression, expansion, and lightening of the surface, i.e. transparency." Renzo Piano, *The Renzo Piano Logbook* (London: Thames & Hudson, 1997), 24.

18 | See Dini, "Renzo Piano," 26. A look at Piano's work at large reveals that reinforced polymer composites did not singularly define his outlook or approach. Studio Piano and, later, Renzo Piano Building Workshop engaged with advanced material and processing technology in numerous projects, using many different types of materials. Generally, though, the possibility of architectural form was seen as concomitant to the technological instruments for its making and had to be controlled and used in an intelligent and innovative fashion.

19 | An isotropic material or substance is one in which a physical property has the same value when measured in different directions. *Anisotropic* means that it has different properties when measured in different directions. Fiber-reinforced polymer composites are generally anisotropic and heterogeneous since they consist of different and discreet elements; their anisotropy would have to be assessed with respect to each element in a textile system. The design of textile systems may consider the anisotropy of micro-mechanical, elasticity, strength, and stability properties as well as patterns. The geometry of advanced textile systems has been referred to as "deterministic" as opposed to the biased stochastic geometry of so-called nonwoven fabrics, where the exact organization can only be modeled based on predictability and conjecture. Simple fabric assemblies are in fact so complex in their internal geometry that they have until now defied precise modeling and simulation of mechanical behavior. This is because the fiber orientation in simple nonwoven fabrics is arbitrary and models of properties and behavior must take this into account—the exception being pultruded products, where all the fibers are aligned with the axis of the product.

20 | This is measured by the Fiber Volume Fraction (FVF), which is given as a percentage of the total volume. The FVF is the indicator of how closely packed the fibers are in the textile. The following three variables affect the FVF: degree of coarseness of the fibers, gaps between the fibers, and fiber diameter. The composite system's strength peaks at about 60–70 percent FVF. Above this value, the strength generally decreases although tensile stiffness may continue to increase. The lack of sufficient resin to hold the fibers together under stress leads to the decline in strength.

21 | L. Hollaway, "Polymers and Polymer Composites," in *Construction Materials: Their Nature and Behaviour*, ed. J. M. Illston (London: E & FN Spoon, 1994), 323.

22 | The question of material system geometry can also be pursued on smaller scales. For instance, the interface bonding between resin and fibrous elements are partly determined by geometry or the coarseness of the fiber's surface. In the case of carbon fiber, one method uses precursor fibers made from polyacrylonitrile (PAN). These are folded graphite sheets layered along the longitudinal axis of the fiber, which explains carbon fibers' structural properties (high strength or high modulus).

23 | There are four principles for achieving lateral cohesion in basic fiber assemblies. One method is by adhesion; the others are all geometric conditions produced through various processes. These can be seen as selective deformations of the initial linear condition of the fibers and fiber bundles. The three geometric methods to achieve frictional interaction are twisting, wrapping, or entanglement. Although one of these may be the principal method for a given assembly, such as a yarn, more than one mechanism is usually in operation to create the required lateral cohesion: "A yarn...is a self-locking structure in which the harder the pull the more tightly the fibers are held together, so that yarn failure must be initiated by fibre breakage." John W. S. Hearle, "Mechanics of Yarns and Nonwoven Fabrics," in *Textile Structural Composites*, ed. Tsu-Wei Chou et al. (Amsterdam: Elsevier, 1989), 31.

24 | Various complex and hybrid textile products exist, such as noncrimp and 3-D fabrics. It is beyond the scope of this brief introduction to textile systems to introduce these and explain their respective structures in relation to commonly known textiles.

25 | In advanced fiber assemblies, the directionality is known but presents a set of criteria that tends to increase in complexity with more advanced arrangements. This results in nonlinear and dynamic mechanical behavior in the textile or fiber preform and the behavior cannot be mapped proportionally in relation to the applied stress. The relatively high flexibility in the fiber preforms gives rise to this behavior.

26 | A corresponding categorization exists for reinforced composites. In this case, the different scalar levels pertain to the fiber/textile and matrix interface (micro-) and the structure of the composite part (macro, e.g., layered/laminated).

27 | This model complies with Deleuze and Guattari's theory of the smooth and the striated. The system is at once characterized by two conditions that are fundamentally different but not mutually exclusive within a given whole.

28 | "Consistency in behavior throughout the composite piece," writes Scardino, "requires preservation of filament yarn properties during orientation and integration of the filament yarns into the desired assemblage or preform and requires uniform distribution of the resin matrix. The high modulus yarns should be oriented and integrated into the finest structural unit cells according to the nature and direction of stresses to be encountered.... Uniformity and fine cell size are the prerequisite for consistent behavior and reliability." The key words here are *orientation* and *integration*, where the latter also pertains to how the meso-geometric condition of the unit cell is integrated with the macro- and global conditions of, respectively, the specific type of the reinforcement and the global form of the composite part. See Frank Scardino, "An Introduction to Textile Structures and Their Behaviour," in *Textile Structural Composites*, 24–25.

29 | In his keynote lecture at the Permanent Change conference, Greg Lynn proposed precisely this. Meanwhile, a number of bad attempts at reformulating tectonic theory have been launched, including the idea of "digital tectonics," which for the very immateriality of the digital is absurd. This, of course, is not to say that computers and computational processes do not affect tectonics. On the contrary, this is exactly the point. But there are fundamental differences between tools, methods, material conditions, and architectural theory.

30 | The material group is rarely accounted for in reviews of tectonic theory and frequently not rostered as architectural material. Its stigma is partly transferred to its reinforced composite counterparts.

31 | The relation between parts and jointing is key to traditional tectonics. The composite paradigm does not eradicate these concerns; gluing composite elements together is not categorically different from bolting them. It is merely a question of technique and degree of articulation. Ironically, composites based on industrial polymers are all glue, since this is the main function of the polymer matrix. A common example is the glue Araldite, which is equivalent to a two-component epoxy resin.

fig. 1 | *Mae West*, by Rita McBridge, Munich, 2010

Plastics as Structural Materials

Werner Sobek with Wolfgang Sundermann and Martin Synold

Contemporary engineering is constantly seeking to extend its palette beyond traditional materials, driven by a desire in architecture for irregular shapes, increased lightness and transparency, and surfaces with novel tactile qualities. There have certainly been technological advancements over the decades related to concrete, metal, and wood, but there are things that even those materials cannot do. Plastics—especially fiber-reinforced plastics—hold the promise of expanding the palette and pushing the envelope of material possibility. For many years, the authors of this essay have been researching and developing new plastics for the structures we engineer. Some of those developments involve polyethylene terephthalate (PETP) or glass-fiber fabrics, carbon fibers, epoxy-paper-sandwich elements, or polycarbonates as load-bearing structures.

The following text is based on various papers we have previously published. It describes our work and experiences in the use of structural plastics, using particular built structures as examples.

The *Mae West* Sculpture by Rita McBride

The redesign of the Effnerplatz in Munich is part of the Eastern Central Ring tunneling project. It is the result of an invited competition, in which eight artists were invited to design a sculpture—with any material—for the Effnerplatz. The winning design was by the American artist Rita McBride. She called her sculpture *Mae West,* after the famous American film actress in the 1930s. The hyperbolic shape of the 52-meter-high sculpture with its diagonal twisted pipes and different diameters (bottom is 32 meters; middle is 7.5 meters; top is 19.5 meters) is to remind one of the dress of a dancing woman. | fig. 1

The project was completed in 2010 and it is possibly the tallest structure yet built using carbon-fiber-reinforced pipes as its primary structural elements. The straight structural struts are bound by two horizontal rings, which stiffen and stabilize it. | fig. 2 The lower ring is formed as a sharp-edged welded box section made of steel, while the upper ring is a Vierendeel beam (an open-web girder) of tubular cross sections. The cross sections of the inclined struts taper upward—the strut diameter is 280 millimeters at the bottom and 220 millimeters at the top. The entire structure is made of carbon-fiber-reinforced plastic (CRP), yet due to the risk of a derailed streetcar colliding with the structure, the lower third of the pipes were made of steel sheathed with nonstructural CRP.

The connections between the two stiffening rings and the inclined CRP tubes are made with coupling pipes. These pipes are fixed to metal in-liners, which are laminated to the inner sides of the CRP tubes; they are also fixed by hollow bolt screws between the CRP tubes and the in-liners. | fig. 3 This fixture is also used to connect the tubes to each other, which happens at four levels in total. These levels lie between the lower and the upper stiffening rings. At each level there is a total of sixteen connections. A pin joint connects the lower steel pipes (sheathed with CRP) to the stiffening ring and to the raft.

Testing the structure extensively in a wind tunnel was integral to the design process. The structure was also tested for its acoustic quality. Without a proper design, the close vertical pipes may be subject to aero-acoustic resonance effects, in the case of strong winds, emitting a humming noise. The structure was also tested for the possible formation of ice. To avoid the accumulation of icicles on the two metal rings, both have specially integrated heating elements. Since the erection of the structure in 2010 no problems concerning icicles have been observed.

The *syn chron* Sculpture by Carsten Nicolai

syn chron is a sculpture designed by the artist Carsten Nicolai and developed with LIN architects and Werner Sobek for the New National Gallery in Berlin, as well as other museums around the world. | fig. 4 To date the structure has been

figs. 2 and 3 | Detail views, *Mae West*, 2010

fig. 4 | *syn chron*, by Carsten Nicolai, Berlin, 2004

reerected five times in other venues. The sculpture served simultaneously as an acoustic structure, a resonance room, and a projection surface. Electronic music composed by the artist generated modulated lighting by means of a laser that digitally projected moving patterns onto the skin's translucent surfaces, and acoustic activations caused the interior of the sculpture to function as a synchronized loudspeaker. | fig. 5

The crystal-like structure consisted of a spatially irregular polygonal framework made of hollow profiles for a lightweight structure. | fig. 6 It was 12 meters long and 8.6 meters wide, and designed to be easily assembled and disassembled at its various exhibition sites. The steel base frame could be dismantled into tubes and intersections through the use of nodal connectors. To hide any distracting elements, the welded nodes were screwed to the tubes via internal plug connections.

The panels were two centimeters thick and made from a core of corrugated aluminum laminate between two covering layers of glass-fiber-reinforced epoxy resin. They had a flexural strength of 2,600 sq. Nm/m and could transfer a bending moment of 2.5 kNm/m with a negligible dead weight of only 3.9 kg/sq. m. This structure had the same stiffness as a steel plate but a dead weight that was 80 percent lower.

figs. 5 and 6 | Detail views, *syn chron*, 2004

Cut pieces of polyoxymethylene copolymer (Polyacetal or POM-C) allow for joints with various dihedral angles between the panel surfaces. This hard and tough material is used for gearings and snap fasteners in precision mechanics (i.e., lightweight engineering) and mechanical engineering because of its outstanding resilient properties and high fatigue resistance. Polyacetal also has a very high aesthetic and haptic quality on account of its surface properties and smoothness.

Velcro connections made from polypropylene were used to fix the epoxy-resin panels to the molded parts. This easily applicable (and detachable) connection not only made for easy assembly, but also allowed for a very simple and effective compensation for slight inaccuracies in assembly.

fig. 7 | Makrolon pergola structure, by Helmut Jahn and
Werner Sobek, Bayer AG, Leverkusen, Germany, 1998

The three-centimeter-wide Velcro strips have a shearing strength of up to 250 N/cm, giving the entire structure a considerable bearing capacity.

There were two main challenges when designing the *syn chron*: no supporting structure was to be visible from inside the crystal, and no fastenings were to be visible from the outside. The structure designed for this purpose was very successful and evidenced the high potential of plastics for structural use, and especially for deployable lightweight systems.

Bayer AG's Corporate Headquarters

The pergola at Bayer AG's new corporate headquarters in Leverkusen, Germany, embodies the architectural possibilities offered by Bayer's translucent Makrolon polycarbonate. Designed by Helmut Jahn and Sobek, it runs a total length of 117 meters along Kaiser-Wilhelm-Allee. | fig. 7 Its roof rests on twenty tapered steel columns that have structurally rigid joints at their base and are set in a grid of 13 meters by 18 meters. The wind loads on the pergola were ascertained in wind tunnel tests and applied with a gust reaction factor in order to consider the system's dynamic response to the rigidly jointed columns.

The pergola's louvers are made of highly transparent Makrolon, a material invented by Bayer and characterized by high impact strength and long-term durability. | fig. 8 The Makrolon louvers have been formed to a 40-centimeter-high and 32-centimeter-wide hollow box-type girder with a diamond-shaped cross section. The boxes are stiffened by an internal Vierendeel web made of stainless steel. The Vierendeel web takes the constant vertical loads, and the external box made of Makrolon stabilizes the web and partially absorbs vertical and horizontal wind loads.

The Makrolon box simultaneously offers weather protection for the internal webs and carries the optical elements of dichroitic glass that are inserted into the Vierendeel beam web openings. These optical elements generate an intense, permanently changing color effect. The impression of changing colors, according to the sun's

fig. 8 | Detail view, Makrolon pergola structure, 1998

figs. 9–11 | Main Entrance Trumpf Headquarters,
by Barkow Leibinger and Werner Sobek, Ditzingen,
Germany, 2010

position and angle of incidence, as well as the visitor's standpoint, is also reflected on the brightly illuminated floor in the approach area.

The Makrolon box is heat-bent on three corners. It is connected to the upper chord of the Vierendeel beam so that the web and the box may expand independently in the longitudinal direction. Ventilation openings are provided in the bulkheads, in order to enable balancing of humidity between the element's interior space and the surrounding air. A heating tape is located in the lower chord of the Vierendeel web to prevent the building up of icicles.

Main Entrance of Trumpf

For the new main entrance of the company Trumpf in Ditzingen, Germany, architects Barkow Leibinger and Sobek designed a highly transparent glass facade situated beneath an extremely slender cantilevered roof. | fig. 9 The glass facade is double-layered using structural glazing technology with statically bearing silicone glue. The main elements of this facade are polymethyl methacrylate acrylic (PMMA) fins that act as stiffeners for the glass panes. | fig. 10 The PMMA is sufficiently strong so that the posts can be far more slender than if they were made of tempered glass. | fig. 11

Translucent Textile Facades Using Vacuumatics Technology

Building skins must be able to meet changing environmental conditions, increasingly complicated user demands, and ever more complex design concepts. Since they can be understood more or less as clothing for buildings, it is obvious to think about textiles and foils when conceptualizing new approaches to their design and materials. They must provide shelter from environmental influences, but also allow for translucency and adaptability.

Structural membranes need to be stabilized by curvature, mechanical pre-tension, or air pressure. While pressurized air has been employed in pneumatic structures for decades, it is very rare to see a vacuum stabilizing the structural system of a permanent building. But recently, together

with the Institute for Lightweight Structures and Conceptual Design (ILEK), Sobek has investigated and developed a new design methodology termed *Vacuumatics* that makes use of a (partial) vacuum to give strength and form to different combinations of lightweight materials. The Vacuumatic cases realized thus far have been analyzed with regard to their load-bearing behavior, light transmission, insulating properties, and connections to the primary structure. This has yielded important results for other projects using membranes for the creation of multilayer (and multifunctional) facades.

Until recently, multilayered membrane structures were generally designed with added mass in order to meet thermal and acoustical requirements, but this typically also led to a loss of transparency. An alternative solution was explored at the Suvarnabhumi Airport in Bangkok. | fig. 12 The concourses linking the main building and the gates are enveloped by a membrane structure with a three-layer assembly specifically developed for this project. While the outer polytetrafluroethylene (PTFE) coated glass-fiber membrane controls influences from the environment, the transparent middle layer reduces noise to a comfortable level. Both layers form a pneumatic cushion that improves the load-bearing behavior for short-term loads. Thus, this assembly takes advantage not only of the specific behavior of each layer but also of the additional effects of the synergy between them. | fig. 13 The radiative emissivity of the microperforated inner textile membrane is greatly reduced due to a special low-emittance (low-e) coating. With this assembly the required comfort level in the passenger-occupied zones can be maintained, while the building skin remains translucent. | fig. 14

A different approach was chosen for the trade show stand of the company MERO Structures in 2002, designed and engineered by Sobek. | fig. 15 The wall shell was covered on both sides by a sandblasted polyethylene foil that was stabilized by the application of a vacuum. | fig. 16 The resulting folds in the foil were intentional and produced a very specific surface texture. This simple solution resulted in stunning aesthetic and haptic qualities. | fig. 17

fig. 12 | Aerial view of Suvarnabhumi Airport, by Murphy/
Jahn and Werner Sobek, Bangkok, 2005

Plastics as Structural Materials

Werner Sobek with Wolfgang Sundermann and Martin Synold

figs. 13 and 14 | Exterior and interior views, Suvarnabhumi Airport, 2005

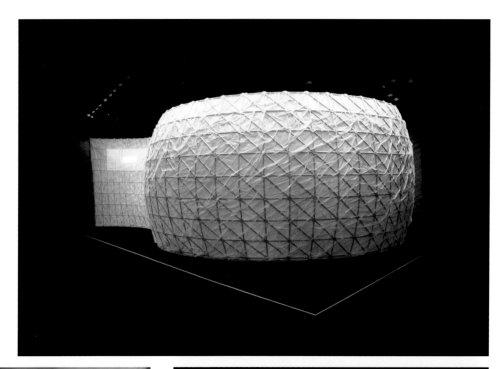

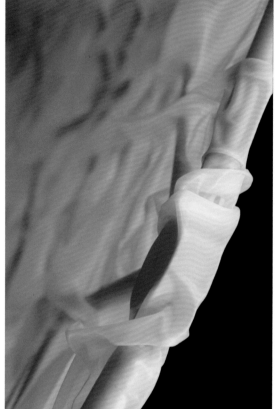

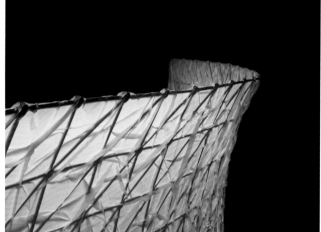

figs. 15–17 | MERO trade fair stand, by Werner Sobek,
Stuttgart, Germany, 2002

Plastics as Structural Materials

Werner Sobek with Wolfgang Sundermann and Martin Synold

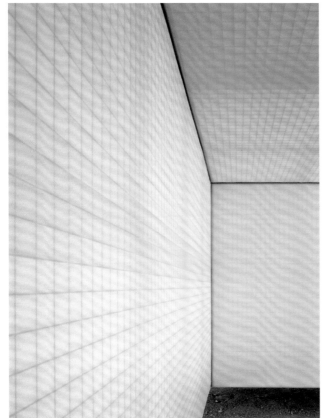

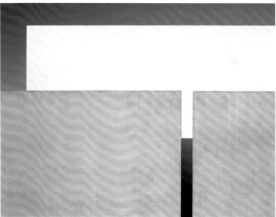

figs. 18–20 | Station Z, by HG Merz and Werner Sobek,
Oranienburg, Germany, 2005

fig. 21 | Facade element based on the Plusminus-System,
by Institute for Lightweight Structures and Conceptual
Design, Stuttgart, Germany

Based on these experiences, the first vacuum-stabilized facade for exterior use was developed together with the architecture firm HG Merz in 2005. The objective was to create a structure providing shelter for the memorial site Station Z in Oranienburg, Germany. Spanning over the ruins of a demolished concentration camp and touching the ground at just a few points, the white sharp-edged box responded to the design objectives with a minimal and simple structure. | fig. 18 The steel space framework is clad on both sides by structural gratings, which are covered with a translucent protective envelope. A slight underpressure is maintained between the inner and outer membranes, holding the pre-tensioned membranes close to the grating. The result is a smooth, planar appearance of all surfaces. | fig. 19 Minimum suction performance suffices due to an active pressure regulation. To produce a formally reduced, almost abstract cuboid, not only the supporting structure but also all edge details of the membrane were moved to the interior of the construction, thus rendering them invisible to the visitor. | fig. 20

The Plusminus-System
The research on inflatables done at ILEK has yielded many interesting structures made of air-inflated thin-film plastic pipes. | fig. 21 But the sometimes-surprising load-bearing capacities of these structures always leave one question: how to create an enclosure that is simultaneously a skin and a structure. Thus, a key objective in the research was to achieve a clear demarcation between interior and exterior. We did not look for perfect transparency, but for selective views in and out: not clear enough to discern what was inside, but still transparent enough to understand the outside.

With these ideas in mind, a system of tubular elements arrayed in a chaotic, overlapping fashion was conceived to provide irregular views in and out through the gaps in the wall. It was further desired to dematerialize the walls as much as possible, to enhance the dichotomy between the enclosed inner space and the glimpses allowed through.

This vision could only be realized by employing translucent plastic film for the skin elements of the facades, which were given their form using a unique pneumatic system. The conceptual dualism of the project was perhaps most boldly articulated by combining pressurized and vacuum-stabilized pneumatic components. Foil tubes were inflated to form the wall's elements, while two clear encapsulating foil layers bound the system together via low pressure. The final result was a visual, tactile, constructive symbiosis that perfectly met the design intentions.

In conclusion, building construction with plastic-based materials allows for highly interesting applications, although as yet these applications still lie mainly in specialized areas. A great deal of research must be done to identify materials best suited for various techniques and environments. This is due to the specific behavior of the materials, dependent on many parameters. Special care must be taken with regard to the detailing, which has to be adequate for each material. Another issue that still merits further study is the longevity of the materials being used.

1 | Wolfgang Sundermann, Werner Sobek, Martin Synold, and Heiko Trumpf, "Plastic Materials: New Approaches and Applications," *Shell and Spatial Structures: Structural Architecture—Towards the future looking to the past* (Venice: IUAV, 2007).

2 | Martin Synold, Timo Schmidt, Werner Sobek, "Translucent Structural Skins: Vacuumatics and Adaptivity," *Shell and Spatial Structures: Structural Architecture—Towards the future looking to the past* (Venice: IUAV, 2007).

3 | Werner Blaser, *Bayer Konzernzentrale / Headquarters* (Basel: Birkhäuser, 2003).

4 | Helmut Jahn, Werner Sobek, Matthias Schuler, *Suvarnabhumi Airport Bangkok, Thailand* (Ludwigsburg: avedition, 2007).

5 | Werner Sobek, Thomas Winterstetter, Holger Hinz, "Das schwebende Dach. Die neue Hauptpforte der Firma Trumpf in Ditzingen," *Stahlbau* 78, no. 11 (Berlin: Ernst & Sohn, 2009): 869–72.

6 | Timo Schmidt, Christine Lemaitre, Walter Haase, Werner Sobek, "Vacuumatics—Bauen mit Unterdruck," *Detail* 2007/10: 1148–58.

7 | Walter Haase, Thorsten Klaus, Fabian Schmid, Timo Schmidt, Klaus Sedlbauer, Werner Sobek, Martin Synold, "Adaptive textile und folienbasierte Gebäudehüllen," *Bautechnik* 88, no. 2 (2011): 69–75.

North Sails Three-Dimensional Laminates

Bill Pearson

In the early 1990s, North Sails, now North Technology Group, developed a process for manufacturing large membranes for the sails of boats at full size, in three dimensions, and in one piece, using giant articulating and reconfigurable male molds. Without question, three-dimensional laminate (3-DL) has been *the* seminal development in sail making since the change from woven textiles to laminates roughly forty years ago. It has made possible a sail that is better in every regard. It has more modulus, is stronger yet lighter, more flexible, and able to carry very high loads across its surface.

As is often the case in a technological revolution, the metamorphosis was accompanied by, or driven by, a new approach to the medium. | figs. 1 and 2 In the case of this change from panel assembly to monolithic structure, the transformation happened all at once, rather than in evolutionary steps. It was a giant leap out of the textile paradigm into the modern world of composite fabrication.

As the boundary between textiles and composites has blurred, the term "flexible composite," once an oxymoron, has become the norm, at least in the sail-making industry. Composite fabrics built in three-dimensional shapes were first developed for the sails of racing yachts, and since then they have been sparking much interest in other fields (although not yet finding too many specific applications). But the time has finally come for these materials and structures to enter the world outside performance sports. The future potential of textiles and fibrous systems in architecture and building construction is appearing significant, as it offers both appealing aesthetics and high performative capacity.

The historical foundations of the sail-making business are embedded in the textile industry. From the woven palm-leaf sails on dugout canoes thousands of years ago to flax fiber, cotton textiles, modern manufactured performance textiles such as polyester and nylon, and on into para-aramids (such as Kevlar) and liquid crystal polymers, sails have been produced from industrial roll goods.

No matter how high performing the technical base fiber, *textile* was until recently defined as gridlike and symmetrical. Today, however, this notion is anachronistic in performance sports. The symmetry of the 0–90 grid (warp and weft) has been replaced by varying spatial fiber density and seemingly random orientations. Nowadays, one-piece molded sails are seamless, unitary structures employing continuous, uninterrupted fiber paths.

Bespoke Fiber Placement

The placement of fibers in modern sails reflects anticipated wind loads and variations in the stress field as the boat moves through the waves. The variation in fiber density and orientation allows us to optimize locally for desired strength and stiffness. The bespoke fiber placement process performed using our custom fabrication robotics allows hybrid blends of different fibers to be used in varying trajectories, densities, and orientations, as required. The greatest fiber densities are clustered in the corners. This requires fiber orientations in modern sails to be asymmetric, as opposed to the formal, symmetrical microstructure of a textile. In traditional textile manufacturing, the symmetry of the 0–90 grid requires fibers to be positioned evenly throughout, not because of the specifications of the structure or product, but because of the constraints of the textile manufacturing process.

The new paradigm—placing fiber only where it is required—allows for better material economy, which in turn allows for reduced weight of the finished part, resulting in the lightest structure possible for a given application. These membranes are built as unitary, monolithic structures in three-dimensional space with complex curvatures—that is to say, in the shape they will assume when they are flying on the boat. Fiber runs corner-to-corner, uninterrupted by seams or joins. Chemistry replaces mechanical assembly; covalent bonds and van der Waals force are the new seams, gluing, and stitching. The fiber is laid in three-dimensional space, in the spatial location it will be in when the sail is inflated. In this process there is no longer any distinction between the sailcloth and the sail. The two are fabricated simultaneously,

fig. 1 | *Dark Shadow*, 105-foot Wally yacht racing off of St. Tropez with her North 3-DL mainsail and North spinnaker

fig. 2 | Around the World Race yacht powering upwind through heavy seas with her one-piece molded 3-DL sails

and they are indistinguishable and inseparable. Surface and structure are integrated. Thus, even though it is still laminated to a film substrate—which I will explain further in the next section—the finished product becomes a composite. Even though there is a visible distinction between surface (the clear Mylar film) and structure (the fiber)—which will disappear in the next-generation 3-Di sail technology—it is nearly monocoque.

Three-Dimensional Molding

The equipment we are using for this bespoke fiber placement is unique and unconventional. The heart of the invention is an articulating mold that can be adjusted in three dimensions to match the complex curvature of a custom sail configuration. The surface contour of the mold is achieved with dual pneumatic actuators controlling up to 350 pantograph armatures driven by an attached vertical screw, one-quarter turn at a time, moving its lifter one millimeter per turn. This adjusts a segmented surface structure made of parallel pultruded battens and supporting crossbars, covered by closed-cell neoprene foam that provides an insulating base layer for the layup. The foam tool bed is covered with a loosely fitted metalized nylon sheet that reflects through the part during infrared heating and curing.

This is a push-button operation, with the actuators firing in rotation to configure a surface area up to 500 square meters in about five minutes, sail-to-sail on a bespoke basis. A number of overhead gantries run the length of building, serving nine individual molds of varying sizes and geometries. A robotic arm descends from the gantry and a number of different tools for varying stages of manufacture can be plugged in. An automated fiber placement system with a PLC-controlled six-axis head is suspended from the gantry, which lays down the fiber architecture. For the structure of a sail, the head precisely follows the three-dimensional curve of the mold surface and the fiber head "draws" a pattern in yarn that matches anticipated loads in each location. Fibers that run continuously from one corner to another provide the

structure's backbone to carry the specified primary structural loads. | fig. 3

After the structural fiber is in place, a secondary film is applied, and before lamination begins, a vacuum bag is built around the laid-up sail. | fig. 4 In a process that is similar to the one used in the manufacture of rigid composite parts, the lamination system involves pulling a vacuum between two layers of the thin film that encase the fiber structure and resin matrix. | fig. 5 This forces the components together, consolidating the laminate, drawing out any air that would create voids in the finished product, and locking individual fiber tows into three-dimensional spatial locations.

Automation and Mass Customization

This process broke through a centuries-old technology wall, in which individual sections of symmetrical woven material had to be stitched or glued together mechanically. But we are already anticipating the next step beyond technical textiles and flexible composites—a second manufacturing revolution that will move beyond the industrial revolution's idea of mass production toward realities of individualized production and rapid customization.[1] The process is the same in each production cycle, but each sail is unique in terms of geometry, structure, and aerodynamics. The visualization of aerodynamic ideas will be fluidly exported as information to control fabrication robotics such as fiber placement and tool paths for lamination systems.

Twenty years after the invention of the 3-DL process, the specificity of the design and manufacturing technique is still representative of the most radical advances in the fields of textiles and composites.[2] The process and the product are still unique, even in their mature state. Today, for better or worse, the formal visual language of asymmetrical fiber architecture and load path structures is the defining feature of a modern sail.

The Next-Generation Technology (3-Di)

The next generation of laminate technology eliminates the film or substrate from the composite laminate package to

fig. 3 | An operator follows the progress of the fiber placement head in the North Technology Group factory.

fig. 4 | A large sail on a mold nears completion in the fiber placement process.

fig. 5 | Sophisticated fabrication robotics lay the structural fibers in place.

create a sail membrane made from fiber and resin only—to be specific, pre-impregnated spread fiber filament tapes. | fig. 6 What we think of as an individual strand of fiber or yarn (or tow, in the case of carbon fiber) is in fact a bundle of individual filaments ranging from 5 to 19 micrometers in diameter, depending on the fiber type. (The width of a human hair is about 25 micrometers). Depending on the material, a fiber can have 2,000 to 24,000 filaments in the tow. With our new 3-Di technology, we take that fiber or tow and break it down into its base component, the individual filament. We then produce a unidirectional spread filament tape, which is in effect a yarn or yarns, but in a different format that imparts higher performance to the finished product through more efficient use of the base materials. A spread filament tape is thus a deconstructed filament bundle (yarn), with filaments spread out side by side and combined with adhesive on a paper backer. Carbon fiber "pre-pregs" for composites are the same filament-level tape construction. However, our process and the end result are unique in terms of both the very light fiber areal weights achievable and the use of high-elongation polyester thermoplastic adhesives that allow the finished fiber and resin matrix membrane to remain flexible. | fig. 7

The 3-Di process constructs a sail out of a multiplicity of layers of these unidirectional (UD) "pre-preg" tapes. This produces a unitary surface with integrated structure and makes the film substrate redundant in the finished part. The same technology and fabrication strategy is already being used for other high-performance composite parts, such as hulls, masts, and racecars. The difference between a sail and a traditional composite part is that a sail needs to be flexible, as explained earlier.

This new fiber architecture is based on a philosophy quite different from that of 3-DL. Its structural typology is quasi-isotropic, rather than based on load path. Fiber, and hence modulus, runs in all directions instead of just in the directions of the primary loads. The resistance of the fabric to stretching is thus much improved. | fig. 8

Pre-preg tapes are deposed with the automated placement head in the orientation dictated by the sail designer for the application. A typical sail will have four to six layers of tape in the body of the membrane, all aligned along different axes, and up to 150 layers stacked in the corners. All of the reinforcing parts, which on a "normal" sail are mechanically fastened to the surface of the laminate (corner patches, batten pocket ends, reef tie-in points) are now located inside the membrane as integrated components of a thermoformed monolithic structure.

By carefully configuring the constitution of each layer, sail designers can prescribe the mechanical properties of the resulting composite. Since material is placed on an as-needed basis, it becomes possible to produce a lighter and more efficient structure for a given application. This process, whereby a finished part retains some properties of a textile but is produced using the materials technology and fabrication strategies of composite manufacture, is unique across all industries.

The architect and sailor Greg Lynn, an early adopter of the new technology on his own sailboat, put the material to use in a series of superlight hanging seats commissioned for the *Hyperlinks: Architecture and Design* exhibition at the Art Institute of Chicago. | fig. 9 The soft seating has a rigid-looking form when unloaded and "at rest," and transitions from a compression structure to a tension structure as it deforms when "loaded" with a human body. An individual seat weighs around one pound and can carry a load of about one thousand times its own weight.

1 | Susan Brown, "Textiles: Fiber, Structure, and Function," in *Extreme Textiles: Designing for High Performance*, ed. Matilda McQuaid (New York: Princeton Architectural Press, 2005): 34–65.

2 | Ibid.

fig. 6 | A large infrared (IR) lamp is plugged into the gantry robot arm and travels over the curved surface of this 3-Di molded sail.

fig. 7 | Lamination of the sail is achieved using IR heat to flow the thermoplastic adhesive while the membrane is under vacuum pressure. Above, an operator checks the temperature of the laminate underneath the IR lamp.

fig. 8 | An operator assists in laying the fiber architecture on a molded sail.

fig. 9 | 3-Di Chair (Hammock seat) at the Art Institute of Chicago, designed by Greg Lynn using carbon fiber and Dyneema hybrid pre-preg 3-Di tape produced for sail membranes

fig. 1 | A new road bridge with glass-fiber-reinforced polymers decks, by Knippers Helbig Advanced Engineering, Friedberg, Germany, 2010

Polymers in Architecture and Building Construction: Potentials and Challenges

Jan Knippers

Plastics have become indispensable in everyday life, industry, and medicine. But even though they are highly developed and efficient in a huge array of applications, in architecture they are still relegated mainly to secondary uses, such as sheeting, insulation, paints, and floor coverings. The vast array of available options can make plastics daunting to architects and engineers, but this is their decisive advantage. In the case of traditional materials, it is the material that determines the construction technique, whereas with plastics, the technique can come first, and then the designer can choose or adapt the particular type of plastic best suited for those mechanical, visual, or structural building requirements. It is the material itself that is designed by the architect; this expands the opportunities for design and is a significant departure from working with all other building materials.

Despite all the variations, there are some properties common to all plastics, such as their relatively low weight per volume, low thermal conductivity, and moldability. Indeed, synthetic materials offer remarkable advantages over conventional building materials and are increasingly used for load-bearing structures and building envelopes, where weight, durability, form, color, and translucency are key concerns.

Potentials

Weather resistance and overall durability are critical for external applications. In contrast to metals, many plastics are resistant to acids and alkalis. They have therefore been used for many years in sewage treatment tank covers, chemical pipes and vessels, and walkways and platforms in offshore constructions, to name a few. As environmental conditions become increasingly aggressive, this resistance becomes even more important in the construction sector. For example, extensive research is ongoing regarding bridge decks made from glass-fiber-reinforced plastics (GFRP).[1] | fig. 1 These are resistant to frost and deicing salts, which in combination with moisture are the main causes of corrosion damage (and the resultant repair costs) to reinforced and prestressed concrete bridges. In the early days of building with synthetic materials, ultraviolet (UV) light caused considerable damage to synthetic materials because it attacked the bonds between carbon atoms. Nowadays, UV light–absorbing stabilizers and reflective coatings provide reliable protection.

The low thermal conductivity of plastics, which is very similar to that of timber and far lower than glass, concrete, or metal, is particularly useful for the design of building envelopes. The thermal conductivity of a plastic can be reduced still further by foaming it up, making possible insulation values even better than that of stationary air. Foams made from polystyrene and polyurethane are undergoing constant optimization, especially with respect to infrared radiation permeability, volatile organic compound (VOC) emissions, and porosity. Phenolic resin foams with very low thermal conductivity—approximately 0.153 BTU-in/hr-sq. ft.-F—are currently at an advanced stage of development.

Thermoplastic materials, mostly polyvinyl chloride (PVC) and polyamide, have been in use for a long time as window frames because they are ideal thermal breaks. They are less stiff than conventional materials, however, and PVC frames need greater widths and/or metal inserts, which affects their thermal properties. Intensive development is currently being pushed forward in the use of GFRP for windows and facades because, apart from its low thermal conductivity and durability, it can also be used as a load-bearing material. In addition, pultruded GFRP sections with a glass fiber content of about 70 percent exhibit a coefficient of expansion that is similar to that of glass. Consequently, it is possible to create a rigid adhesive bond between the glazing and the GFRP without causing significant stresses that result from disparate expansion-contraction behavior. It is thus no longer necessary to provide an elastic layer between the glass and its frame. Many window and facade manufacturers are currently working on such developments. The use of GFRP could result in slimmer frame widths compared with other materials, especially wood or PVC—a considerable bonus from the architectural viewpoint.

Many synthetic materials can be more easily molded and shaped than metal, glass, timber, or other conventional building materials, enabling simpler production of complex components and opening up new design options. The Walbrook, a London office and retail development, is the first instance of GFRP used on a large scale.[2] Its louvers were initially designed as aluminum profiles, a very common material used for facades. However, it proved impossible to meet the specific requirements regarding the quality of the surface. The 155,000-square-foot facade is shaded entirely by GFRP lamellas with brilliant surface properties. GFRP can be molded into any shape and employed as lightweight, delicate elements with high weather resistance. Vertical strips break up the facade and support the horizontal sun-shading louvers positioned every one meter up the side of the building. Direct sunlight is screened depending on the time of year and time of day, and the metallic paint finish on the surface reflects scattered light into the interior. The louvers are elliptical in section and measure 50 by 12.5 meters on the south-facing side and 20 by 6.2 meters on the north side. | figs. 2 and 3

The geometry of the building envelope was developed in a digital, parametric three-dimensional model, which specified a large number of different molded parts and generated the data required for fabrication. The facade elements were manufactured in three steps: The original molds were made from CNC-milled rigid polyurethane foam. From these, the GFRP negative molds for the louvers were formed, and the textile-fiber reinforcement was laid into the molds and manually impregnated with polyester resin. A pressure bag was used to give the GFRP its final form while still wet; each louver is made of two half-shells. The tolerances due to the manual lamination work were compensated for by the CNC milling. Some 4,000 louvers and 750 lesene elements were manually produced in this way. There is a remarkable contrast between the digital design process and high-tech

figs. 2 and 3 | The Walbrook, by Foster + Partners,
London, 2010

appearance of the GFRP lamellas, and the way they were
actually produced in small and medium-sized shops across
Europe. The louvers were attached to aluminum facade elements in the factory to create fully prefabricated subassem-
blies. | figs. 4 and 5

New Applications

Glass-fiber composite materials are very flexible, combining
high tensile strength with low bending stiffness. Although
for most applications in building construction, these characteristics are unfavorable, they can be functional for new
types of pliable structures. Convertible systems in architecture are usually based on a combination of stiff elements or
soft textiles connected by hinges. GFRP allows large, elastic
deformations and enables a completely new interpretation
of convertible structures. The concept of using bending
for kinematic adaptation is rather uncommon in building
construction, but it is commonly found in nature, mainly in
plants.[3] The kinetic facade of the Thematic Pavilion of Expo
2012 in Yeosou, South Korea, was based on advanced bio-
mimetic research. The designers began with an investigation of plant movements and developed their ideas through
several levels of abstraction until a feasible technical solution was achieved, transforming their architectural vision of
an adaptive and smoothly swaying facade into built reality.
This facade covers a length of about 140 meters and a height
between 3 and 13 meters. It consists of 108 kinetic lamellas
supported at their top and bottom edges. The facade had
to be designed for the very high wind speeds on the South
Korean coast. The wind loads were derived from wind tunnel
tests. | figs. 6–10

The complex elastic deformation is induced by a small
vertical compression force at the top and bottom supports. A
computer addresses each lamella individually within a specific
logic of movements, choreographies, and operation modes.
The maximum opening of a thirteen meter lamella takes about
seven seconds. In case of very high wind speeds, the facade
closes and locks automatically in a "parking" position.

figs. 4 and 5 | Manufacturing process of GFRP lamellas for
the Walbrook

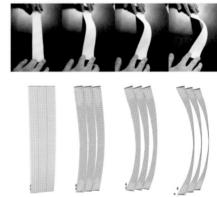

figs. 6–8 | Thematic Expo Pavilion, by SOMA Architects, Yeosou, Korea, 2012

fig. 9 | Kinetic facade, Thematic Pavilion, 2012

fig. 10 | Principle of the facade's elastic deformation, Thematic Pavilion, 2012

Trends

When building with plastics, reinforcing fibers, fillers, and additives can very easily be varied in numerous ways. The visual and haptic qualities can also be specifically controlled. The ability to select and control the material components represents new and demanding responsibilities for architects and engineers. Interesting visual effects can be achieved by adding thermochromic, phosphorescent, or photochromic pigments. Light permeability is an important design element and in the case of synthetic materials can often be adjusted.

Plastics are the only materials that allow the construction of load-bearing and simultaneously light-permeable structures. A light permeability of approximately 40 percent can be achieved with polytetrafluoroethylene (PTFE) fabrics for tensile structures, and with fiber-reinforced thermosetting plastics, values of up to 85 percent are possible. Research into such options for "smart" building envelopes, which can be further adapted to suit the outside temperature or UV radiation, are still in the early stages of development. The same applies to the integration of materials that store heat or moisture. Combined with transparent plastics, this can result in tremendously interesting visual and physical building characteristics.

The processing of synthetic materials often takes place at comparatively low temperatures and pressures, making it possible to integrate functional elements with relative ease. For example, it is fairly simple to incorporate light-channeling glass or polymer fibers for lighting effects into fiber composites. | fig. 11 The integration of sensors for measuring temperature, strain, or cracks is important in aerospace applications. Embedding these in the material protects them against external influences and enables the measurement of variables within the component itself, and not only on its surface. The use of piezoceramics is very common in aircraft. These convert strains into electrical voltages to enable permanent monitoring of the mechanical actions within a component. Fiber-optic sensors represent another form of technology that is currently being developed for

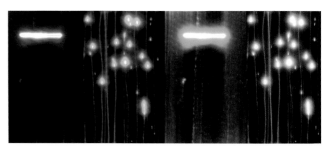

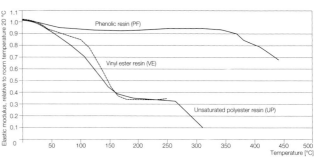

fig. 11 | Light-channeling fibers laminated into GFRP panels, ITKE University of Stuttgart

fig. 12 | Diagram showing the change in the elastic modulus of thermosets exposed to temperature

aircraft; the first applications are undergoing trials. Even though the diameter of these fibers is much larger than that of the glass fibers used to reinforce the material itself, they are related, and the two types are easily combined.

The next step in development is the use of actuators for the active control of component geometry. Piezoelectric or electrostrictive materials are used for the actuators, which, in a reversal of the sensors, convert an electrical voltage into an elongation and can therefore actuate a deformation of the component. They are mostly integrated into the fiber-reinforced synthetic material in the form of thin plates just a few tenths of a millimeter thick. Piezoelectric actuators are currently being used primarily for high-frequency vibration damping functions. A typical example of this is controlling the vibrations of helicopter rotor blades. One future application could be active acoustic facades. Research into other actuators is currently ongoing. Shape-memory materials—which are already being used in medical technology applications in the form of wires or fibers—are metals or polymers that have different basic shapes at different temperatures, to which they always return after cooling or heating. Consequently, with temperature control, large active elongation is possible at low frequencies, in contrast to piezoelectric materials. Polymer gels could also be suitable for actuators. These are carbon compounds that, in damp media, react by exchanging ions and varying their volume. One possible application could be "artificial muscles" for the active control of sun shading elements in facades.

Challenges

All these developments open up numerous opportunities, many of which have only been used tentatively so far and are still being researched. But there are also some obstacles that prevent the widespread application of plastics in architecture.

Plastics are made from organic polymers and are therefore combustible, even though this is hardly possible in practice for some fluoropolymers, such as PTFE and ETFE. Even the addition of flame retardants does not render plastics entirely incombustible, and these additives often increase the toxicity of the fumes. It is thus sometimes impossible to use plastics if the specification calls for noncombustibility or fire resistance. Familiar solutions from steelwork—for instance cladding with mineral fiber boards or applying intumescent paint finishes—have generally proved to be unsuitable. More research is required into the development of active and passive fire protection measures for synthetic materials.

Decreases in stiffness also cause difficulties. On a warm summer day in New York, say, the loss of stiffness of GFRP is about 30 percent. In a fire, temperatures of more than 500 degrees Fahrenheit are reached within minutes, and under these temperatures GFRP does not show *any* load-bearing capacity. Thus, even if polymer materials can be prevented from catching fire, they cannot be used as load-bearing elements in constructions with fire protection requirements.[2] | fig. 12

One challenge is to develop materials that have polymer-like construction and processing properties, but are not combustible, meaning that they are not based on mineral oil but on ceramic mortars or inorganic binders. These will be tested for the first time in the refurbishment of Berlin's State Opera. To enhance the acoustic properties of the auditorium, the entire roof will be lifted by a few meters. The additional space of the reverberation gallery will be covered by a grid structure, which forms a visually closed ceiling but allows sound waves to pass through. Many options were investigated to construct this grid, including extruded aluminum profiles and timber lamellas, but only plastics can produce a net with varying member width and thickness to provide the artistic appearance that appealed to the architect. After many discussions with representatives from the chemical industry, a type of phosphate cement reinforced by glass fibers was found, which will be used here for the first time ever in building construction. It is treated and processed at an ambient temperature in a manner very similar to thermoset resins. Its mechanical properties, however, are not as wide-ranging as those of GFRP. Data does not yet exist on long-term behavior, so durability tests will commence shortly. | figs. 13–17

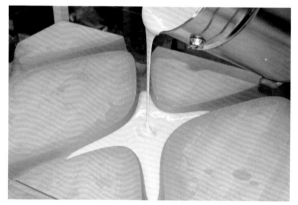

figs. 13 and 14 | Reverberation gallery, Staatsoper Berlin,
by HG Merz, Berlin, 2013

figs. 15–17 | Fabrication of mock-up for panel in the
reverberation gallery at the Staatsoper Berlin, by ITKE
University of Stuttgart

Depending on the application, components made from synthetic materials score differently in ecological audits. There is an urgent need for research into the problems that plastics cause at the end of their life cycle. This applies especially to fiber composites made from virtually inseparable and chemically resistant components. Increasingly stringent environmental legislation makes it more and more difficult to dispose of such products in landfills. Natural fibers made from flax, hemp, or ramies are currently being used as substitutes for glass fibers in the linings of vehicles and rolling stock, and also in the furniture and sports industries. But these natural fibers are still embedded in conventional petrochemical plastic, which limits their ecological advantages.

Replacing petrochemical plastics with resins based on natural materials is even more difficult. Biopolymers such as polylactic acid (PLA), which is made from starch, are already being used in great quantities for containers and packaging. But the development of natural plastics made from starch, sugar, or vegetable oils that provide the high mechanical strengths and levels of durability required for buildings is still at a very early stage. Currently, some automotive manufacturers are testing molded parts made from bioplastics for vehicle bodies. To what extent bioplastics might be suitable for load-bearing or enclosure components in buildings, with the end goal of using them instead of finite raw materials, is as yet unclear. It will be one of the key challenges for materials researchers in the coming years.[4]

1 | J. Knippers et al., "Bridges with Glass Fibre Reinforced Polymers Decks—The new Road Bridge in Friedberg, Germany," in *Structural Engineering International* 20, no. 4 (2010).

2 | J. Knippers et al., *Construction Manual for Polymers + Membranes* (Basel: Birkhäuser, 2011).

3 | J. Lienhard et al., "Form-finding of Nature Inspires Kinematics for Pliable Structures," in *Proceedings of the International Symposium of the International Association of Shell and Spatial Structures (IASS), Spatial Structures Temporary and Permanent, Shanghai, China*, ed. Q. Zhang et al. (2010), 2545–54.

4 | C. Koehler, "Natural fibre-reinforced polymers and bioplastics," in *Construction Manual for Polymers + Membranes* (Basel: Birkhäuser, 2011).

All-Plastics (In-Building)

Billie Faircloth

For the past several years I have collected feats of material derring-do. These are stories in which the lead characters manifest undeniable cases of monomaterial-mania, or obsession with one material and its ability to do everything: win a war, usher in a cultural revolution, sustain a colony in a foreign land, or provide a glimpse of the future.

The diagnosis, monomaterial-mania, is formed simply by inserting the word *material* into the psychological condition "monomania." Defined as an obsession with a single thought or idea, *monomania* literally means "one paranoia" or "one delusion."[1] While inserting the word *material* between "mono" and "mania" may force a pejorative association onto the concept of a "one-material delusion," aligning the word *material* more closely with the prefix "mono" suggests the notion that a single material can do everything. And "everything" in the context of architecture can mean structure, space, skin, form, aesthetics, performance, and beyond. One material is everything, and one material cures everything.

I have, to date, collected seventy-eight such stories, and the materials implicated in roughly fifty of these stories are plastics. The fact that all fifty of these proposals happen to be about houses is quite revealing. They are, in fact, fifty proposals for all-plastics houses.

All. Plastics. Panacea or provocation? | fig. 1

I have also collected eleven publications with two juxtaposed words, the first being *plastics* and the second, *building*. *Plastics* is a noun; *building* may be a noun or a verb. Interposing one article of speech, *in*, may force the grammatical hand. Shall we mean "plastics in building," noun and noun? As in, "Are there plastics in that building?" Or shall we mean "plastics in building," noun and verb? As in, "Did you build this house out of plastics?"

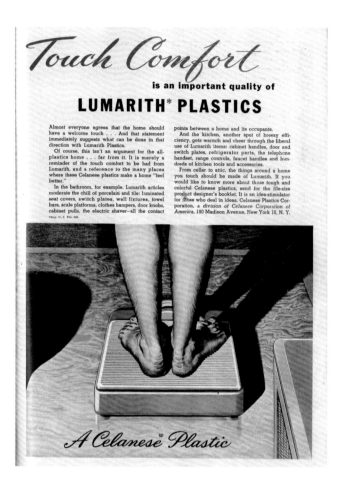

fig. 1 | Advertisement, Celanese Plastic Corporation, *Architectural Forum*, January 1946

The use of plastics materials in building

EEUA handbook no. **31**

Published for
The Engineering Equipment
Users Association
by
Constable and Company Ltd

fig. 2 | Reprinted front cover of *The Use of Plastics Materials in Building*, EEUA Handbook no. 31, Conference Proceedings

Plastics. In. Building. Fact or process? | fig. 2

At first glance the phrases "all-plastics" and "plastics in building" may seem nonspecific. Yet, as the material constraints of plastics became known, codified, and applied as the use of plastics in architecture emerged, both phrases headline repeatedly in architectural journals, meeting reports, and industry publications, organizing efforts to determine plastics' use. Material intentions are succinctly captured by these phrases, as "all-plastics" may be applied more to wholes, and "plastics in building" may be applied more to parts. And each phrase presently carries generative potential, as plastics' relationship to architecture may be said to be simultaneously inert and constantly emerging.

I will explain. Let us begin with "all-plastics."

All-Plastics

The phrase "all-plastics" is literal and applicable precisely because plastics are transmutable—in other words, capable of changing from one nature or substance to another form or condition—from liquid to solid, for instance, and seamlessly fusing geometrical trajectories. A washing machine tub, previously assembled from thirty-two metal parts, may be assembled from two plastic parts, thanks to plastics' transmutability. An "all-plastics" anything—be it a house or a washing machine tub—offers a challenge: to make that thing from the least possible number of parts. Make that house a single shell.

Conversely, the phrase "all-plastics" might refer to another challenge altogether, one equally dependent on the transmutability of plastics: namely, to use as many plastic products as possible in the making of that house. Plastic products—doorknobs, wall base, or floor tile—are dependent on plastic's capacity to resemble other materials. An "all-plastics" house might be assembled from many different "all-plastic" products.

The architect T. Warnett Kennedy asserted that his all-plastics house proposal in the October 1941 issue of *British Plastics and Moulded Products Trader*—which he described as an experiment in prefabrication—was the first. "It is safe to say," he declared, "that this will be the first attempt in any part of the world to erect an all-plastics house." The desire for such a house was known, acknowledged, sometimes derided, and most certainly debated. For instance, the Celanese Corporation promoted plastics' application for small elements, such as switch plates and doorknobs: "Almost everyone agrees that the home should have a welcome touch … and that statement immediately suggests what can be done in that direction with Lumarith Plastics. Of course, this isn't an argument for the *all-plastic home* … far from it."[2]

The Celanese Corporation may have known of the Vinylite House: a mise-en-scène that included sea-foam green and yellow vinyl floor tile and moldings, which appeared at the Chicago World's Fair in 1933, in the Chemistry Division of the Hall of Science. Referred to as the "House That Chemistry Built," it portended a plastic future.[3]

But it was a house designed and built by the architect Ionel Schein and sponsored by the French Chemical Company Charbonnages de France that would receive recognition as officially the "first." Prototyped in 1956, the All-Plastics House was rationalized into a frame and fill system. Semimonocoque in its construction logic, it deployed its plastics diversely—as structure, building envelope, and interior finish materials.

Amid the working-out of the plastic house prototypes, which was quite public, various national plastics organizations utilized industry publications as a platform to debate the pragmatics of an all-plastics house. For instance, the British Plastics Industry specifically addressed "all-plastics" as point number eighty-five of a bulletin enumerating the contribution of plastics to postwar rebuilding efforts. Citing the Vinylite House as an example, it stated, "There is a world of difference between an exhibition model, designed to attract attention regardless of cost or practicability, and a house intended for permanent use."[4] In the United States in the mid-1970s, when plastics had become normalized

as building products, there was certainly still controversy surrounding plastics' use in architecture. The Society of the Plastics Industry directly addressed the potential of an all-plastics house in the pages of *Progressive Architecture*: "The SPI emphatically states that an all-plastics house is not an industry goal. There are situations for which plastics are most sensible and those which are not."[5]

Plastics in Building

The problems concerning those working toward "all-plastics" were not the same as the issues facing the people working out plastics' specific uses in building systems—work that would fall under the phrase "plastics in building."

Fact. Not process.

When the Society of the Plastics Industry reiterated its position against an "all-plastics" house to an architectural audience in 1975, it indirectly referenced twenty-plus years of applied plastics research, the emergence of a market for plastic building products, and defining plastic's use through two industry-supported endeavors: the National Academy of Sciences' Plastics Study Group and the aptly titled "A Model Chapter on Plastics for Inclusion in a Building Code."

The United States National Academy of Sciences and the National Research Council (NAS-NRC) jointly formed the Building Research Institute (BRI) in 1952 "to promote the advancement of building technology by bringing together those engaged in improving the design and construction of buildings."[6] In 1954 the BRI held a conference titled "Plastics in Building."[7] Based on the conference's success and the recognized potential to apply plastics to a myriad of uses, it convened the Plastics Study Group in 1955. The Plastics Study Group facilitated a national conversation among architects, engineers, the academy, and industry, specifically concerning the use of plastics in building. Conference presenters, especially those in the first five meetings, regardless of vocation, were working out the building systems to which plastics could be applied—roof, structure, interior, utilities, and building envelope—and attempting to agree on the essential engineering parameters to be met in each context. Presenters were likewise working out the performance potential of particular plastic products, such as pipes, tiles, light-fixture lenses, panels, wall coverings, trim, skylights, windows, and bathroom fixtures.

Although the Group's effort of authoring a *Plastics Handbook for Designers*—initiated in 1960—was never realized, the intention was explained: "About two years ago several of us became concerned by the fact that plastics were not being used to their fullest extent in building. Designers were steering clear of plastics, just as they tend to with any new material, but here the language was confusing them and they were being misled by advertising claims.... We felt that just as the *Steel Handbook*, the lumber data books, etc., have become acceptable standards for reporting information on these well-known materials, we could start on a similar project for plastics."[8]

Yet, a handbook of sorts already did exist, though its intended audience was the product manufacturer rather than the designer. "Technical Data on Plastics," published by the Manufacturing Chemists Association as early as 1948 ,described the physical properties of plastics as related to fabrication, mechanical tests, and durability. The Society of the Plastics Industry jointly worked with the Manufacturing Chemists Association in the mid-1950s to propose "Technical Data"—which was regularly updated and expanded—as the numerical foundation for "Model Chapter."[9]

In booklet form, "A Model Chapter on Plastics for Inclusion in a Building Code" was distributed to attendees of the Plastic Study Group meeting in December 1956, where its purpose (ultimately life safety) and adoption process was discussed. "Model Chapter" categorized plastics' maximum allowable use according to the type of construction and building component in question: interior finish and trim, wall panels, roof panels, skylights, light-transmitting panels in monitors and sawtooth roofs, light-diffusing systems in ceilings, partitions, exterior veneer, awnings and canopies, greenhouses, signs, fences, and so on.[10] The booklet

was also intended for code authorities who needed a way to assess such plastic building products as acrylic skylights and vinyl tile specified by architects and showing up on construction sites.

"Model Chapter" coalesced the then twenty-six materials described in "Technical Data" into one category: plastics. "Model Chapter" defined plastics for architects and code authorities per their function and form. Frederick J. Rarig, assistant secretary and attorney for Rohm & Haas Company of Philadelphia, later reflected in the pages of *Progressive Architecture*, "The architects made it clear that they wanted plastic materials dealt with as plastics and indexed as plastics. They did not consider it practical to endeavor to establish in building codes separate provisions for individual classes of plastics that would be identified by esoteric generic terms identifying classes of polymers and copolymers."[11]

Efforts to facilitate a conversation on plastics' use in building and a plastics code followed a trajectory from product experimentation toward product codification, and not translation. The relationships between material, form, and technique became increasingly fixed and normalized. For instance, architectural journals, NAS-NRC publications, and industry conference proceedings solidly demonstrated the degree to which extruding thermally treatable materials became essential to realizing profitable plastic building products, which in turn engendered a die-to-form relationship and fixed the scale at which plastics in architecture are tenable.

These efforts were not charged with working out whole prototypical architectures; they were not wrestling with the relationship between plastic "parts" and plastic "wholes."[12] For instance, those involved in drafting the "Model Chapter" did not foresee an immediate future in which plastics might be considered a structural material.[13] Rather, architecture's scale was broken down into discrete and separate plastic parts, a standardization strategy that was tenable given the numerous plastic materials being developed and the components they could become.

"We have fallen blindly in love with the word 'plastics.'" These are the words of Frederick J. McGarry, associate professor of building, engineering, and construction at the Massachusetts Institute of Technology, at the third meeting of the Plastics Study Group in 1956. His continuation of this statement precisely captures the tenuous relationship between "all-plastics" and "plastics in building":

> We believe that in plastics we can find answers to all our problems. Our major difficulty is scale—the transition between little things and big, structural things. The impetus is there—manufacturers like the building market—architects like the physical properties. But let's be more candid—let's tell architects not to make the units too large, as yet. Let's back off for a while and express plasticity in terms of flat sandwich panels and workable things until we can control additional uses more adequately. The plastics industry just hasn't the experience and equipment for the large units that the architect desires.[14]

All-Plastics-in-Building
The phrases "all-plastics" and "plastics in building" continue to provide a way of thinking about plastics and plasticity's relationship to architecture. Both phrases embody potential, as plastics' relationship to architecture may be said to be simultaneously inert and constantly emerging. That such a paradoxical state is possible can be ascertained with a simple experiment. Pulling twenty-five articles from the pages of popular architectural press spanning nearly eighty years, three phrases are constantly repeated, regardless of the era:

> "Plastics are the future."
> "Plastics are difficult to decipher."
> "Plastics are not substitute materials."[15]
> Inertia.

This 1925 definition of *plastic* may be useful in resolving exactly why this is the case: "The commercial name of any of a class of substances, such as celluloid or viscose, which are worked into shape for use by molding or pressing when in a plastic condition."[16] Plastics, then, were from the outset assumed to be "worked materials." And while I suspect that the notion of "worked" arises from plastic's origins in cellulose, horn, milk, cotton—materials with immediacy, some immediately transformable into homogeneous, fluid, and formable resources—it does allow architects to let down their guard, and recast the definition of *plastics* to include *all* organic materials that might manifest heat- and pressure-induced plasticity.

The working of horn—or the natural polymer keratin—into a snuff box or hair comb, and the working of crude oil into granules of polycarbonate—which in turn, are extruded into a cellular sheet—allows us to observe that the present disequilibrium that exists in sourcing very large organic molecules from one source (oil) and the equipoise that might be gained with biomass, as well as the continued creation of a "smart" polymer class, only typifies plastics and therefore plasticity's condition; it has and always will be constantly emerging and requiring much "working."

Plastics were then and are now the future; they are difficult to decipher and are not just substitute materials. Plastics' constant emergence and ceaseless redefinition, requiring both continued codification and translation, renders its "all-plastics" proposition inert in the context of "building."

Still, there is the potential that plastics' undecided relationship to architecture could be entirely upended, and that the phrases "all-plastics" and "plastics in building" will fall into disuse by repelling the very thing architects are said to have desired. Architects are said to have wanted "plastics dealt with as plastics and indexed as plastics."[17] Since the early 1940s, roughly 135 separate materials, classified as plastics, have been associated with architectural production via the context of the architectural journal.[18] We might proceed to separate, rather than continue to coalesce. We might approach plastics as they really are: thousands of different materials, each one with a range of distinct and diverse properties.

1 | The *Oxford English Dictionary* defines *monomania* first as a mental illness and second as "an exaggerated or fanatical enthusiasm for or devotion to one subject; an obsession, a craze." "monomania, n," *OED* Online, www.oed.com.

2 | Celanese Plastic Corporation, Advertisement for Lumarith Plastics, in *Architectural Forum* (January 1946).

3 | "Synthetic Houses," *Scientific American* 149 (1933): 180. Here reporting of the conference uses the phrase "The house that chemistry built," which was presumably a slogan.

4 | British Plastics Federation, "On Plastics and Building," in *Plastics* (London: His Majesty's Stationery Office, 1944), 6–8.

5 | "Pandora's Plastic Box," *Progressive Architecture* 56 (September 1975): 86.

6 | Proceedings from each conference regularly include BRI's purpose statement. Over several publications, BRI maintains concerns with communication across industries and profession, integration of building technologies, and dissemination of technical information. See Building Research Institute, *Plastics in Building* (Washington, D.C.: National Academy of Sciences–National Research Council, 1955), 149.

7 | Ibid, 137–46. This conference, the first exploring the application of plastics in building, was sponsored by the Society of the Plastics Industry, the Manufacturing Chemists Association, and the Building Research Advisory Board. The names of over 500 attendees can be found on these pages of the proceedings.

8 | William F. Reardon, "Roof Materials and Assemblies," in *Information Requirements for Selection of Plastics for Use in Building* (Washington, D.C.: National Academy of Sciences–National Research Council, 1960), 4.

9 | The 1948 edition of "Technical Data on Plastics" includes twenty-three sections, each one addressing a separate plastic material. The 1952 edition (mine a 1955 reprint) includes twenty-six sections. The difference between 1948 and 1955 is subtle. For instance, by the 1952 edition, the section on cellulose acetate eliminates "rods" and "tubes," and adds separately titled sections "plastic films" and "foamed plastics." The 1952 edition was presumably the basis for the "Model Chapter."

10 | See "A Model Chapter on Plastics for Inclusion in a Building Code," reprinted as Appendix D of "Chapter 3: Building Codes and Regulations" in *Plastics in Building*, ed. Irving Skeist (New York: Reinhold Publishing Corporation, 1966), 34–37.

11 | F. J. Rarig, "Plastics and the Building Codes," in *Progressive Architecture* 51 (1970): 97.

12 | A significant exception is noted at the Plastic Study Group's second meeting. Held in July of 1956 at Massachusetts Institute of Technology, a portion of the meeting program was dedicated to the discussion of the Monsanto House of the Future. Titled "Engineering of the Monsanto House of Tomorrow," it was presented by Albert G. H. Dietz.

13 | See the transcription of an exchange between Mr. Rubenstein and F. J. Rarig where Mr. Rubenstein queries the "acceptance of reinforced fiberglas in the building code." *Plastics in Building*, 102.

14 | Building Research Institute, Report of a meeting at the Illinois Institute of Technology, Chicago, Illinois, December 5–7, 1956: 11.

15 | This observation was made after reviewing two hundred articles published in architectural journals between the years 1934 and 2010.

16 | "Plastics—A Definition," in *Modern Plastics* 1 (1925): 20.

17 | Rarig, "Plastics and the Building Codes," 97.

18 | In more than 200 articles published in architectural journals between 1934 and 2010 approximately 135 plastics are named by their chemical name (e.g., cellulose acetate) or acronym (CA).

Recycling to First Principles: Back to Atoms

William F. Carroll Jr.

The two major types of plastic, based on their processing dynamics, are thermoplastics and thermosets. Thermoplastics soften when heated. Thermosets do not soften when heated but rather their molecular chains become stiffer and more highly structured through the development of crosslinks, which convert single-dimensional chains into two-dimensional nets and potentially three-dimensional structures. Thermosets char when heated but will not melt. Certain foods provide a good analogy. Butter is like a thermoplastic: it can be melted or softened and remolded. Bread, on the other hand, is like a thermoset: it dries, toasts, and eventually chars when heated, but obviously does not melt. Most of the plastic articles we see on a daily basis are thermoplastics. Oil paint, epoxy resin, and fiberglass are thermosets.

There are four classical steps in the recycling process: collection, separation, reprocessing, and resale. The most common recycling process for plastics—and the dominant technology for recycling thermoplastics—is material recycling. In material recycling, the four classical steps translate to collection of mixed recyclables, separation of plastics, further separation by identity and possibly color, shredding or grinding, washing and drying, and finally thermal reprocessing (melting and reforming) into a pelletized raw material that can be used by plastics processors.

To illustrate thermoplastics recycling, consider "recycling" as a large box of used, broken crayons. It would be possible to separate them by color, remove the labels, melt them, and pour the melted material into a crayon mold. Adding a fresh label would make the recycled crayon largely indistinguishable from a new one. Material recycling takes into account the different kinds of plastics commonly in use and their different chemistry and characteristics, with the goal of maximizing their value directly back into products made from those same materials. It is advantageous for a number of reasons. Firstly, it preserves the energy investment and

reduction in entropy associated with the polymerization process. This is because material recycling processes generate usable material with lower energy investment than synthesis of new, virgin material. Secondly, material recycling is minimally capital intensive, as it is a physical process rather than a chemical process. But material recycling of thermoplastics has its limits. The physical properties of thermoplastic molecules are generally related to the length of the molecule, and excessive thermal or shear history can "wear out" a thermoplastic molecule by breaking and shortening it.

The tool kit for material recycling of thermosets is somewhat limited. Because they cannot melt, they cannot be reprocessed as themselves into new articles. They can only be reground to a fine particle size and mixed with virgin materials so that new polymer forms around the reground particles. A useful analogy is recycling concrete from building materials. Concrete is a composite of cement, sand, and a stone aggregate. While not a plastic, concrete is a thermoset in that it cures as it ages and dries. In fact, the curing process goes on long after the visible water is gone, creating more crosslinks over time. When recycled, concrete is pulverized and the resultant material is used as new aggregate with added cement. Because concrete never really stops curing, the pulverized material retains some reactivity and adheres well to the new cement. Similarly, adhesion of thermoset plastic particles to a new matrix is critical to obtaining useful physical properties.

Thus, to overcome these limitations for thermosets or worn-out thermoplastics, a recycler may wish to consider a chemical means for recycling. Schemes for converting plastics to "oil" by some sort of pyrolysis and using that oil to synthesize new petrochemical raw materials are not new. But they do come with difficulties. Generally, these schemes have involved mixed plastics or soiled streams of material. In either case, before processing the "oil" in a finely-tuned industrial device, extensive cleanup processes are needed to remove impurities such as compounds containing halogens, nitrogen, sulfur, and metals. Alternatively, processes have been developed to convert waste of various kinds, including plastics and cellulosics, to a chemical raw material called "synthesis gas," which consists of carbon monoxide and hydrogen.

Synthesis gas is made industrially, via coal, oil, or natural gas. From coal, the most common reaction is the water-gas shift reaction:

$$C + H_2O \rightarrow CO + H_2$$

While apparently simple, this reaction involves a large investment of heat. More common is the creation of synthesis gas from natural gas and water:

$$CH_4 + H_2O \rightarrow CO + 3H_2$$

While still energy intensive, after separation of the gases this reaction is the most common industrial source for hydrogen. Under the right conditions, virtually any material that finds its way into garbage—from cellulosics such as wood and paper to plastics—can, in principle, be converted to synthesis gas. A demonstration project of the German utility Lurgi did just this, generating synthesis gas to feed a methanol production operation.

From there, synthesis gas can become the raw material for a number of chemical streams, the most relevant of which, for plastics, is the Fischer-Tropsch synthesis of hydrocarbons.

$$(2n)H_2 + nCO \rightarrow n(CH_2) + nH_2O \, (Fe, Ru, Co \text{ as catalysts})$$

In this reaction, $n(CH_2)$ represents a hydrocarbon that is purified and then used as a raw material in a process called cracking, which results in ethylene, the most common raw material for plastics. Virgin hydrocarbons used in cracking include ethane, natural gas liquids (derived from natural gas), or naphtha (derived from oil). The energy investment in making hydrocarbons in this way, known as coal-to-liquids (CTL), or gas-to-liquids (GTL), is not trivial. The standard assumption for CTL plants is approximately 50 percent efficiency. This translates to one ton of bituminous coal yielding about two barrels of liquids, with approximately half the heat value of the coal being expended in the process. There is a similar energy investment in GTL plants.

Over the course of the twentieth century, at least two countries have found themselves isolated from normal trade, and poor in petroleum resources but rich in other sources of carbon. As a result, they became proficient at synthesizing petroleum-related products from nonpetroleum sources. In World War II, the German government was obviously not participating in normal trade. Earlier in the century, German scientists had worked out the process for synthesizing hydrocarbons from coal resources via synthesis gas. Developed during the 1920s and commercialized during the 1930s, this synthesis became a production reality during the war, and it provided 10 percent of the fuel for the war effort as well as 25 percent of the motor fuel for the German government. Later in the century, the government of South Africa developed commercial capacity through the company Sasol to produce gasoline by this method, which became particularly important when the country found itself isolated from mainstream trade as the world boycotted its policy of apartheid. Today, Sasol licenses know-how for its "coal-to-chemicals" process in areas of the world such as central China, where petroleum resources are obscure but coal is available.

While the process is quite energy intensive, Sasol sees it as an important commercial opportunity using other raw materials as well. A barrel of oil has a heat value of about 5.8 million BTUs. One thousand cubic feet of natural gas has a heat value of about one million BTUs. Thus, if valued for thermal processes only, the ratio of prices of these two commodities should be about six. At the time of this writing, however, a barrel of oil costs approximately $100 and 1,000 feet of gas costs about $5—a ratio of approximately twenty. As a result, Sasol has purchased an interest in a shale gas concern and announced GTL plants for North America with the plan of using natural gas to produce diesel fuel by their

219

Recycling to First Principles: Back to Atoms
William F. Carroll Jr.

gas-to-liquids process, more economically than it can be produced via the normal route, from petroleum.

Why would one go to all this trouble instead of material recycling? Chemical recycling could be part of an overall resource management program if there was a desire to keep materials out of landfills or incinerators—a variation on the "cradle-to-cradle" concept espoused by the architect William McDonough. It could be used to recover materials landfilled previously, or, as mentioned earlier, to recover difficult-to-recycle materials, such as mixed waste or thermosets.

But recycling carbon in this way also points to a less obvious fact. For all the discussion of "running out of" petrochemical resources such as oil and gas, it should be recognized that carbon is an abundant chemical element in the Earth's environment. Use and reuse of carbon as a raw material, given an abundant nonfossil-based source of energy such as solar, nuclear, or geothermal, is a sustainable strategy for the twenty-first century. Consider that all the strategies involved in fuel cells or the hydrogen economy involve intensive use of very rare metals, such as platinum. There may not be a sufficient abundance of platinum upon which an energy economy can be based. Even the so-called rare earth elements, while significantly more abundant than platinum-like metals, are substantially less abundant than carbon. Nature recycles carbon, and as a result, it is difficult to imagine running out of it. If we can make the energy investment make sense, we should think about it as well.

References

"Advanced Recycling," American Chemistry Council Plastics Division, http://www.americanchemistry.com.

Arpe, H. J., Industrial Organic Chemistry, Fifth Edition (Weinheim, Germany: Wiley-VCH Verlag GmbH & Co., KGaA, 2010).

Dutch, S. I., "Periodic Tables of Elemental Abundance," in Journal of Chemical Education 76, no. 3 (1999): 356–58.

"Fischer-Tropsch Archive," www.fischer-tropsch.org.

Fleischer, M., "The Abundance and Distribution of the Chemical Elements in the Earth's Crust," in Journal of Chemical Education 31, no. 9 (1954): 446–55.

Liebner, W. et al., "Multi-Purpose-Gasification (Mpg) Process Acquired from Svz Schwarze Pumpe" (paper presented at Gasification Technologies Conference, San Francisco, California, October 8–11, 2000).

McDonough, W. et al., Cradle to Cradle: Remaking the Way We Make Things (New York: North Point Press, 2002).

"Natural Gas Units and Conversion Tables," http://www.natgas.info/html/natgasunitsconversion.html.

Sasol, "Unlocking the Potential Wealth of Coal: Introducing Sasol's Unique Coal-to-Liquids Technology," http://www.sasol.com/sasol_internet/downloads/CTL_Brochure_1125921891488.pdf.

"Sasol Announces a Further CAD $1,050 Million / ZAR 7,413 Million Acquisition in Canada—the Company's Second in the Montney Basin," http://www.sasol.com/sasol_internet/frontend/navigation.jsp?articleTypeID=2&articleId=30000002&navid=4&rootid=4.

Schrag, D, "Coal as a Low-Carbon Fuel?" Nature Geoscience 2 (2009): 818–20.

Stranges, A. N., "Germany's Synthetic Fuel Industry 1927–45," (paper presented at American Institute of Chemical Engineers 2003 Spring National Meeting, New Orleans, Louisiana, January 22–24, 2003.

Strong, A. B., Plastics—Materials and Processing, (Upper Saddle River, New Jersey: Prentice-Hall, 1996).

Toman, M. et al., "Unconventional Fossil-Based Fuels: Economic and Environmental Trade-Offs," Rand Technical Report Series (Arlington, Virginia: RAND Corporation, 2008).

Witcoff, H. A. et al., Industrial Organic Chemicals, (New York: Wiley-Interscience, 1996).

fig. 1 | Mercedes-Benz Daimler AG Headquarters, by Renzo Piano, Sindelfingen, Germany, 1997

Plastic Fantastic

Hartmut Sinkwitz

Plastic in its many forms has certainly influenced architecture in important ways, but it has truly captured the imaginations of designers of automobiles, and automobile interiors in particular.

At Mercedes-Benz, all of the designers' ideas must exhibit the highest possible consistency with established brand values. New ideas are understood as expressions of modernity, but within a specific context and value system. The design philosophy combines historical and future values; outside observers should be able to piece the new together with the familiar, like a puzzle. Designers at Mercedes-Benz always aim to bring technical innovations onstage, whether through headlamps or interior displays, for example. | fig. 1

What does plastic mean to designers, engineers, and, last but not least, automobile buyers? Our customers associate Mercedes-Benz with materials that are traditionally understood as "valuable," such as leather, metal, and wood. Not plastic. But the use of plastic in automotive interior design has led to boundless freedom in the creation of free, complex, and organic shapes. Looking at a Mercedes-Benz interior, one can still believe that only traditional materials were used. | figs. 2 and 3

Customers know that leather seats are more costly than synthetic ones, so we love to indulge them in the illusion that they are sitting in a vehicle furnished completely in leather, even when they are not. We enjoy discussing high-quality processed plastics that perfectly imitate the feel of natural materials. Leatherlike radii, a haptically pleasant softness, and an avoidance of the noises of plastic create a holistic sense of well-being that a customer expects from a premium vehicle. During the implementation of a new series, a dozen designers on our team will work to coordinate and harmonize the many plastic parts in terms of color, touch, and degree of gloss in relation to their adjacent components. The use of the most precisely suitable plastics for each part creates enormous complexity, especially considering the company's numerous production sites worldwide. The detail-oriented designers may spend years in development to ensure that an interior composed of about fifty different materials will be experienced as a unified composition. | fig. 4

Plastic is also used in aspects of the vehicle design that are not necessarily visible, for instance on the bottom of the chassis. Recyclates are employed where the customer does not come directly into contact with plastics, yet they contribute to his or her protection and safety. As a newly established brand, Smart Car introduced a paradigm shift to automobile manufacturing through the specific use of visible plastics. The colored body panels of the car's outer form are made of plastic, and the visible parts of the passenger compartment are made of steel; the latter takes on the function of visually indicating the safety of the automobile. In terms of strength and durability, including the ability to withstand impact, the body panel plastics are vastly superior to metal and were specifically created for the first car in the world that was designed not only for driving, but especially parking. This radical concept was an invention of the Mercedes-Benz design team. By treating plastics as an expression of modernity without the ballast of traditional expectations, they turned the material into a symbol for innovation, not only in the concept of the automobile but for an entire brand. Plastics have surpassed steel as an indispensable part of the smart identity. | figs. 5 and 6

New light-emitting diode (LED) headlights and ambient light concepts for the interior are beautifully functional, and they also serve as symbolic expressions of technical competence and an innovative use of brand power. The more distinctive and aesthetically pleasing the light elements become, the more the materials used to make them will come to embody the peak of creative art. | figs. 7 and 8

The German word for plastic, *Kunststoff,* translates as "art material," which couldn't be more apt, at least in automotive design. While plastics in architecture are often associated

fig. 2 | First foamed dashboard in the R107 Model, 1980

fig. 3 | C-Class model dashboard, 2011

fig. 4 | Diagram of material complexity in the C-Class model

fig. 5 | Recycled plastics used in the A-Class model

fig. 6 | Plastics used in the Smart Car model

with the creative utopias of the postwar period, their importance in automobile manufacturing is constantly increasing. They accommodate not only an ever-expanding range of customer needs and desires, but also the dreams of the automobile designers. In the future we will surely see plastics making possible the invention of bionic structures covered with translucent fabrics. With today's options for light design, this transformable material will continue to evolve its own enviable identity. What remains as the fascinating momentum for the customer is the light itself in its aesthetic form, rather than the plastic as an independent material.

fig. 7 | Headlight showing precision of materials in Smart Car model

fig. 8 | Visible lightweight constructions for high-performance materials

fig. 1 | Unilever Headquarters, by Behnisch Architekten, Hamburg, Germany, 2009

Improving the Sustainability of High-Performance Plastics in Architecture

Erik Olsen

Plastics are ubiquitous, but usually invisible, in modern buildings. As a climate engineer I am not expected to have expert knowledge in plastics, nor can I claim such. Examination of our work, however, reveals the importance of plastics—at all scales—in implementing our ideas and achieving our performance goals.

Plastics often enable achievement of performance that otherwise would be unobtainable. Performance has many possible measures: structural, acoustical, electrical, thermal, optical, et cetera. (For my purposes here, thermal and optical properties will be used as surrogates for any of the properties of interest in a building material.) The engineered, chemical origin of plastics, which provides many of their performance benefits, also often leads to great difficulty in their recycling. This environmental critique provides the context for my non-expert examination of plastics, which poses three questions relating to the use of plastics in architecture:

1. Is there a recyclability advantage to using plastics on a large scale in architecture?
2. Are design for performance optimization of plastics and design for subsequent separation of plastics conflicting goals?
3. Can we improve the environmental performance of plastics by extending their life cycle?

Each of these questions presents a rich area for study by industry, academia, and practitioners.

Is there a recyclability advantage to using plastics on a large scale in architecture?

Plastics in modern buildings are mostly invisible because they are used for hidden, utilitarian functions such as insulation on electrical wires, thermal insulation, window frames, curtain wall thermal breaks, piping, and roof membranes. Although many of these plastics are actually recyclable if properly collected and separated, their highly heterogeneous application often makes this nearly impossible. This problem is analogous to the difficulty in postconsumer plastic recycling, in which value is often lost because plastics are not sufficiently separated by type.

There are, however, examples of large-scale use of fairly homogeneous materials. Extruded polystyrene (XPS) insulation is a utilitarian candidate, but there are other, more visible ones as well. An example with growing popularity is ethylene tetrafluoroethylene (ETFE). A single layer of ETFE forms the exterior skin of the double facade on the Unilever Headquarters in Hamburg. | fig. 1 The performance demands on the exterior skin are quite low, as its main purpose is to provide an acoustic buffer from the adjacent harbor, allowing occupants to use natural ventilation without disturbance from harbor traffic. Because ETFE has 1 percent the weight of glass, the structural demand for supporting this second skin is also greatly lowered, further reducing the building's overall use of materials.

The lack of high-tech performance requirements allows the application of pure, unmodified ETFE material. Whether ETFE, XPS, or something else, the use of homogeneous plastics on a whole-building scale presents an interesting opportunity for recycling. At the end of the building or material's life, a recycler can potentially collect a large amount of material at a single building site. With the challenge of geographically distributed, heterogeneous use eliminated, is there a greater incentive for recycling? Currently a major barrier to recycling these materials is a lack of recycling infrastructure, which generally doesn't exist because the low cost of the materials prevents recycling from being cost-effective. Would careful design, enabling easy collection of large quantities of a recyclable material, change this equation? This potential leads to a second question.

Are design for performance optimization of plastics and design for subsequent separation of plastics conflicting goals?

Homogenous application of ETFE or XPS is an exceptional situation. More frequently, plastics are coated, used as coatings, processed, laminated, or otherwise used in composite materials in order to achieve a certain performance. Suvarnabhumi Airport in Bangkok, for instance, includes a triple-layer membrane roof spanning across the primary concourse spaces. | figs. 2–6 The outer layer is PTFE-coated (polytetrafluoroethylene) glass-fiber fabric. Its high solar reflectance reduces solar heat gains transmitted to the space below while still allowing a controlled amount of daylight through. The transparent polycarbonate middle layer provides acoustic protection from the high outdoor noise levels. The interior layer of low-e coated glass fiber changes the indoor thermal sensation by reflecting back the cool temperature of the radiant floor below, further controls daylight transmission, and provides interior acoustic absorption through the open weave.

At Suvarnabhumi Airport, the material is still fairly homogenous in plan. But the ETFE roof of the Dolce Vita shopping center in Lisbon, where plastic properties are also varied in plan, has a greater degree of discontinuity in the material. | figs. 7–9 Here the individual roof cushions are treated in order to achieve performance similar to a north-facing roof monitor. White ETFE with a reflective coating is used on the south-facing part of the pillow, providing near opacity to block the direct sunlight, while transparent ETFE with a solar-control coating is used on the north-facing part of the pillow to admit diffused daylight. As with Suvarnabhumi Airport, a low-e coating is applied to the underside to reflect the cool temperatures of a radiant floor.

The introduction of nonhomogeneity to enhance performance doesn't only occur on the large scale of these examples. The best-insulating spacers used for the edges of insulating glass units are a composite of stainless steel and polypropylene; high-performance, thermally insulated

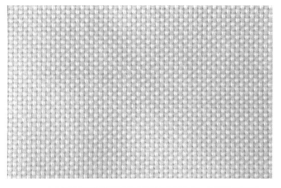

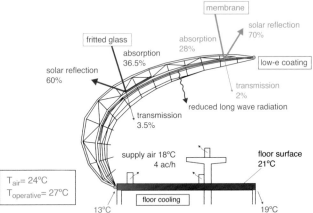

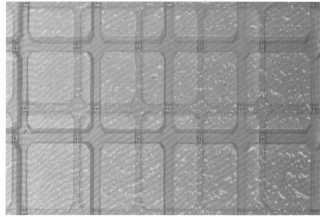

fig. 2 | Concourse, Suvarnabhumi Airport, by Murphy/
Jahn, Bangkok, 2008

fig. 3 | Climate diagram, Suvarnabhumi Airport, 2008

fig. 4 | Outer layer, Suvarnabhumi Airport, 2008

fig. 5 | Middle layer, Suvarnabhumi Airport, 2008

fig. 6 | Inner layer, Suvarnabhumi Airport, 2008

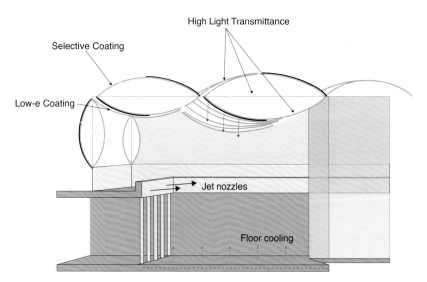

Selective Coating

Low-e Coating

High Light Transmittance

Jet nozzles

Floor cooling

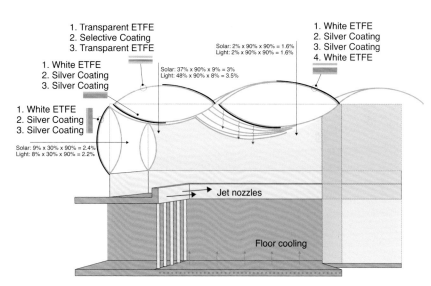

1. Transparent ETFE
2. Selective Coating
3. Transparent ETFE

1. White ETFE
2. Silver Coating
3. Silver Coating

1. White ETFE
2. Silver Coating
3. Silver Coating

1. White ETFE
2. Silver Coating
3. Silver Coating
4. White ETFE

Solar: 2% x 90% x 90% = 1.6%
Light: 2% x 90% x 90% = 1.6%

Solar: 37% x 90% x 9% = 3%
Light: 48% x 90% x 8% = 3.5%

Solar: 9% x 30% x 90% = 2.4%
Light: 8% x 30% x 90% = 2.2%

Jet nozzles

Floor cooling

fig. 7 | ETFE cushion roof, Dolce Vita shopping center, by RTKL, Lisbon, Portugal, 2010

fig. 8 | Daylight and solar control strategy diagram, Dolce Vita shopping center, 2010

fig. 9 | Roof composition diagram, Dolce Vita shopping center, 2010

fig. 10 | Deconstructed Herman Miller chair

fig. 11 | Building deconstruction

curtain walls are composites of aluminum and several types of plastic; and slab-integrated radiant heating and cooling results in a nearly inseparable composite of PEX (cross-linked polyethylene) tubing and concrete. Although these are applications for enhancement of thermal performance, similar examples may be named in nearly all aspects of building construction and performance, such as biaxial hollow concrete slabs, which are essentially composites of plastic balls, steel reinforcement, and concrete.

Unfortunately, all of these examples generally result in materials that cannot easily be separated into their constituent components. The building industry lags behind others, which have already begun careful design for later disassembly, as in the often-cited example of task chairs that break down into homogeneous components. At a typical building deconstruction site, extreme effort is required to separate out even the most rudimentary construction materials. | figs. 10 and 11

Is it possible to create high-performance materials using unmodified plastics that can still be easily separated for recycling or reuse? What are the benefits of such an approach? One possible benefit is increased ease of assembly. Warmboard is a radiant flooring product, primarily for residential use, consisting of aluminum sheeting bonded to a plywood substrate with prerouted channels to accept radiant tubing. Although designed for fast and easy assembly, this approach also makes future recovery and recycling of the radiant tubing feasible. | fig. 12 But examples of such synergies remain unusual. How else can the entire life cycle of architectural plastics be addressed?

Can we improve the environmental performance of plastics by extending their life cycle?

If plastics must be modified or used in composites, the clear alternative to recycling is simply extending their life cycles. Changing the expectations for the life of a material can have a dramatic effect on its environmental impact. A typical residential building in New York, for example, could choose from many different types of insulation, all with different thicknesses and different estimated global warming potential over their entire life cycles. | fig. 13 The global warming potential considers both the emissions resulting from space heating and the embodied global warming potential of the insulation.

Foam plastic insulation such as XPS is manufactured with a blowing agent in order to create the foam. Some blowing agents, such as HFC-134a, have very high global warming potential, which means there is a point at which using additional insulation increases the global warming potential due to the embodied emissions of the insulation, even though the heating demand is reduced. Substituting a lower-emissions blowing agent such as CO_2 is the best solution, but the impact can also be reduced if the insulation is simply used for a longer period of time; extending the life from fifty to 150 years shifts the preferred insulation level from just over R-20 to over R-35 when using HFC-134a. When environmentally preferable alternatives with similar performance (such as cellulose insulation) are not available, extending the product life cycle is indeed the best solution to minimizing the life-cycle impact of a plastic.

This leads to a final question: Is it better to produce the highest-possible performance materials, perhaps with limited recyclability, and use them in high-quality buildings that will stay in use for hundreds of years? Or is it better to accept reduced performance if it allows for easy reuse of materials? Regardless of the answer—or the ideal solution, in which both architectural performance and recyclability are achieved simultaneously—plastics have already achieved ubiquity in buildings. Yet, as with nearly all materials, many questions must still be addressed in order to achieve their most sustainable application.

The solutions require close collaboration, as exhibited in the above case studies, between design professionals, manufacturers, and installers, perhaps more frequently and intensely than in current practice. The growth of life cycle assessment as a technical discipline will allow its gradual integration into this process, in the same way that expert-led

climate-responsive design has gradually become a part of many design processes. We see the first steps on this path in our own practice today—when challenging materials and methods we may perform a simple life cycle assessment, or turn to experts in special circumstances. Although integrated materials may or may not be desirable, the increasingly integrated design process is fundamental to finding the solutions.

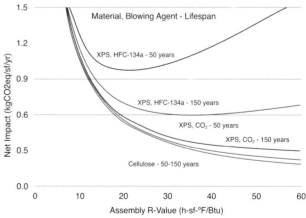

fig. 12 | Prerouted aluminum/plywood radiant floor substrate

fig. 13 | Diagram of life-cycle global warming potential of various insulation types

Cultural Effects

Plastic Music

Brian Kane

Music and plastic met and collided well before the 1960s. Long before Andy Warhol's *Exploding Plastic Inevitable,* the conceptual supergroup Plastic Ono Band, or Jefferson Airplane's "Plastic Fantastic Lover," music's material was plastic.

Philosophers and theorists of music are often fond of using the phrase "musical material" to describe the notes, tones, chords, and formal schemata from which composers build their compositions. But the phrase always sounds an oxymoronic note, for what could be less material than the evanescent vibrations that constitute music's stuff? Is it true that musical material, like plastic, has its own limits of malleability, and temporary and permanent deformation, beyond which the material cannot accommodate without breaking? Sounds, especially when coupled with digital signal processing, can be molded, morphed, and manipulated in infinite ways. They can be stretched, compressed, granulated, and filtered. Furthermore, musical material is inexpensive in the sense that an endless supply is found in the composer's imagination and the surrounding urban and natural soundscape. Moreover, since musical material cannot be defined without considering the coconstitutive role of the auditor, habits of listening—whose very plasticity is at question in many forms of experimental and new music—cannot be neglected.

The plasticity of musical material has been part of an aesthetic of music that has argued for its transcendence. The infinite malleability of music renders it a medium that meets minimal conditions of materiality. According to Hegel, sound vanishes as soon as it appears and is the proper medium to present the infinite interiority of unexteriorized spirit. Both spirit and sound have minimal formal properties. They adapt and conform to any instance, lacking the resistance and persistence of stone, wood, or pigment. Music's essential plasticity puts its materiality under erasure.

Sometimes musical transcendence encounters other forms of "plastic" that are much more literal than the encounter

of the musical mind with sound's evanescent plasticity. Music encountered plastic quite directly, for instance, at the famous Jazz at Massey Hall concert in 1953, where Charlie Parker played on his iconic white plastic mouthpiece, a Brilhart Streamline, and also on a Grafton plastic saxophone.[1] | figs. 1 and 2 Whether the sound of the plastic saxophone is noticeably different from that of the metal saxophone is hotly debated; it may have *felt* different to Parker, but many listeners cannot *hear* any difference. Yet in the lore that surrounds this performance, the ostensible cheapness of Parker's plastic sax is always noted in the cliched, mindlessly uttered praise, "Bird could have played a piece of junk and it would sound good." The logic of such statements is always recuperative; the degree of musical transcendence is contrasted with the poverty of the materials. Cheap plastic is redeemed into great music. The genius overcomes the resistance of the materials by impressing them, and thus transforming them, with *spirit*.

That same plastic saxophone, the Grafton, was used at the end of the decade by Ornette Coleman, and in his hands it became a signifier of his avant-garde status. As one of the inventors of free jazz, Coleman came to electrify the New York jazz scene from Fort Worth by way of Los Angeles. His compositions and solos prolonged Parker's musical logic, albeit in an idiosyncratic and singular manner. More importantly, his sound was different. That strange sound, which was inextricably associated with his plastic saxophone, became iconic, signifying his difference from the rest (although he soon replaced it with a white-plated metal Selmer horn). The image of Coleman holding his white alto on the cover of *The Shape of Jazz to Come* seemed to interject the very liminal, cheap plastic materiality of his instrument into his music. | figs. 3 and 4

The relationship between music and plastic is most significant in music's commoditization. The vinyl record was the main medium for the distribution of music throughout the twentieth century. While the production of music depended on metal disc cutters and lathes, copper masters, and magnetic tape, the malleability and durability of vinyl allowed for

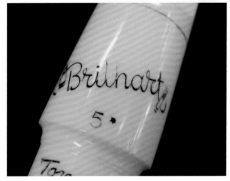

fig. 1 | Charlie Parker playing a white Brilhart mouthpiece

fig. 2 | Brilhart white plastic mouthpiece

music's mass distribution. For decades, the American living room (and, more importantly, the American teenager's bedroom) held a veritable stockpile of fetishized vinyl, housed in cardboard sleeves and covered with images. The plastic discs required a disciplined ritual of maintenance and care, of wiping down and brushing off. The material inscriptions on the vinyl records effectively became codes for the formation of identity, the construction of class and generational divides, and the accessing and sharing of cultural knowledge.

Perhaps music's use of plastic has subsumed a potential expressive program to the pragmatics of replacing systems already in place. In architecture, plastic has over the decades silently replaced other materials in the manufacture of paint, coating, plumbing, siding, and windows. With records, it is likewise true that vinyl replaced other materials, such as shellac, largely because it was lighter and cheaper and would not shatter in shipping. But thinking of vinyl in this way promotes a kind of musical phantasmagoria, in which the recording becomes simply the container of the musical inscription and is somehow separate from the work's essence; in this mindset it is just the music's pragmatic form, necessary for the reproduction of the work but inessential to the work itself.

But vinyl does more than grant durability to the musical commodity; it changes its very sound. Vinyl records have a lower surface noise level than shellac records, and thus their material properties help to hide the noises, pops, and clicks that act as sonic signifiers of the recording's materiality. In other words, they contribute to an ideology in which noise is the enemy, and the most desired recording is the one that reveals its medium the least.

Also interesting is the fact that the opaque, obsidian color of most vinyl records comes from mixing carbon black into transparent PVC, which increases the disc's strength and makes it less resistant to scratches. Yet the carbon black itself has magnetic properties that attract dust to the disc's surface. The perpetual ritual of running a brush over a vinyl disc before playing it, the care that goes into maintaining the silence that preserves the work's ostensible autonomy, is a material effect of the use of carbon black. Transparent colored discs have not been all that uncommon over the decades, but their garish reds, blues, and oranges often signified that they contained music that understood itself a commodity, aiming for quick consumption with little aspiration to becoming part of music's imaginary canon. The sound quality of these records is likewise less fetishized.

The quality of the vinyl makes a difference in the sound of the music. The thin-sounding audio of many recordings from the 1970s is due not to the processes of studio recording used at that time, but to the widespread industry habit of pressing new records on recycled ("reground") vinyl, or to novelties such as RCA's (temporary) switch to Dynaflex, a thin and flexible type of vinyl record that was touted as more user-friendly but probably was inspired by a corporate desire to save money on materials. Today these experiments are much despised by audiophiles, who prefer recordings on heavy-duty 200-gram virgin vinyl.

Is the plasticity of musical material halted when fixed into a recording? Solid as a commodity, the recording circulates seemingly unaffected by its consumption. Yet, the true metaphysician of music's plasticity, the collector who refuses to play his or her records, knows this is not the case: each time the needle draws its spiraled path from perimeter to center, the inscription changes ever so slightly. The collector's fetishism is rationalized by a simple economic formula: exchange value equals sound quality. But that is not the reason. There is no difference for this gramophonic Platonist between the act of reproduction and reinscription. To play is to rewrite; to rewrite is to defile. No manifestation lives up to the original impression, and the impression must be protected from the tone arm's mechanical scribbling. Unlike Parker's cheap plastic saxophone that lets spirit speak because of its shoddiness, the spirit written into the unplayed, spiral groove is fragile as flesh. Scratched into a material world, the soft groove of spirit made sound is always ravaged by the diamond-hard tip of the needle.

1 | The Grafton was an ivory-colored plastic saxophone that began manufacture in 1950.

fig. 3 | Ornette Coleman and Don Cherry, Newport Jazz Festival

fig. 4 | Record cover for Ornette Coleman's *The Shape of Jazz to Come*

This real-life Recycling robot, collects trash and measures atmospheric pollutants.

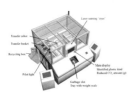

fig. 1 | The Great Pacific Garbage Patch

fig. 2 | PennDesign's Recycling Robot

Plasticity

Winka Dubbeldam

The Great Pacific Garbage Patch, which has one of the highest known levels of plastic particulate suspended in the upper water column, is one of several oceanic regions where researchers have studied the effects and impact of plastic photodegradation in the neustonic layer of water, and how it impacts the environment and ocean life. | fig. 1 The Great Pacific Garbage Patch has existed since about 1950, weighs around 3.5 million tons, and 80 percent of it is plastic.

The University of Pennsylvania School of Design has been developing robotic systems to search for and collect the plastic particulate in the ocean. Along existing ship routes, the robotic systems collected materials become free construction material, recycled into building panels that are watertight and indestructible. | fig. 2 Though experimental and small in scale and effect, this work is seen in light of a half century of economic and urban change in the United States, where consumer products and an economy based in consumption fueled the tremendous rise in plastics as both household item and eventual waste product. Even slightly reversing these equations requires an examination of not just the plastic waste itself but the decades-long production of infrastructure and economic investment in American urbanization. The production of a consumer landscape was altered and enabled by changes in gender roles, labor and household income structures, and ultimately an emergent urban/suburban model where consumption and production were separated geographically. The recycling of materials, and the creation of new biodegradable materials, helps to reduce the need for new production of what would eventually become more waste.

The past fifteen years of design practice have often relied on spatial models; plastic figures whose shape and surfaces have been sought in part for the promise of their continuity. In the 1912 "Technical Manifesto of Futurist Sculpture," Umberto Boccioni provides what still seems to be a refreshing promise: "new forms which connect [a sculpture] invisibly and mathematically to the visible plastic infinite and to the interior plastic infinite." Boccioni was not concerned with waste or plastics but his formulations instigated in design work a search for linking diverse forms, temporally distinct by way of a higher dimensional mathematics. The new mathematics produced, but more so enabled, a new continuity of sculpture in time and in space. In seeking to link the plastic particulate suspended in the oceans back to a mode of production for future architecture and urbanization, we have been inspired by Boccioni and by architectural experiments based on his work. In the Greenwich Building, we introduced a habitable folded-curtain wall as a three-dimensional glass building formation, which optimizes the traditional experience of facade or building envelope. | figs. 3 and 4 Thus an architectural and sculptural model of space becomes an environmental model for production and for social change.

fig. 3 | View within the inhabitable curtain wall, Greenwich Building, by Archi-Tectonics, New York, 2004

fig. 4 | View of curtain wall from street, Greenwich Building, 2004

fig. 1 | Solar Cooker online advertisement, from the research project "The Other Plastic Soup: Recycling in Haiti," by Engineers Without Borders at the University of Minnesota, 2010–2011

Plastic Soup

Lydia Kallipoliti

Lost, the unprecedentedly popular TV series that ran from 2004 through 2010, transported its audience to an uncanny island that was unmappable in geographic space or linear time, and perpetually in flux in terms of its location. A key question tormented viewers: where the line might be drawn between reality and science fiction. Could an island really exist outside of our "perception" in the conventional sense?

What scientists today call the "plastic soup" is not so unlike the island in *Lost*. Famously known as the Great Pacific Garbage Patch or the Pacific Trash Vortex, the plastic soup is a moving island of pelagic plastics, chemical sludge, and other debris that has coagulated and is trapped by the currents of the Pacific Ocean. This physical accretion, located in the center of the North Pacific Ocean, originally formed in the mid-1990s and is now about twice the size of Texas.[1] The phenomenon of the plastic soup was partially caused by the chemical properties of polymers, particularly thermoplastic polymers, which when heated, soften and fuse into new formations. It also relates to the photodegradation of some plastics, which when exposed to the sun disintegrate into smaller pieces while remaining polymers at the molecular level.

In 2010 the group Engineers Without Borders at the University of Minnesota researched the possibilities of using solar cookers to melt piles of plastic waste and remold them into new products. Referencing the Great Pacific Garbage Patch, they termed their research the "plastic soup." After the devastating earthquake that year in Port-au-Prince, Haiti, plastic waste became ubiquitous. The smell of burning plastic was everywhere, and the city was covered almost entirely in plastics, like confetti, not to mention other forms of debris.[2] Engineers Without Borders intervened by collecting plastic waste aggregates and converting them into new useful products like shoes. Remolding this waste was envisioned as a possible strategy of *détournement*—in other words, an opportunity to take tactical advantage of the fundamentally adhesive properties of plastics at the molecular level in order to harvest new life. | fig. 1

The plastic soup opens our eyes to a phantom condition: namely, an entire island that satellites cannot see.[3] Nor do any of us *wish* to see it. The plastic soup is an unintentional island that grew out of the metropolis; it is an invisible by-product of technological progress in the urban sphere, growing without control and beyond our sight. The plastics that comprise it contaminate our water and the air we breathe.

As a vision of horror and the object of fascination, the plastic soup serves here as an entry point for a discussion of plastics since the late nineteenth century. This discussion began when the German architect Gottfried Semper spoke of rubber as a material so potentially useful to the industrialized world that contemplating its possibilities left him speechless with excitement.[4]

Throughout history, mystery has always surrounded the metamorphic properties of some materials. Material transitions evoke infinity, through the perpetual transformation of matter. The Roman poet Publius Ovidius Naso, known to the English-speaking world as Ovid, began his epic on *metamorphoses* (fifteen books using Greek and Roman myths) by claiming: "Of bodies changed to other forms I tell."[5] And as much as he was interested in the mythological transformation of creatures into new bodies and forms, he was also using the same techniques in his writing, by transforming one myth verbally into the other. For many artists "infinity was rooted in the alchemical, elemental, and metamorphic power of materials and their mercurial effect on another, whether they are chemicals reacting to moisture or substances or phenomena-including, for example, sound transformed through an encounter with another."[6] In this viewpoint, matter does not come to an end, it is not wasted; instead it changes state.

Technically speaking, thermoplastic polymers, which are linear polymers rather than network polymers, can be formed and reformed, yet all variations originate from the same substance. This is due to their chemical composition at the micro level, since in a linear structure, individual molecules have no permanent chemical links. Rather, they are held in place by weak secondary bonds that can be temporarily broken and rearranged into new positions. Such materials reach a malleable *mesophase* until a shape is given. In this process, matter never ceases to exist, but only changes states. The plastic soup exists in the physical state of a semi-liquid; beyond simply being a collection of plastic materials, the soup actually *represents* the idea of its own transformation.

At the same time, the plastic soup is a disturbing vision; it is an environmental hazard that kills ocean life and migrating species of birds that mistake the island for a natural source of food. It is also an incidental accretion of plastic matter, defying any precise definition of form and representation. It is neither possible to map or draw the soup in its current state, nor to predict and map its evolution. There is no control over its formation.

In the discipline of architecture, this realm of impossibility, the moment when representation fails to be descriptive of the form of objects, is both magical and terrifying. An analysis of the plastic soup can serve as the entry to a particular history, a "stocktaking" (to paraphrase the architectural critic Reyner Banham) of five material experiments with plastic matter in the postwar period.[7] The projects failed, according to their architects, because they never quite formed as expected or forecast; they were experiments of direct action challenging the limits of representation. None of the projects were drawn. Instead they were all shot with a spray gun, which deployed plastic polyurethane foam onto some kind of scaffold, in most cases chicken wire.

1972: Charles Harker, founder of Tao Design Group in Austin, juxtaposed Le Corbusier's "Machine for Living" of the early twentieth century with a new concept for habitation that he titled the "Soft Machine." Tao, an experimental group of architects, sculptors, and artists associated with the University of Texas at Austin, explored the application of new plastic materials in architecture and published their molded shelters as environmental paradigms for a "soft future" in *Architectural Design* and the *Domebooks*.[8] | figs. 2 and 3

figs. 2 and 3 | Earth House, by Tao Design Group, Hill Country, Texas, 1972

figs. 4 and 5 | Foam House, by Felix Drury, Langdale, Alabama, 1971

We are in the midst of a Socio-Psychological, Cybernetic, Mass-media and Space Age revolution. The architect must respond to these influences and must discover the path to a "soft machine." We should create a softer, more fluid and exciting physical environment, understanding form as the articulation of a set of interacting forces.[9]

In his manifesto for the "Soft Machine," Harker outlined an alternative definition of matter as patterns of energy that eventually solidify. He spoke of matter that could be remodeled in numerous ways and materials that could be composed morphogenetically, via the transformation of substance, rather than morphologically, via the transformation of form. For Tao Design Group, it was key to dispense with firm tectonic divisions such as structure, envelope, and roof in order to envision an environmentally friendly, "soft" future. They employed the term *soft* both literally, meaning the use of plastic materials, and conceptually, meaning the projection of an elastic understanding of tectonic conventions.

1970: The architect Felix Drury designed a corporate guesthouse for the West Point-Pepperell headquarters at Langdale, Alabama. | fig. 4 The house was literally shot out of a spray gun, and according to Drury it represented just the beginning of many exciting new applications for foamed plastics—urethane foam, to be precise—as structural material in housing. The forms were inflated after being stapled to the formwork of concrete floor slabs. They were then sprayed from the outside with urethane foam of about three pounds per cubic feet in density. Nevertheless, environmental conditions like ambient air temperature and wind velocity are decisive parameters that affect both the density and the adhesion of foam. An ideal temperature is 70 degrees Fahrenheit, while adverse circumstances, like cold weather, slow down chemical reactions and compromise the application and the desired formation of continuous surfaces. Such was the case for Drury's foam house. | fig. 5

After the prototype house was completed, Drury evaluated the result as "entirely unsatisfactory."[10] It seems that certain chemical reactions that took place during the spray-foaming created layers of polypropylene fiber, leaving an irregular interior surface with open pores and niches. Even though Drury was frustrated with the result, he mentioned in subsequent interviews that "this technology is only a crude start. It is not the magical material, but it can do things no other material can do, such as to freely work with curved surfaces. As drastic changes occur in man's use and sense of time, scale and place, foam allows the architect to experiment with conditions which might accommodate these changes."[11]

1967: The German architect Rudolf Doernach was one of the chief early pioneers of plastics in architecture, according to Arthur Quarmby in his 1974 book *Plastics and Architecture*.[12] He was regularly featured in the pages of *Architectural Design*'s "Cosmorama" section between 1966 and 1969, publicizing a peculiar socio-spiritual material discourse that strategically positioned organic and plastic matter as the primary foundation upon which, and by which, a city could grow.[13] In one such project titled Biotecture, "contractible and reusable organic matter" would become a universal building material, invented and programmed by environmental scientists, or, as he called them, "comprehensive architects."[14] | fig. 6 Doernach envisioned animated matter as a tool for social reform, and he was obsessively searching for ways to extend matter spiritually, beyond its physical limitations. | fig. 7

1965: The artist Gunnar Aagaard Andersen coagulated layers of plastic foam in the manner of a Surrealist automatic drawing to create the *Armchair, a portrait of my mother's Chesterfield Chair*. He used polyurethane, a material developed in World War II, which is "thermosetting," meaning that it effervesces to a fluid state and spreads as a floating mass.[15] Thus, the armchair was a product of chemical reactions that took place without the formal control of the artist. As a brownish-colored, viscous-looking pile, the armchair has often been described as repulsive and disturbing. In "Cosmorama," for instance, it was featured with the caption "Blobs of Gulp."[16] Andersen was intentionally experimenting

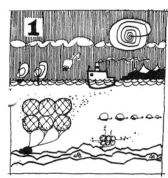

Take net and cables to hold pneumatic bubbles below surface of sea. Maritime micro-organisms colonize everything: Bubble system and captain Smoky's boat.

A tourist arrives to conquer this selfgrowing submarine shell—he perforates some of the Plastic bubbles as he has learned, when he left his mother or when he deflorates. Soon he has bigger inner spaces in INNER SPACE: living-room, bedroom and the whole works.

Provolution
R + D (or Rudolph Doernach)

Interdisciplinary micro-macro-game

How to grow a maritime city?
How to grow a fur for society?
How to grow Biocity edible city?
How to regain PARADISE?

While captain Smoky's boat slows down and loses speed because of algae crust, the bubble matrix grows a live space frame of optimal loadbearing capacity—huge macro bone. Oysters and shells climb to this submarine Bio and nibble from it, not knowing yet that or they get nibbled themselves.

The bubble - over - perforator - deflator - deflorator loosens some of these cables to let his house mate with the sun in summer, when the sea keeps quiet. He also re-uses some bubbles to grow more space for bubbling companions. Among them his friend Delphine, who hauls in breakfast every morning and some fabulous sea lettuce too.

Edible City keeps growing because one tourist found out how to use fluid plastics and fibrous plastics to reinforce Edible City's liv space frame. Another started to fool around with a perforated hose simply because he likes to play with all round-long things; this wa he discovered how to feed the big sea bubbles with all kinds goodies from EDY Chemical Co. At the same time he used th invisible plastic hose to cool his HAPPYTAINER. One day a bott of whisky caught fire; the cooling system acted as a fire patro One day Rudolf—called R + D—brought a little atomic breede for Edible City. You should have seen all these animals going-nut growing-huts in the warm sea.

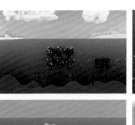
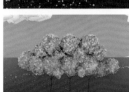

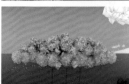

fig. 6 | Provolution, by Rudolph Doernach, *Architectural Design*, "Cosmorama," February 1966

fig. 7 | Creative documentation of Rudolph Doernach's Provolution, redesigned by Saeed Arida and Lydia Kallipoliti

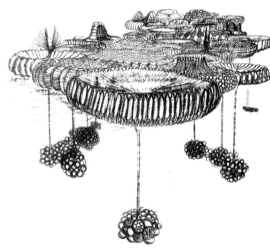

fig. 8 | *Armchair (Portrait of my mother's Chesterfield Chair)*, painted polyurethane foam, by Gunnar Aagaard Andersen, 1964–65

fig. 9 | Gunnar Aagaard Andersen creating an armchair at Dansk Polyether Industry, 1964–65

fig. 10 | *Chemical Architecture*, by William Katavolos, Visionary Architecture exhibition, the Museum of Modern Art, New York, 1960

with the idea that industrially produced objects must be mechanical assemblies of parts. | figs. 8 and 9

1960: William Katavolos's "Chemical Architecture" is canonized as the "Organics Manifesto" in Ulrich Conrad's collection of twentieth-century modern manifestos, and is featured in the Museum of Modern Art's exhibition Visionary Architecture. In the curatorial statement, Arthur Drexler wrote that the featured projects were all unbuilt, either because they were technically unfeasible at the time they were designed, or because society could find neither the justification nor the money for their construction.[17] In his project description, Katavolos envisioned cities as being designed via the microscopic manipulation of materials, and he imagined a city that would grow "softly" rather than being designed as an end product. His manifesto predicted the evolution of "deterministic design" into something more democratic and sustainable. | fig. 10 He wrote:

> A new architecture is possible through the matrix of chemistry. Man must stop making and manipulating, and instead allow architecture to happen....We are rapidly gaining the necessary knowledge of the molecular structure of chemicals, which will have a specific program of behavior built into them in a sub-microscopic stage. Accordingly, it will be possible to take minute quantities of powder and make them expand into predetermined shapes, such as spheres, tubes, and toruses. Visualize the new city grow moulded on the sea, of great circles in which plastics pour to form a network of strips and discs that expand into spheres, and further perforate for many purposes.[18]

Across these five episodes, we witness a persistent preoccupation with matter undergoing evolutionary transformations, as well as with the aggregative molecular qualities of plastics as models for social reform. For many architects, plastic objects and environments mediated, in many respects, a reconciliation between natural and artificial production methods. First, techniques of shaping plastics allude to organic processes, such as metabolism and growth, and therefore direct nature to the chemical laboratory: the transference of value systems from undisturbed natural ecosystems to artificially controlled synthetic environments. Second, molding, spraying, and engineering plastics constitutes an open construction process, one that allows the object under formation to depend on environmental parameters, such as local winds, temperatures, and other contingent meteorological phenomena.

The word *plastic* can also be reviewed in light of what Reyner Banham identified as a gradual repudiation of deterministic thinking in design. Banham's 1965 article "A Clip-On Architecture" evaluated the notion of "unpredictability" as imminent in the British tradition of architectural underground currents in the mid-1960s.[19] But Banham's analysis of indeterminacy was founded on a different material logic, one that was adjunctive and linear, based on Gerhard Kallmann's interpretation of endlessness as a combinatorial multiplicity of units.[20] On the other hand, plastic stands opposite to the orthodoxy of repetition and standardization, putting forward the evolution of the cellular unit itself. The episodes imply a physical, transformative process of accretion, deriving from the chemical properties of the materials deployed in relation to variable environmental parameters.

The kinds of experimentation for which these authors advocated, enmeshed as it was with all of their wonders, obsessions, blemishes, and personal values, seems quite obscure in its directions and purposes when compared to the scientific definition of the *experiment*. Usually, an experiment is conducted in order to verify or prove wrong a hypothesis, or in order to research a causal relationship between phenomena. Moreover, an experiment should be replicable under certain conditions and in a particular number of steps or phases. The fuzzy, nonlinear nature of much of the design process doesn't fit this description. One could argue that design experiments are "hypothesis-less" and highly contingent, with outcomes determined by constellations of factors related to the interaction of materials and how they are deployed. Peter Cook, in his influential book *Experimental Architecture*, writes:

> It is difficult to define "experiment" in the architectural sense. One is now forced to admit that design has so far been tantalizingly imprecise as a science. While there are bodies of knowledge, such as structural theory, weather protection and fabrication, these are a mere technical backup and have limits as a support as a theory of architecture.[21]

While Cook acknowledges that "a practical problem could lead to a piece of pure inventiveness" and praises technological innovation for detouring architecture as a discipline from the fetishization of buildings, he denies that technical innovation is purely experimental and classifies this kind of expertise in the traditions of the problem solver and the "boffin" designer.[22] There are many ambiguities in Cook's analysis, such as the role of invention in design practices, yet he clearly states that in order to perform the most "precise" architectural experiments, one must look toward other disciplines. Even today, the idea of "experimenting" in architecture and design connotes something not quite scientific—a transgression of techno-rational and functional traditions. Indeed, it suggests a willful immersion in unfamiliar territories with the specific goal of attaining results that represent improvements, but which could never have been predicted.

The types of material experiments discussed here—utilizing techniques such as spraying and molding foam—opened up alternative means of production in architecture and design that disengaged the prevailing conventions (and limitations) of architectural drawings. | fig. 11 The model of "direct action" put forward in the five aforementioned episodes stimulated major design debates, the echoes of which are still vibrant in contemporary practice. At the same time, material experimentation has often occasioned denigrating critiques, depending upon the subjective aesthetic criteria of

the authors. Certain individuals who were less than sympathetic to open-ended exploration—or even wished the experimenters to fail because of disagreements with their agendas for the field—disparaged these experiments for their formal vulgarity. Even in the pages of "Cosmorama," one of the most progressive—even radical—forums of the sixties and seventies, there was a deeply ingrained unwillingness to look beyond form: "The sculptured house has always been a bit of a freak."[23]

The five episodes outlined here, which we might alternatively term at this point the "plastic freak show," do not simply narrate a counterhistory of "formless" experimentation. Because of the properties of polymers to form and reform, to change phases and crystallize, plastics have come to recount strategies of architectonic reduction: the demise of assembling parts—the "death wish," if you will, of tectonics. However, the story does not end with the negation of tectonic principles in favor of unpredictability and "monomateriality." Rather, it starts anew by questioning the emerging tectonic principles of the "gun-shot." In engineering, the term *splat* describes the basic building block in thermal spray technology when a droplet impacts a surface. Many overlapping splats solidify and adhere to one another to form layers, and then spread to fill interstices.[24] | fig. 12 Along these lines, the underlying belief in the "plastic freak show" was that an architect could design by orchestrating and directing matter at the molecular level. But this was an impossible charge, as these substances are neither free-form nor amorphous rather their shape and form emerges from their material properties on the microscale.

Despite the misinterpreted reception of such projects, the "plastic freak show" entails a short-lived subversion of the belief in representation as an exclusive mode of spatial production, putting forward an agenda of "direct making" without necessarily having a strong formal intent. These experimental schemes, beyond being historically informative, narrate stories, wonders, obsessions, blemishes, and personal values that haunted their authors. In many cases,

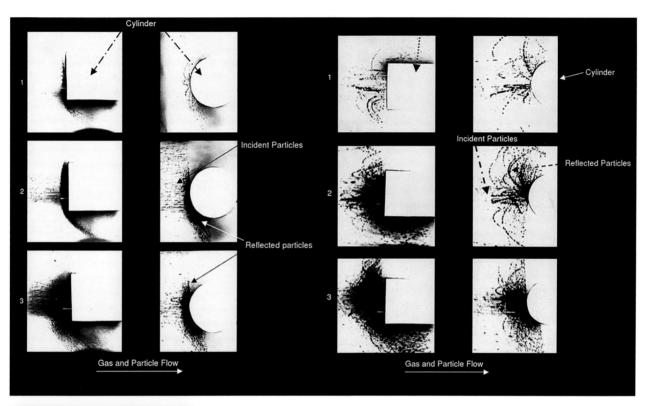

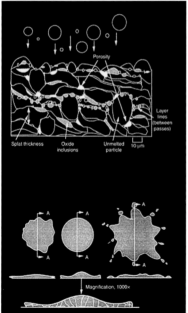

fig. 11 | Laser sheet photographs illustrating the trajectory of particles around a cylinder and a cube

fig. 12 | Thermal spray coating microstructure and typical thermal spray structures

the projects were very crude in form, leaving their authors unsatisfied or in anxious search of the materialized visions they could not somehow pin down. Many experiments utilized erratic material interactions and therefore defied established definitions of representation; there was little tectonic control over their formation. As such, these architects were prisoners of their visions, openly willing to fail. Latent in the punctuated lineage of this experimental trajectory is the disciplinary inclination for ongoing, unceasing production; a production so self-indulgent that it might "devour" the heroic architect and remind us all of the fragility of precious concepts before one yields to the action.

1 | John Elkington, "Plastics Pollution—Not Just a Drop in the Ocean" in the *Guardian Professional Network*, June 1, 2011. See http://www.guardian.co.uk/sustainable-business/sustainability-with-john-elkington/plastics-pollution-collaboration-ocean.

2 | "The Other Plastic Soup: A Haitian Recipe," posted on July 23, 2010, http://www.theplasticfreetimes.com/news/10/07/23trash-patch-other-plastic-soup-haitian-recipe.

3 | The term *island* is used loosely to describe a dense collection of tiny floating pieces of plastic, most of which are not on the surface. In reality, the Pacific Gyre Vortex is not a compact island, as a tight mass; rather, it is a collection of pieces that forms and reforms in a specific region of the ocean. The gyre is invisible to satellites due to the fact that several pieces are below surface level and the overall mass is constantly reforming.

4 | See Gottfried Semper, *Style in the Technical and Tectonic arts, or, Practical Aesthetics* (Los Angeles: Getty Research Institute, 2004), 184.

5 | Ovid, *Metamorphoses*, translated by A.D. Melville (Oxford: Oxford University Press, 1986), Book 1, 1.

6 | Richard Flood and Frances Morris, eds., *Zero to Infinity: Arte Povera 1962–1972* (Minneapolis: Walker Art Center; Distributed Art Publishers, 2001), 17.

7 | See Reyner Banham, "Architecture after 1960, Stocktaking 1," in *Architectural Review* 127 (January 1960): 9–10; Reyner Banham, "Stocktaking 1960: Tradition Technology," in *Architectural Review* 127 (February 1960): 93–100; Reyner Banham, "Stocktaking 1960: The Science Side" and "Human Sciences," in *Architectural Review* 127 (March 1960): 183–90; Reyner Banham, "Stocktaking 1960: The Future of the Universal Man," in *Architectural Review* 127 (April 1960): 253–60; Reyner Banham, "Stocktaking 1960: History and Psychiatry" in *Architectural Review* 127 (May 1960): 325–32; Reyner Banham, "Stocktaking 1960: Propositions," in *Architectural Review* 127 (June 1960): 381–89.

8 | See "Soft Future" in "Cosmorama," *Architectural Design* 43, no. 10 (October 1973): 617. See also the work of the Tao Design Group in ed. Lloyd Kahn, *Domebook 2* (Bolinas, California: Shelter Publications, a non-profit educational corporation, 1971) and ed. Lloyd Kahn, *Shelter* (including *Domebook 3*) (Bolinas, California: Shelter Publications, a non-profit educational corporation, 1973).

9 | Ibid; See also Charles Harker's manifesto statement for the "soft machine," written retrospectively in 2006.

10 | Clinton A. Page, "Foam Home" in *Progressive Architecture* 52, no. 5 (May 1971): 100–3.

11 | Ibid., 103.

12 | Arthur Quarmby, *Plastics and Architecture* (New York: Praeger Publishers, 1974), 170.

13 | See Rudolf Doernach, "Biotecture," in "Cosmorama," *Architectural Design* 36, no. 2 (February 1966): 4–5.

14 | Ibid., 5.

15 | See Sebastian Hackenschmidt and Dietmar Rubel, "Formations of the Formless" in ed. Peter Noever, *Formless Furniture* (Vienna: MAK; Hatje Cantz Verlag, 2008), 17–23.

16 | "Blobs of Gulp," in "Cosmorama," *Architectural Design* 35, no. 11 (November 1965).

17 | Arthur Drexler, "Curatorial statement for Visionary Architecture", at the Museum of Modern Art in 1960, MoMA archives, New York. Other featured architects included Frederick Kiesler, Buckminster Fuller, Paolo Soleri, Kiyonori Kikutake, and many others.

18 | William Katavolos, "Organics" (1960), in ed. Ulrich Conrads, *Programs and Manifestoes on the Twentieth Century Architecture* (Cambridge, Massachusetts: MIT Press, 1970), 163.

19 | Reyner Banham, "A Clip-On Architecture," in *Architectural Design* 35, no. 11 (November 1965): 534.

20 | See Gerhard Kallmann, "Man Made America," in *Architectural Review*, (December 1950).

21 | Peter Cook, *Experimental Architecture* (New York: Universe Books, 1970), 16.

22 | Ibid., 11–12. The definition of a "boffin" is a scientist or technician engaged in military research.

23 | "Blobs of Gulp," *Architectural Design*, 1965.

24 | Joseph R. Davis, *Handbook of Thermal Spray Technology* (Materials Park, OH: ASM International, 2004), 47. Thank you to Deborah Ferrer for this reference.

246

The Plastic Paradox and Its Potential

Craig Konyk

Plastic is a material that can be engineered to last 400 years, and yet we freely throw it away. It can also be engineered to last only a few months, like bio-bags that are made from corn-derived polymers. While most plastics are engineered to be durable, many will eventually degrade when overexposed to sunlight. Plastic can be made to assume any form and is often employed as a substitute for natural materials, mimicking leather, wood, and others. This plastic paradox has had significant impact on the production of art and architecture.

In *A Girl* (2006), the sculpture of a giant newborn by Australian hyperrealist artist Ron Mueck, plastics in the form of polymers and silicones are used to simulate flesh, similar to the paintings of obese nudes by Lucian Freud. | fig. 1 The object was to create an authentic rendering of flesh, veins, and follicles, where the synthetic materials create the "real," even as its scale and context are severely altered.

Claes Oldenburg's *Soft Toilet* (1966) takes a differing tack. | fig. 2 A toilet has a hard surface, made of vitreous glazed ceramic. However, when it is rendered in the soft, flaccid vinyl, we immediately sense the disassociation. It exists somewhere between recognizable and unrecognizable. Even though the sculpture is made at the same scale as an actual toilet, our expectation of the object is immediately altered by the simple substitution of vinyl for vitreous china.

Beginning in the early 1920s, artists began to incorporate newly invented plastics into their artwork, making it one of the first creative fields to employ the material. Yet these early varieties of plastic were inherently unstable materials. Plastics have been used in the art world for decades now, and with that, a new paradox has revealed itself through the material degradation of critically acclaimed works of plastic art. This issue has become significant, as many of these artworks are represented in museums and private collections. Indeed, the issue is of such importance that the French insurance group AXA produced a manual entitled "Plastic Art: A

Precarious Success Story."[1] In the brochure, scientists, engineers, and art restorers and historians address the risk of irreversible—that some works will be irretrievably lost—but advise clientele on known restoration techniques and other prescriptions for the preservation of plastic artworks.

Rhodoid was a highly flammable precursor to Plexiglas made of cellulose acetate and widely used in motion picture film. Russian constructivist Naum Gabo used it in his work *Construction in Space: Two Cones* (1936). In 1967 curators at the Philadelphia Museum of Art noticed irreparable degradation in the piece of discoloration, cracking, and a vinegar odor and contacted Gabo, who blamed poor archival storage conditions.[2] Ultimately he offered to refabricate the piece for $7,000, which was its art market value at the time. The curators instead hired a professional art restorer to refabricate the piece, substituting Plexiglas for the rhodoid.

The natural tendency of early formula plastic to degrade has created some unanticipated consequences. Duane Hanson, a contemporary of postmodern artists such as Cindy Sherman and Robert Longo, created lifelike figures of ordinary people, circa the 1970s. Hanson did not plan for the degradation of his vinyl, polyester, and fiberglass creations. Unlike *The Portrait of Dorian Gray*, these lifelike figures have actually "aged," albeit differently than anticipated. Hanson's works appear as if they were just pulled out of a time capsule, yet have such advanced degrees of degradation that they are strangely corpse-like, rather than the day-in-the-life portraits as originally intended. | fig. 3 In fact, curators of the Wallraf-Richartz Museum in Cologne had Hanson return to "age" his *Woman with Handbag* (1974), adding age spots and thinning her hair.[3] Yet since Hanson's death in 1996, they are left to decay, more lifelike (or lifeless-like) than anyone had ever anticipated.

For some artists, the use of plastics liberated their formal strategies, such as the Danish furniture designer Gunnar Aagaard Andersen, in the making of his *Armchair* (1964). However, it was not until the embrace of the impermanence of these materials by a new generation of artists that the use

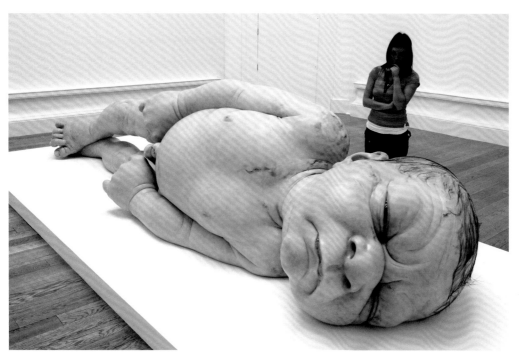

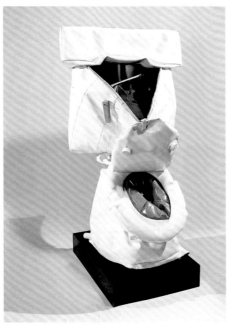

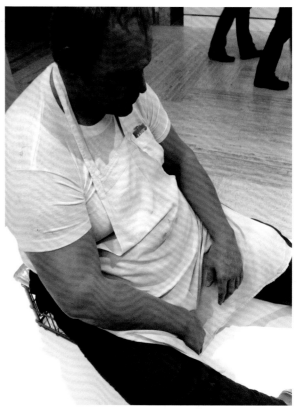

fig. 1 | *A Girl*, by Ron Mueck, 2004

fig. 2 | *Soft Toilet*, by Claes Oldenburg, 1966

fig. 3 | *Dishwasher*, by Duane Hanson, 1974

fig. 4 | Eva Hesse looking through her Rubberized
String and *Untitled (Rope Piece)*, *Life* magazine, by Henry
Groskinsky, 1969

fig. 5 | First plastic house, architect unknown, circa 1960s

of plastics sought deeper intentions of meaning. Eva Hesse felt that these new, unstable materials perfectly represented her state of mind, seen through her *Untitled (Rope Piece)* (1970), only months before her death from a brain tumor. | fig. 4 Hesse wanted to attain something different than pure representation. She stated in 1968, "I wanted to get to non-art, nonconnotive, nonanthropomorphic, nongeometric, non, nothing, everything, but of another kind, vision, sort, from a total other reference point."[4] The nature of plastic and polymers to degrade was considered part of the process in her work: "Some of my work is falling apart....If and when I can, I repair it. If not, so what? They are not wasted. I went further in the work that followed."[5] For Hesse, each work was not an end in itself, but merely a waymarker on a journey to something more. She accepted the work's lack of permanence. Thus plastic was the perfect medium, as it facilitated this creative self-destruction. One of Hesse's last quotes, given in an interview between brain surgeries for her inoperable tumor was, "Life doesn't last, art doesn't last. It doesn't matter."[6]

Within this idea of a material that can creatively degrade, there may be a new potential for architecture. The perpetual architectural quest for permanence has come under new suspicion, as plastics allow for a new way of thinking about the evolutionary lifespan of buildings. This new architecture might look similar to the plastic houses of the 1960s, when no one really understood how long plastic was going to last, once exposed to the realities of the world. | fig. 5 This may still be the future potential for plastics in architecture.

1 | See Stefan Albus et al., "Plastic Art—A Precarious Success Story," (Cologne: AXA Art Versicherung AG, October 2006).

2 | See Sam Kean, "Does Plastic Art Last Forever?" *Slate* magazine, July 1, 2009.

3 | Ibid.

4 | Cindy Nemser, in *October Files: Eva Hesse*, ed. M. Nixon (Cambridge and London: MIT Press, 2002).

5 | Exhibition statement, Chain Polymers exhibition (New York: Fischbach Gallery, 1968).

6 | Taken from a 1970 interview with Cindy Nemser when Hesse was already quite ill. See Cindy Nemser, *Art Talk: Conversations with 12 Women Artists* (New York: Scribner, 1975).

Plastic Life

Galia Solomonoff

In the mid-1950s, plastics held a promise of expansion and lightness that was later betrayed by their association with industrial mass production, rather than the more localized practices of artisans, artists, and architects. The "plastic promise" was one of total design—the idea that plastic would become the immersive and expansive material of our everyday living environments. | fig. 1 Plastics have indeed reshaped and retextured everything, yet we persist in viewing them in a fundamentally different way than glass, steel, concrete, or brick, which we consider noble, durable, and time-tested. Plastic is often dismissed as easy and temporary—practically already a waste material at the moment of its making—even though it can be very long lasting and is found everywhere in the construction industry.

In 2001 Fabian Marcaccio and Greg Lynn installed *The Predator,* a temporary piece commissioned by Jeffrey Kipnis, at the Wexner Center for the Arts in Columbus, Ohio. The production involved extensive use of vacuum-formed plastic and silicone. It felt bravely new, suspended somewhere between architecture and painting. The piece was conceived as a temporary installation and now is on permanent display at the Museum für Moderne Kunst in Frankfurt. *The Predator*, made of silk-screened and painted vacuum-formed plastic, is a painting-architecture hybrid that transforms filmic special effects into effects of painting and architecture that visitors can walk through.

Dia:Beacon, the minimalist museum completed with OpenOffice in 2003, was designed to give permanent placement to a group of minimalist works. | fig. 2 The space provides the framework for artists such as Michael Heizer, Fred Sandback, and Bruce Nauman to take risks, rather than the structure. | fig. 3

Andy Warhol, whose work is also in the Dia:Beacon collection, expanded the art field and its awareness of "tasteful" comfort. The Warhol/Factory/Pop idea was that

fig. 1 | *99 Cents*, Andreas Gursky, chromogenic color print, 1999

fig. 2 | Gallery (with Michael Heizer sculpture), Dia: Beacon, by OpenOffice, Beacon, New York, 2003

fig. 3 | Gallery, Dia:Beacon, 2003

fig. 4 | Installation view, *Defective Brick*, by Galia
Solomonoff, Artists Space, New York, 2000

fig. 5 | View of *Defective Brick* unit, made of Hydrocal,
multiple production views, *Defective Brick*, 2000

anybody could do anything. In April 1966 Warhol rented a Polish community center in the East Village in New York, known as the Dom, to present a mixed-media event called *The Exploding Plastic Inevitable,* a combination of performance, art installation, and interior design. Audiences were bombarded with floor-to-ceiling projections of Warhol films, such as the disturbing and abrasive *Vinyl* (1965). At center stage, the Velvet Underground performed their discordant music, enveloped in Warhol lighting effects and surrounded by inflatable silver Mylar plastic pillows. It is easy to romanticize the event, yet the actual experience was probably a bit pathetic or uncomfortable. It probably felt improvised, unscripted, formless, informal, and plasticky. This unexpected and sometimes ridiculous feeling is central to the expansion of ideas, yet practitioners are often reluctant to delve into it.

Artists are often interested in things everyone else considers useless; they are motivated by the idea of seeking something uncertain, probably unnecessary to most, yet deeply needed by someone. *Defective Brick* was a collaborative project that aimed to share these values. It was first developed in the digital realm, and in 1999 it was installed at Artists Space in New York. At that time Artists Space was directed by Claudia Gould, who organized annual architectural shows, the previous of which had been by Greg Lynn.

The participating architects were asked to create full-size installations, which demanded a different type of engagement and risk than just drawings or models. It is easier to look dignified in the digital realm than in a physical installation. *Defective Brick* and *Predator* were a kind of three-dimensional sketch. | fig. 4 Normally, in architectural production, the architect draws and others execute. Here, a group of colleagues and students was enlisted to actually build. | fig. 5 The project room was populated with "defective bricks" made from Hydrocal—a plasticized compound of gypsum that cures with water—layered together with vacuum-formed styrene bricks, using silicone as mortar and aluminum tubes as reinforcement. | figs. 6–8

Defective Brick was all about risk-taking in that we actually got to build, rather than drawing things for others to build. Architects do not build whatever we want; we determine what we want by what we can build. The point of engaging architects in places such as Artists Space, Storefront for Art and Architecture, or MoMA PS1 is not to transform architecture into sculpture or art, but to allow a different mechanism to surface in which architects become comfortable with building and risking a more improvised or even ridiculed outcome. It engages a vulnerable aspect of the making process.

Every year 540 billion pounds of plastic are produced, much of which is for items that will be used a single time.[1] Some, for instance medical syringes, are arguably more essential than others, like straws or sandwich bags. From an environmental point of view, plastic waste is a huge problem, but the fact remains that in a world with seven billion inhabitants, plastic is cheap and light—an excellent material to transport, store, and distribute water, for example. Humanity needs plastic more than we need wood, concrete, or steel. It is more fundamental to our survival.

Rio de Janeiro depends on plastic tanks to keep its 5.6 million inhabitants hydrated and safe. In 2010 two students from Columbia University's Graduate School of Architecture, Planning and Preservation (GSAPP), Nick Hopson and Klara Nostrom, developed a proposal for a life-cycle network of tanks, computer terminals, and balloons for the 2016 Rio Olympics.[2] With the help of a topographical alteration, a differentiated totality emerged from a sum of repetitive parts. The parts had overlapping performance cycles, in that they acted as internet cabins, water tanks, and floating dirigible balloons. They were to be arranged in different formations at different times, first for the Olympic ceremony and then later as communal devices. The idea was to overturn one-time use in favor of a chain of uses and to recast the lightness of plastic as a positive characteristic. | figs. 9–11

BOB, a full-scale pavilion produced in the summer of 2011, was developed to provide a communal outdoor space.[3]

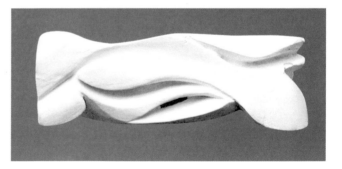

fig. 6 | Installation view, *Defective Brick*, 2000

fig. 7 | Brick rendering, *Defective Brick*, 2000

fig. 8 | Detail of single handcrafted brick, *Defective Brick*, 2000

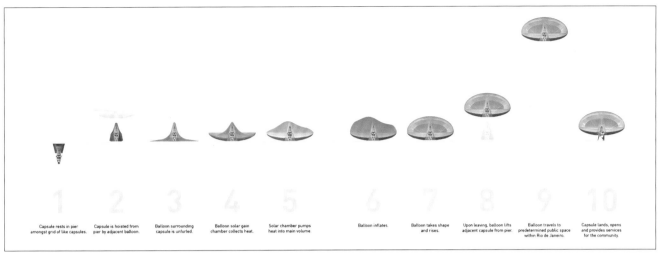

1	2	3	4	5	6	7	8	9	10
Capsule rests in pier amongst grid of like capsules.	Capsule is hoisted from pier by adjacent balloon.	Balloon surrounding capsule is unfurled.	Balloon solar gain chamber collects heat.	Solar chamber pumps heat into main volume.	Balloon inflates.	Balloon takes shape and rises.	Upon leaving, balloon lifts adjacent capsule from pier.	Balloon travels to predetermined public space within Rio de Janeiro.	Capsule lands, opens and provides services for the community.

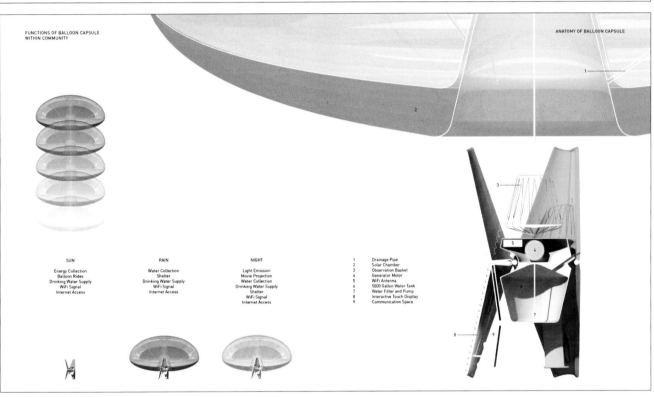

FUNCTIONS OF BALLOON CAPSULE WITHIN COMMUNITY

ANATOMY OF BALLOON CAPSULE

SUN	RAIN	NIGHT
Energy Collection	Water Collection	Light Emission
Balloon Rides	Shelter	Movie Projection
Drinking Water Supply	Drinking Water Supply	Water Collection
WiFi Signal	WiFi Signal	Drinking Water Supply
Internet Access	Internet Access	Shelter
		WiFi Signal
		Internet Access

1 Drainage Pipe
2 Solar Chamber
3 Observation Basket
4 Generator Motor
5 WiFi Antenna
6 5000 Gallon Water Tank
7 Water Filter and Pump
8 Interactive Touch Display
9 Communication Space

fig. 9 | Balloon metamorphosis study, by Nick Hopson and Klara Nostrom, at Columbia GSAPP, New York, 2011

fig. 10 | Balloon capsule details study, 2011

fig. 11 | Balloon installation rendering, 2011

fig. 12 | Installation view, BOB, by Columbia GSAPP/Galia
Solomonoff, Nathan Carter, Liam Gillick, New York, 2011

fig. 13 | Illuminated at evening, BOB, 2011

The outcome was an inflatable plastic white cloud above a public bathroom and forum, sited on the Columbia University campus. | figs. 12 and 13 Historically, the pavilion has been a place to instrumentalize, deploy, or promote a specific cultural, corporate, or national projection or desire. We were interested in the tension inherent in the pavilion as a site for architecture and art, as well as the happenings it might contain. The art and architecture studio had a seminar component in which we discussed historical precedents as well as recent ones, such as the Chanel pavilion, the temporary structures built for the World Social Forum in Brazil, and the Serpentine Pavilion series in London. Because of their temporary nature, pavilions are often considered an architect's opportunity to explore autonomous ideas through building. BOB was an opportunity to discuss public needs and to extend the discussion to the thinly separated public, corporate, and educational territories.

The inclusion of a toilet was due to the constant omission of public bathrooms in the planning of urban monuments. For example, the 9/11 Memorial, which opened in 2011 in New York and cost $700 million in public funds, includes no toilets.[4] Our mantra was adapted from Carl Andre, "A society that does not provide public bathrooms does not deserve public art."[5] By deploying a public bathroom in an academic courtyard, we acknowledged the gap between lofty cultural aspirations versus mundane biological needs. BOB's toilet utilized a system of composting and did not have a septic tank, as would a standard portable toilet. In the proposal, the fan-assisted ventilation of the tank also pressurized a large inflatable canopy and BOB's balloon signaled the bathroom from a distance.

Few projects are realized as they are designed. Experimentation and risk are two sides of the same coin; one cannot experiment without risk. Often, the powers that be are risk averse. Columbia's facilities department reviewed our proposal early in the semester and expressed approval of the scheme. But in April 2011 when construction was well under way, they informed us that the composting toilet was no longer permitted. In the name of public safety, the university prevented the use, but not the display, of the composting toilet.

The BOB discussions had spanned from art to architecture, from the science of health to new technologies. In the end, BOB developed its own character: gentle, steady, aware of the world around it. Our pavilion showed us that humor is as good a tool as reason, that reason alone cannot always change things, and that limits are sometimes invisible. The scarcity of public bathrooms suggests a broader condition of our society. We are invested in projecting a dignified image of ourselves through architecture, yet we are simultaneously reluctant to engage with real conditions.

If art, architecture, or politics are to expand the limit of the known and find new solutions, then they require active engagement and risk taking. As we move forward to address real conditions, such as the access to clean water in Rio de Janeiro or better public infrastructure of sanitary facilities in New York City, we may benefit from considering how something works before considering how it looks. The lightness and variety of permutations of shapes and textures make plastic the first ally in finding solutions to a large range of problems. The Pantheon of our times may be a temporary, expansive, immersive, and inflatable plastic one.

1 | Anne Trafton, "One Word: bioplastics," *MITnews*, November 17, 2009, http://web.mit.edu/newsoffice/2009/bioplastics.html.

2 | Hopson's and Nostrom's proposal responded to an architecture studio brief from spring 2010, calling for a scheme that integrated Olympic uses planned for Rio 2016 back into the city's infrastructure following the event.

3 | BOB was developed and constructed by a collaborative team including myself and Nathan Carter of GSAPP, Liam Gillick of the School of the Arts, and second-year graduate students from both schools. The studio was taught in spring 2011.

4 | David B. Caruso and David Porter, "World Trade Center Memorial Magnificent, But At A Steep Price," Huffington Post, September 9, 2012, http://www.huffingtonpost.com/2012/09/09/world-trade-center-memorial-2012_n_1868462.html.

5 | "A society which cannot afford clean, attended public facilities does not deserve public art." From a written interview with Jack Risley and John Zinsser, "Carl Andre," *Journal of Contemporary Art*, May 19, 1990, http://www.jca-online.com/carlandre.html.

Die Plastik

Mark Goulthorpe

"What is plastik? I have attempted to crack open this concept in its first principles."

—Joseph Beuys

Joseph Beuys interrogated the *condition* of plastic arts and then displaced it: a strategic deconstruction of artwork. His installations, dress, happenings, talks with dead hares, fat/felt/honey material agglomerations, and awkwardly erudite wordiness exposed the raw semantic of disciplinary inheritance and jangled it. The legacy of postwar austerity was embedded in the works' survival-pack logic, bringing artwork off its pedestal and into the arena of social realism, for instance, "Energy Plan for the Western Man," Beuys's 1970 United States tour. In respect of art's profound requalification during this period, it was just as Walter Benjamin had predicted in *Art in the Age of Mechanical Reproduction*, announcing that cold technical change would translate into hot plastic action.

As we negotiate the current adaptation of the plastic arts within an age of now digital hyperproduction, at issue once again is *the base condition of the plastic arts* in respect to technical change: *plastik* as a conceptual as well as physical materiality is the very process of its instantiation-into-being.

Yet this time, beyond the digital paradigm lies a new *material* paradigm, intoxicating plastic arts. Plastic is not necessarily plastic, that is, a polymer or spatial quality. One Main is made of plywood but it is the most plastic work we have realized. | figs. 1–3 The interior was generated as a malleable parametric model of languid complex-curved forms with elements subject to plastic deformation: the ceiling lifted over function, oriented toward light (or pulled toward gravity), and inflected along lines of social flow; the floor curled up to provide seating or to define a zone; the furniture eased to accommodate activity. Even light pockets, ventilation grilles, and door handles all became subject to a universal *pliancy*, power and information outlets as melding pockets in the base elements.

Such apparent formal complexity displaces the tectonics of late-industrial assembly in preference for subtle surface continuity, and is attained with sustainable Finnish spruce plylam milled on a single three-axis CNC machine. Once a series of scripts were developed, the output of toolpath information from the parametric model was essentially automatic, and we provided instruction directly to the machine. There was no intermediary step—no architectural drawings—with over a million linear feet of too path nested into standard plywood sheets ready for rapid, accurate machining. Of note was that functional inflections such as the ceiling air vents or the light pockets were never actually "designed" nor even rendered prior to their manufacture. They were applied by the engineers according to code requirements and simply appeared as vectorial inflections in the final parts—elements that mime their "genetic" occurrence.

The *efficiency* of such a process was strikingly unitary in its material and procedural logic, and carbon negative in its use of wood. Virtually all elements seemed to announce new modalities of practice and new plasticity of formal register. The milling machine prefers a fluid continuity of cut, where the straight line is a localized instance of a generalized curvature; there is no loss of efficiency with curvilinearity. The plastic aspects of form have perhaps often been conflated with aesthetics and perception, or with light. Here the plastic qualities are essentially also highly efficient; evidence of a deeply embedded computational process of formation that is many steps removed from the final product and perceptual experience of the space but nonetheless accessible as the base elements of a newly plastic imagination. Such shape to mass, light to form, and computation to manufacturing capacities *pull* on conceptual thought—creating a newly differential curved accelerometer of cultural thought. They reestablish plasticity (mental and physical) at the heart of matter: plastic bends imagination in its demonstration, proving to be flexible, establishing a *topological variance of material property* as a new mental and material paradigm. A new plasticity.

figs. 1–3 | Interior views, One Main Street, by dECOi
Architects, Boston, 2009

fig. 1 | *Spread Self-Hood*, by Fabian Marcaccio, 1991

Plasticity Formation/Information

Fabian Marcaccio

Traditional modes of art production, such as oil painting, made the realistic representation of flesh possible. The development of photo emulsions made the "instant" image possible. Digitization and the internet made the instant delivery of information possible. And new polymer materials, together with digitally aided technology, have now made a new type of composite corporeality possible. These plastics change the essential relations and sensations of objects vis-à-vis one another and the body. Examples are numerous and range from the intimate (sex toys and medical silicone) to the massive and structural (silicone sealants in glass and steel curtain walls).

Many polymers are used as aids in circulation, for instance, the tubing that connects the body to medical machines, or the gaskets cushioning rigid parts of machinery. In their varied roles as sealant, circulant, cushion, gasket, filler, or prosthetic, new polymers are essential for the successful passage of materials and fluids between bodies and objects, rigid entities and soft ones. They are in the interstitial spaces of everything that matters. And not only do they *form*, but they *inform* as well. Plasticity is present at the level of digital information and the distribution of that information. These new plasticities act as the flexible aura between things, through a type of plastic subjectification.

Since the late 1980s, my work has engaged this "new plasticity" in multiple ways, primarily using silicones and polymers. The curing time of silicone is short, unlike that of oil or acrylics, which makes it a forceful, gestural artistic material. | fig. 1 It is also flexible, so it can be applied on, through, or between different grounds, creating passages between disparate materials. Silicone can be transparent, but it bears physical evidence of the gestural forces that shaped it, unlike glass or resins, which essentially erase the actions that formed them. This transparent directionality can be tinted or fully pigmented; the tinted, semitransparent mass is hyperglazed—a glazing with a body unlike any other paint, however like a limited form of a traditional encaustic.

Silicone can be applied through a form of air painting, by which I mean painting the material onto a temporary or borrowed ground, and then peeling it off and rearranging it on another ground. These parts can be free-form or dammed using stencils or molds. The strongest feature of these disparate techniques of plasticity is that they can be unified, mixed, and glued together to construct either a collage or a continuous, gestural, serial work, as desired. Other methods might involve controlling the flow with a silicone extruder while using hydraulic force or bubbling; the casting of silicone parts from molds; and using compressed air to inflate masses of silicone.

Silicone can be applied in layers to the surface of digitally printed vinyl or canvas. I call these photo-paint composite works *Paintants*. The aim is the integration of indexical and iconic representational information. | figs. 2–4 My *Environmental Paintants* integrate territorialized and deterritorialized material. Sited within and responding to architecture, these works involve silicone accumulation on a large scale, morphing the material with the spaces surrounding it. | figs. 5–10

In the *Rope Paintings,* the silicone bridges the thick gaps of each cross of the woven ground. Silicone is the only paint-like medium that is sufficiently flexible and viscous to work in this hypertextural mode. | fig. 11

The structural canvas works are expressed in three dimensions. Silicone reconnects and reskins the different parts of the unfolded shells that form the complete piece. This type of rigid tailoring is facilitated by the flexibility of the silicone. | fig. 12

The evolution of the humanist flesh of oil paintings to the new silicone medium is a phenomenon of posthuman hyperplasticity. Silicone possesses all the attributes of a supermedium—a medium that can move from a super impasto or surface plating to intricate detail, all in one continuous flow.

figs. 2 and 3 | *The Predator*, by Fabian Marcaccio and Greg Lynn, 2001

fig. 4 | *The Predator*, by Fabian Marcaccio and Greg Lynn, 2001

fig. 5 | *Miami Paintant*, by Fabian Marcaccio, 2004

fig. 6 | *Miami Paintant*, 2004

fig. 7 | *Re-sketching Democracy*, by Fabian Marcaccio, 2004

fig. 8 | Detail, *Re-sketching Democracy*, 2004

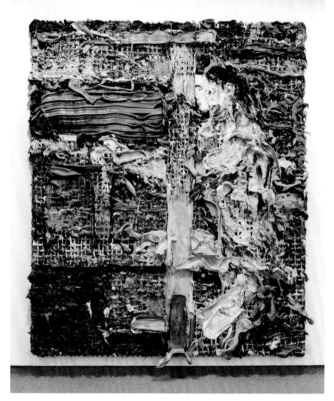

fig. 9 | *Topographical Paintant*, by Fabian Marcaccio, 2006

fig. 10 | Detail, *Topographical Paintant*, 2006

fig. 11 | Detail, *Megan: Rope Paintant*, by Fabian
Marcaccio, 2010

fig. 12 | *Megan: Structural Canvas Paintant*, by Fabian
Marcaccio, 2010

Acknowledgments

Permanent Change: Plastics in Architecture and Engineering is the fourth book in the series originating from the Columbia Conference on Architecture, Engineering, and Materials. The series of conferences and books has worked toward a goal of reinvigorating the academic and professional collaborations between the Schools of Engineering and Architecture. Like the preceding series titles, *Engineered Transparency*, *Solid States*, and *Post-Ductility*, *Permanent Change* also represents an ongoing collaboration between the Columbia University Graduate School of Architecture, Planning and Preservation (GSAPP) and the Fu Foundation School of Engineering and Applied Science.

From the Department of Civil Engineering and Engineering Mechanics, professor Christian Meyer and Chair Raimondo Betti each sustained this partnership, and former dean Feniosky Peña-Mora generously endorsed our shared work and plans for the next stages. *Permanent Change* and the entire Columbia Conference on Architecture, Engineering, and Materials series benefited from the support of Mark Wigley, dean of GSAPP, who initiated the idea for a conference that linked the schools of architecture and engineering, and whose intellectual leadership helped forge the critical relationship with our partners. Michael Bell, the founding chair of the conferences, has been assisted by a scientific committee as well as a wide range of academic and professional advisors.

The Institute for Lightweight Structures and Conceptual Design (ILEK), University of Stuttgart, Germany, joined as a collaborating academic partner for *Permanent Change*. Directed by Werner Sobek, ILEK has contributed to bringing a new scope of research to the conference, and special thanks to Heiko Trumpf of Werner Sobek Engineering and Design for facilitating this relationship.

The Vinyl Institute's engagement with Columbia provided a critical bridge to industry and was undertaken with a deep regard for the traditions of scholarship and practice in our speakers' work. Former president Gregory Bocchi, as well as George Middleton, Sylvia Moore, and Kevin Mulvaney, vice president of marketing and communications, provided direction at every stage of planning. Judith Nordgren, former vice president of marketing and communications, initiated our collaboration with the Vinyl Institute, whose generous support as our Exclusive Sponsor made this event possible.

Permanent Change would not have been possible without the energy, goodwill, and intellectual rigor of our advisors and collaborators, including Johan Bettum, Felicity Scott, and Craig Buckley. Industry advisor William F. Carroll, vice president of industry issues for Occidental Chemical Corporation, generously helped to establish new relations with the field of chemical engineering. Steven Holl, Sanford Kwinter, Matthias Schuler, and Laurie Hawkinson have all been instrumental in expanding the scope and context of the conference. David Hinkle, associate dean of GSAPP, has provided broad support for the entire series of conferences and related books. Stephanie Salomon has been an invaluable editor for all program text. Benjamin Prosky, former director of special events and external affairs at GSAPP, guided all logistics with his team—Lucia Haladjian and Tong

Tong—and was also central to the fundraising and overall direction of the conference. Stefana Simic assisted Benjamin Prosky and Michael Bell on coordination and editorial goals. William Menking, editor; Diana Darling, publisher; and Lynne Rowan of the *Architect's Newspaper*, our exclusive media sponsor, have supported the conference series since its inception.

We are grateful to Mary Kate Murray of Michael Graves Design, who introduced our goals to Michael Graves. Luke Bulman and Jessica Young of Thumb have again provided the complete visual identity of the conference. Frank Heinlein and Andrea Scheufler coordinated ILEK and Werner Sobek's contributions. Special thanks go to the architect Eunjeong Seong, who has been an influential critic, researcher, and editor on each of the four installments of the conference. Greg Lynn provided tremendous energy in working with us to build the conference roster. Sylvia Lavin offered encouragement in taking on the topic of plastics and lent her time, and critical and editorial skills to our planning. Rosana Rubio Hernández conceived inventive exhibits for each of the four conferences, assisted by Mara Sánchez Llorens and Carlos Fernández Piñar for *Permanent Change*.

Our deep thanks also to the architect Yoshiko Sato for creating an installation interrogating conference goals. With her partner Michael Morris, and assisted by Shuning Zhao and John Hooper, Sato employed plastics to transform Avery Hall to create an aura of beauty with a material that is so often seen as artificial. We thank Stretch Marquees and Fabric Structures as well as AZEK for in-kind materials and fabrication support of Sato's installation, and Mark Wasiuta, director of exhibitions at GSAPP, and his team members, Gregory Bugel and Brittany Drapac.

The following additional members of the GSAPP community have provided wide-ranging assistance and talent for this conference. From development, Devon Ercolano Provan and Julia Fishkin both assisted in fundraising on the entire conference series, and Danielle Smoller worked to secure the optimal facilities for the event; for audiovisual assistance, John Ramahlo, Lou Fernandez, Kevin Allen, and student assistants Brendan Sullivan, Michael Christopher Georgopoulos, and Kooho Jung; web designer Gabriel Bach; director of operations Mark A. Taylor; Nathan Carter, Building/Model Shop manager; from the Fabrication Lab, Phillip Anzalone, director, and Brigette Borders, manager; Sal Bernardino, manager of Columbia University Print Services; and Sarah Riegelmann of Highroad Press.

Finally and foremost we thank the entire group of authors who have contributed to making such a strong community of the Columbia Conference on Architecture, Materials, and Engineering, and to everyone at Princeton Architectural Press who has given so much energy and creativity to the book series. Meredith Baber, as editor for *Permanent Change* at Princeton Architectural Press, has been central to raising the book's quality, as has series editor Megan Carey, and Lindsey Westbrook. Jan Haux has provided the book's visual identity in his elegant graphic design, the fourth time he has worked on this series. He has been central to the energy and success of the series. In the GSAPP Books office, the assistance of Jess Ngan and Atreyee Pathe was key in the development of *Permanent Change*.

Contributors

Michael Bell is a professor of architecture at Columbia University's Graduate School of Architecture, Planning and Preservation (GSAPP) and chair of the Columbia Conference on Architecture, Engineering, and Materials.

Johan Bettum is a professor of architecture and program director of the Städelschule Architecture Class in Frankfurt.

Craig Buckley is an assistant professor in the History of Art Department at Yale University. His research interests center on the history of modern architecture and the experiments of the historical avant-gardes, and the publishing and media practices of architects.

William F. Carroll Jr. is an adjunct professor of chemistry at Indiana University and vice president of industry issues for Occidental Chemical Corporation.

Beatriz Colomina is a professor of history and theory and founding director of the program in media and modernity at Princeton University School of Architecture (SoA).

Winka Dubbeldam is professor of practice and chair of the Department of Architecture at the University of Pennsylvania and principal at Archi-Tectonics in New York.

Billie Faircloth is research director at KieranTimberlake in Philadelphia.

Mark Goulthorpe is an associate professor at MIT School of Architecture and Planning, and founding director of dECOi Architects, HypoSurface Corp, and Zero+ LLC.

Michael Graves is professor emeriti at Princeton University SoA and the founder of Michael Graves & Associates and Michael Graves Design Group.

Juan Herreros is chair professor at the School of Architecture in Madrid, professor of practice at Columbia University's GSAPP, and founder of Herreros Arquitectos.

Lydia Kallipoliti is a practicing architect, engineer, and theorist in New York, an assistant professor at Syracuse University, and founder of EcoRedux.

Brian Kane is an assistant professor of music at Yale University and author of the forthcoming *Sound Unseen*, a book on acousmatic sound.

Jan Knippers is a professor at the University of Stuttgart Faculty of Architecture and Urban Design, where he heads the Institute for Building Structures and Structural Design. He is also a partner at Knippers Helbig Advanced Engineering, in Stuttgart and New York City.

Craig Konyk is an adjunct assistant professor at Columbia University's GSAPP and principal of Konyk Architecture.

Christoph a. Kumpusch is an adjunct assistant professor of architecture at Columbia University's GSAPP and founder of c.a.k_LAB.

Sylvia Lavin is the director of critical studies in the architecture department at the University of California, Los Angeles (UCLA) and the director of the design/research group Hi-C.

267
Permanent Change
Contributors

Chip Lord is professor emeritus in the film and digital media department at the University of California, Santa Cruz. He is also a media artist and founding partner of Ant Farm (1968–78).

Greg Lynn is a professor at UCLA's School of Architecture and Urban Design and principal at Greg Lynn FORM.

Fabian Marcaccio is an artist in New York.

Michael Morris is an adjunct professor at Columbia University's GSAPP and Parsons The New School for Design's School of Constructed Environments and principal at Morris | Sato Studio.

Erik Olsen is a climate engineer and managing partner of TRANSSOLAR Climate Engineering in New York.

Jorge Otero-Pailos is an associate professor of historic preservation at Columbia University's GSAPP and an architect, artist, and theorist specializing in experimental forms of preservation.

Bill Pearson is technical director of North Sails, the world's largest sailmaking firm.

Theodore Prudon is an adjunct professor of historic preservation at Columbia University's GSAPP and an architect and principal at Prudon & Partners, a firm specializing in restoration.

François Roche is an adjunct assistant professor at Columbia University's GSAPP, and an architect and founder of New Territories, R&Sie(n).

Yoshiko Sato was a long-standing adjunct associate professor at Columbia University's GSAPP until her death in 2012. She was a partner with Michael Morris in the New York City–based firm Morris | Sato Studio.

Felicity D. Scott is an associate professor of architectural history and theory and codirector of the Critical, Curatorial, and Conceptual Practices in Architecture program at Columbia University's GSAPP.

Hartmut Sinkwitz is director of the interior design center of competence at Daimler AG.

Werner Sobek is a professor at the Illinois Institute of Technology and the founder of Werner Sobek Engineering and Design. He is also the director of the Institute for Lightweight Structures and Conceptual Design (ILEK) at the University of Stuttgart.

Galia Solomonoff is an associate professor of practice at Columbia University's GSAPP and principal at Solomonoff Architecture Studio.

Mark Wigley is an architectural critic and theorist and the dean (2004–present) of Columbia University's GSAPP.

Lebbeus Woods was a professor at the Cooper Union and an architect and theorist.

Credits

Project Credits

Blobwall, Los Angeles, California

Design: Greg Lynn FORM—Jackilin Bloom, Adam Fure, Chris Kabatsi, Daniel Norell

Fabrication and robotic technology: Machineous—Andreas Froech, Jeff McKibban

Distributor: Panelite

Bloom House, Los Angeles, California

Design architects: Greg Lynn FORM—Jackilin Bloom, Brittney Hart, Adam Fure, Chris Kabatsi, Brian Ha, Danny Bazil, Andreas Krainer

Architect of record: Lookinglass Architecture & Design—Nick Gillock, Emil Mertzel

Completion: 2008

Structural engineer: KPFF Consulting Engineers

Mechanical and electrical engineer: Storms & Lowe

Soil engineer: AGI Geo Technical

Survey engineer: R.S. Engineering Company, Inc.

General contractor: Oliver Garrett Construction, Inc., Oliver Garrett, Michael Murbarger

Corian thermoforming fabricator: Complete Fabrication & Machine, LLC (Paul Doak and Brent Nicholson)

Corian cabinetry and installation: Pacific Westline, Inc. (Dan MacLeith)

Corian reseach and development and material donation: DuPont Surfaces (John Sagrati, Trevor King, and Don Nordmeyer)

Fiberglass lantern fabrication: Kreysler & Associates (Bill Kreysler, Ken Anderson, Makai Smith, and Joshua Zabel)

Lantern lighting: Los Angeles Neon & Cathode (Jan Carter)

Window and door fabrication: Pacific Architectural Millwork (Heidi Miley and Mike Honey)

Munch Museum (LAMBDA), Oslo, Norway

Principal architect: Juan Herreros

Director: Jens Richter

Project team: Gonzalo Rivas, Carmen Antón, Ramón Bermúdez, Paola Simone, Margarita Martínez, Diego Barajas, Carlos Bayod, Luís Berríos-Negrón, Carlos García, Spencer Leaf, Verónica Meléndez, David Moreno, Xavier Robledo, Riccardo Robustini, Ángela Ruiz, Joanna Socha, Paula Vega

Local architect: Lpo Arkitekter

Coordination: Advansia AS

General consultant: Kulturplan Bjørvika: Multiconsult—Florian Kosche-Bollinger Grohman, Hjellnes Consult, Brekke og Strand, Civitas

Competition consultant: IDOM

Facades: ARUP

Sustainability: Kan Energi

ICT: Rambøll

Landscape architect—competition: Thorbjörn Andersson

Client: Oslo Kommune

PlayBox Film Headquarters, Madrid, Spain

Project director: Juan Herreros

Architect in charge: Ana Torres

Project team: Carmen Antón, Paula Vega

Completion: 2011

Artists team: Mónica Fuster, Tomás Saraceno

Structure: Eduardo Barrón

Illumination project: Maurici Ginés

Client: Francisco Arango

Hybrid Muscle, Changmai, Thailand
Architect: R&Sie(n)...
Contractor: Christian Hubert de Lisle, ADS
Creative team: François Roche, Stéphanie Lavaux, Jean Navarro
Completed: 2003
Key dimensions: 130 square meters
Cost: $65,000
Client: The Land, Rirkirt Tiravanija,

Shearing, Sommières, France
Architect: New-Territories / R&Sie(n)...
Creative team and associated partners: François Roche, Stéphanie
    Lavaux, Alexandre Boulin, Olivier Legrand
Engineer: Abaca Engineer
Contractor: Christian Hubert de Lisle
Completed: 2003
Key dimensions: 160 square meters
Cost: $160,000
Client: Ami and Judith Barak

Filtration, La Baïse, France
Architect: R&Sie(n)...
Creative team and associates partner: François Roche, Stephanie
    Lavaux, Gilles Desévédavy
Completed: 1997

The Light Pavilion, Chengdu, China
Designer: Lebbeus Woods, Christoph a. Kumpusch
Site: Sliced Porosity Block
Architect: Steven Holl
Completed: 2012
Client: CapitaLand Development

LightShowers, Wilmington, Delaware
Design: Michael Morris and Yoshiko Sato with Paul Ryan
Design team: J. Christopher Forman, Deborah Richards, Jorge
    Salgado, Kasia Ehrhardt, and Vivian Hu
Models and drawings: Deborah Richards
Completed: 2007
Installation area: 111 square meters
Finishing materials: CNC-fabricated Corian, video and LED Lighting,
    aluminum, and Plexiglas
Correspondent: Ma Dong Hee
Editor: Shin Ji Hye
Client: Delaware Center for the Contemporary Arts

Image Credits

Cover

© Phillips de Pury & Company
Thyseen-Bornesmisza Art Contemporary, Vienna

History and Theory

"Neither: Plastic as ~~Concept~~, Plastic as ~~Material~~"
fig. 1: courtesy of *Architectural Review*; fig. 2: courtesy of Whitney
Museum of American Art; fig. 3: © The Richard Avedon Foundation;
fig. 4: © Museum of Modern Art/Artist Rights Society; fig. 5: source
unknown

"Pollution, Plastics and the Sealed Interior"
fig. 1, 4, 5: courtesy of Avery Architectural Library archives; fig. 2:
courtesy of Wellcome Library, London; fig. 3, 6: courtesy of J. S.
Redfield, Clinton Hall; fig. 7: source unknown; fig. 8: courtesy of
Art Institute of Chicago; fig. 9, 10: courtesy of Holabird and Root
Architects; fig. 11: © François Dallegret

"Plastic Atmospheres, 1956 and 2008"
fig. 1: Canadian Center for Architecture; fig. 2, 3, 12: source unknown;
figs. 4–7, 9, 10, 13, 14: courtesy of Francis Loeb Library, Harvard
University; fig. 8: © Simon Smithson; fig. 11: FRAC Centre;
fig. 15, 22: courtesy of SANAA; fig. 16, 17: © Ivan Blasi; fig. 18, 19:
© Museum of Modern Art, New York; fig. 20: courtesy of Diario Oficial
de la Exposición Internacional de Barcelona; fig. 21: Gaspar Sagarra
y Torrents/ADAGP; fig. 23: © Ramon Pratt

"Structural Experiments in Inflatability"
fig. 1: © Matthew Waxman; figs. 2–14: © Chip Lord

"Plastic Man Strikes, Again (and Again)"
fig. 1: courtesy of *A Plastic Presence*; fig. 2: © Museum of Modern Art/
Artist Rights Society; figs. 3–8: © Les Levine

"From Boat to Bust: The Monsanto House Revisited"
fig. 1, 2, 5, 6: courtesy of Monsanto Company Records, University
Archives, Department of Special Collections, Washington University
Libraries, St. Louis, Missouri; fig. 3, 4: MIT Museum and Photography,
Katherine Malishewsky; fig. 7, 8: courtesy of Theodore Prudon

"The Plastic Line"
fig. 1, 2: courtesy of the Library and Archives of Canada;
figs. 3, 4, 10, 13, 15–18, 20–23: courtesy of R. Buckminster Fuller
Estate; fig. 5: courtesy *Japan Architect*; fig. 6, 25: © Corbis;
figs. 7–9: courtesy North Carolina Digital Collection; fig. 11, 24:
courtesy *Architectural Forum*; fig. 12: courtesy of North Carolina State
University; fig. 14: © Museum of Modern Art; fig. 19: © Architectural
Press Archive / RIBA Library Photographs Collection

"Good-Bye Tectonics, Hello Composites"
figs. 1, 3-6, 8-19, 22–37, 40–49: courtesy of Greg Lynn FORM;
fig. 2: source unknown; fig. 7: courtesy of Greg Lynn FORM ©
Ari Marcopolous; fig. 20, 21: courtesy of Greg Lynn FORM ©
Carlo Lavaroti; fig. 38, 39: courtesy of Greg Lynn FORM ©
Richard Powers

Projects

"Blobwall and Bloom House"
pp. 114–19, 123–24: courtesy of Greg Lynn FORM; pp. 120–22: courtesy
of Greg Lynn © Richard Powers

"Plastic Man Goes to Market"
fig. 1: © DC Comics; figs. 2–5: source unknown; fig. 6: Arch. Ignazia
Favata/Studio Joe Colombo, Milano; fig. 7, 10: © Aldo Ballo;
fig. 8: courtesy of Ray and Charles Eames; fig. 9: courtesy of George
Nelson/Vitra Design Museum; figs. 11–26: courtesy of Michael
Graves Design Group; fig. 27: courtesy of Michael Graves

"LAMBDA + PlayBox"
pp. 138–43: courtesy of Juan Herreros Arquitectos

"The Song of the S(t)yrene"
figs. 1–13: courtesy of François Roche

"The Light Pavilion"
pp. 151–57: courtesy of Steven Holl Architects and Christoph a.
Kumpusch © Iwan Baan; pp. 158–59: courtesy of Steven Holl
Architects

"LightShowers"
pp. 161–67: courtesy of Morris Sato Studio

Structure and Energy

"Structuring Plastic Flow"

fig. 1, 8, 15: courtesy of Johan Bettum; figs. 2, 3, 5–7: courtesy of Renzo Piano Building Workshop; fig. 4, 9, 10: courtesy of Markus Hudert; fig. 11: Markus Hudert with Johan Bettum; fig. 12, 13: Mari Amservik with Johan Bettum; fig. 14: Valerie Kerz with Johan Bettum; fig. 16: various with Johan Bettum

"Plastics as a Structural Material"

figs. 1–3: © Sabine Haubitz + Zoche; fig. 4, 6: courtesy of Christian Gahl; fig. 5: © Uwe Walter; figs. 7–9: © Rainer Viertlböck; figs. 10–12: © Werner Sobek; figs. 13, 14: © Roland Halbe; figs. 15–19: © Zooey Braun; fig. 20: © Udo Meinel; fig. 21: courtesy of ILEK

"North Sails Three-Dimensional Laminates"

figs. 1–9: courtesy of Bill Pearson

"Polymers in Architecture and Building Construction: Potentials and Challenges"

fig. 1, 9: courtesy of Knippers Helbig Advanced Engineering; fig. 2, 3: courtesy of Foster + Partners; figs. 4, 5, 10, 11, 14–16: courtesy of the Institute for Building Structures and Structural Design (ITKE), University of Stuttgart; fig. 6–8: courtesy of SOMA Architects; fig. 12, 13: © HG Merz

"All-Plastics (In-Building)"

fig. 1: courtesy of Architectural Forum; fig. 2: courtesy of Engineering Equipment Users Association

"Plastic Fantastic"

figs. 1–8: courtesy of Mercedes Daimler AG

"Improving the Sustainability of High-Performance Plastics"

fig. 1: © Behnisch Architekten; fig. 2: courtesy of Jahn © Rainer Vierltböck; fig. 3–6: courtesy of Jahn; figs. 7–9: © RTKL; fig. 10: courtesy of Herman Miller; fig. 11: Creative Commons; fig. 12: courtesy of Warmboard; fig. 13: courtesy of Eric Olsen

Cultural Effects

"Plastic Music"

fig. 1: courtesy Mark Miller, *Cool Blues: Charlier Parker in Canada*; figs. 2: source unknown; fig. 3: © Lee Friedlander; fig. 4: courtesy of Atlantic Records

"Plasticity"

fig. 1: courtesy of the University of Pennsylvania School of Design; figs. 2–4: courtesy of Archi-tectonics

"Plastic Soup"

fig. 1: courtesy of the Regents of the University of Minnesota; fig. 2, 3: courtesy of Charles Harker and the Tao Design Group; fig. 4, 5: courtesy of John Zimmerman for Progressive Architecture magazine; fig. 6: courtesy of AD magazine; fig. 7: courtesy of Saeed Arida and Lydia Kallipoliti; fig. 8: © Tecta/MAK; fig. 9: source unknown; fig. 10: © William Katavolos; fig. 11: courtesy of Anatolii Papyrin et al., *Cold Spray Technology* (Novosibirsk, Russia: Elsevier Science, 2007); fig. 12: courtesy of Joseph R. Davis, *Handbook of Thermal Spray Technology* (Materials Park, Ohio: ASM International, 2004)

"The Plastic Paradox and its Potential"

fig. 1: © Getty Images; fig. 2: courtesy of Whitney Museum of American Art; fig. 3: courtesy of Philadelphia Museum of Art; fig. 4: courtesy of Portland Museum of Art; fig. 5: © Henry Groskinsky; fig. 6: source unknown

"Plastic Life"

fig. 1: © Andreas Gursky; fig. 2, 3: © Open Office; figs. 4–8, 12, 13: courtesy of Galia Solomonoff; figs. 9–11: courtesy of Nick Hopson and Klara Nostrom

"*Die Plastik*"

figs. 1–3: Courtesy of dECOi Architects

"Plasticity Formation/Information"

fig. 1: courtesy of Kevin Bruk Gallery, Miami, Florida; figs. 2–4: courtesy of Museum für Moderne Kunst Frankfurt am Main, photo: Axel Schneider, Frankfurt am Main; fig. 5, 6: courtesy of the Miami Art Museum; fig. 7, 8: © David Arranz; fig. 9: © Erica Overmeer; fig. 10: courtesy of Second International Biennial of Contemporary Art of Seville, Spain; fig. 11, 12: courtesy of Joan Prats Gallery, Barcelona, Spain